THE CENTER FOR CARTOON STUDIES PRESENTS

HARRIET TUBMAN
TOWARD FREEDOM

THE CENTER FOR CARTOON STUDIES PRESENTS

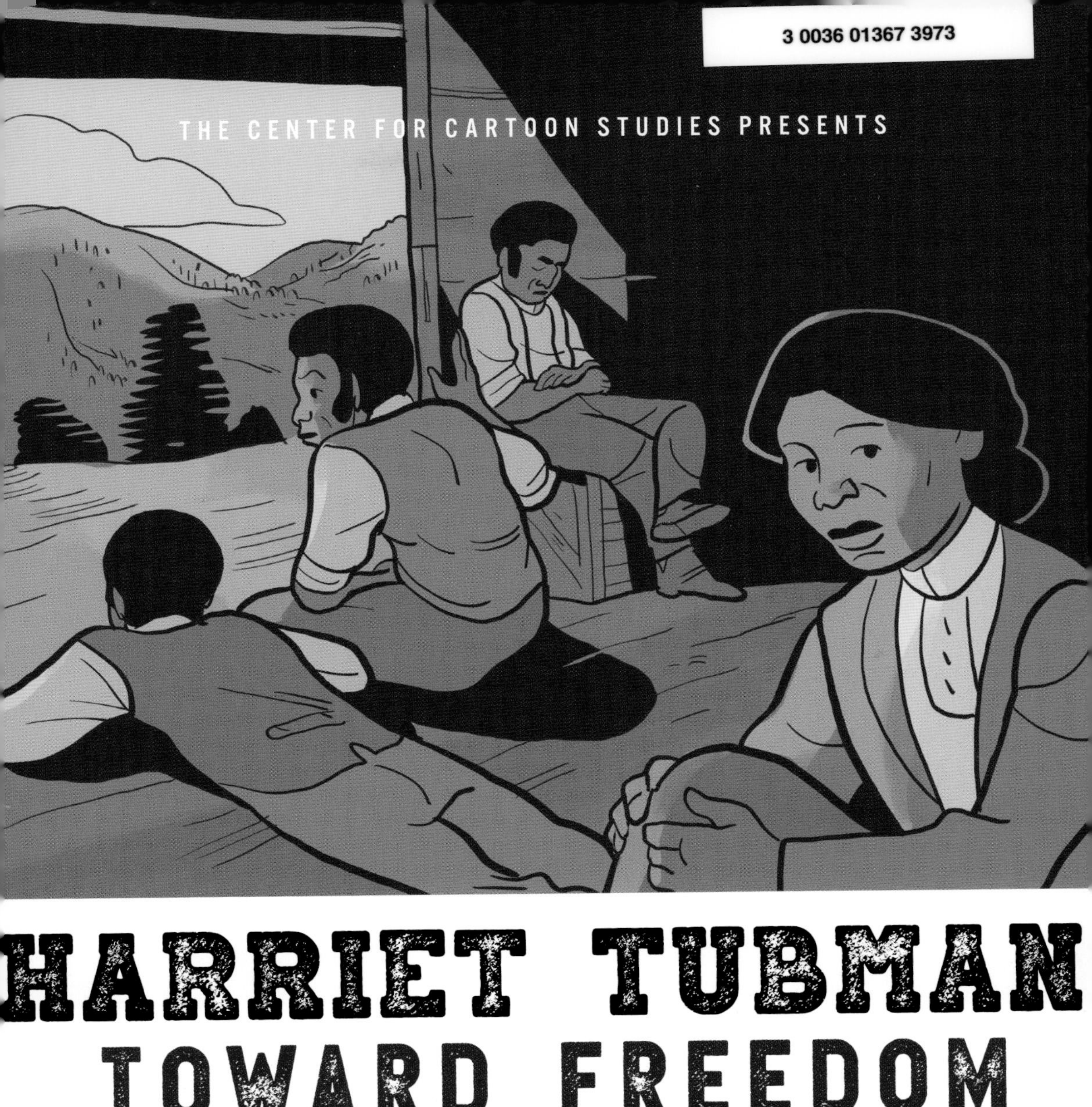

HARRIET TUBMAN
TOWARD FREEDOM

Whit Taylor & Kazimir Lee
With an introduction by Carole Boston Weatherford

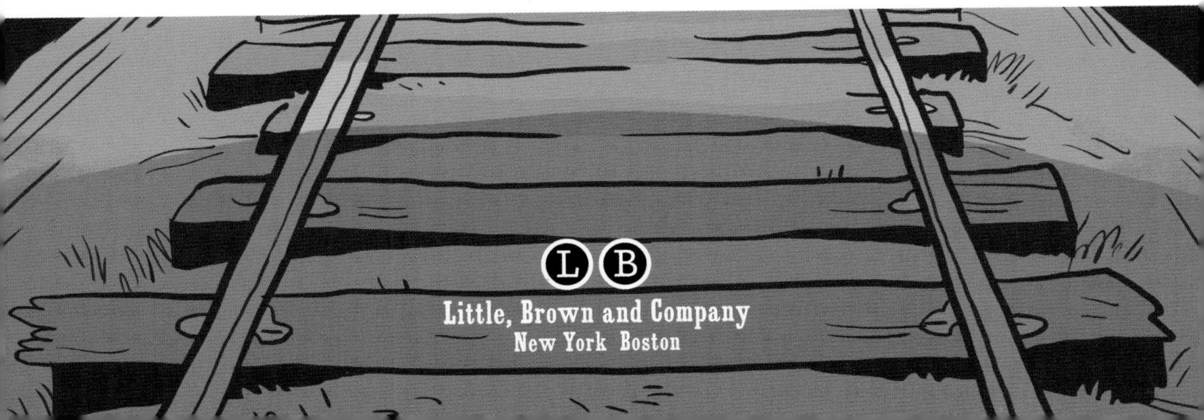

LB
Little, Brown and Company
New York Boston

About This Book

The text was set in Adobe Caslon Pro and Felt Tip Woman, and the display type is Woodblock.

Little, Brown and Company
Hachette Book Group
1290 Avenue of the Americas, New York, NY 10104
Visit us at LBYR.com

First Edition: June 2021

Little, Brown and Company is a division of Hachette Book Group, Inc.
The Little, Brown name and logo are trademarks of Hachette Book Group, Inc.

The publisher is not responsible for websites (or their content) that are not owned by the publisher.

Library of Congress Cataloging-in-Publication Data
Names: Taylor, Whit, author. | Lee, Kazimir, 1986- illustrator. | Weatherford, Carole Boston, 1956- writer of introduction.
Title: Harriet Tubman: toward freedom / Whit Taylor & Kazimir Lee; with an introduction by Carole Boston Weatherford
Other titles: Center for Cartoon Studies presents Harriet Tubman: toward freedom
Description: New York: Little, Brown and Company, 2021. | "At head of title: Center for Cartoon Studies presents." | Includes bibliographical references. | Audience: Ages 10-14 | Summary: "Graphic biography detailing Harriet Tubman's escape from slavery and her efforts with other abolitionists to rescue dozens of those still enslaved" —Provided by publisher.
Identifiers: LCCN 2020043364 | ISBN 9780759555501 (hardcover) | ISBN 9780759555518 (trade paperback) | ISBN 9780759557666 (ebook) | ISBN 9780759555907 (ebook other)
Subjects: LCSH: Tubman, Harriet, 1822-1913—Juvenile literature. | Slaves—United States—Biography—Juvenile literature. | African American women—Biography—Juvenile literature. | Underground Railroad—Juvenile literature. | Tubman, Harriet, 1822-1913—Comic books, strips, etc. | Slaves—United States—Biography—Comic books, strips, etc. | African American women—Biography—Comic books, strips, etc. | Underground Railroad—Comic books, strips, etc. | LCGFT: Graphic novels.
Classification: LCC E444.T82 T43 2021 | DDC 326/.8092 [B]—dc23
LC record available at https://lccn.loc.gov/2020043364

ISBNs: 978-0-7595-5550-1 (hardcover), 978-0-7595-5551-8 (pbk.), 978-0-7595-5591-4 (ebook), 978-0-7595-5766-6 (ebook), 978-0-7595-5549-5 (ebook)

Printed in China

APS

Hardcover: 10 9 8 7 6 5 4 3 2 1

Paperback: 10 9 8 7 6 5 4 3 2 1

Introduction

by Carole Boston Weatherford

Besides my parents, Harriet Tubman was my first hero. I first learned about the famed leader of the Underground Railroad at my all-Black elementary school in Baltimore. I'm not sure whether the study of Tubman was required by Maryland's social studies curriculum or whether my "woke" teachers just pushed Black history (for which I'm grateful).

As a girl in the 1960s, I admired Harriet's fight. As I learned more about her, I sensed her strength, sacrifices, and spirit—the qualities that bore comparison to the biblical Moses.

Despite my early Harriet worship, years passed before I linked her to my own heritage on Maryland's Eastern Shore. One branch of my father's family hails from Dorchester County,

Tubman's birthplace, and another branch was enslaved at Wye House, the same Talbot County plantation where young Frederick Douglass first experienced slavery's brutality. These two bordering counties produced not only my ancestors but also two of the nation's leading abolitionists.

Research for my book *Moses: When Harriet Tubman Led Her People to Freedom* led *me* to Tubman's roots and to her 1869 narrative. That mythic account brought Harriet's faith into focus. For me, Harriet had become mystical and monumental.

Her legacy is enshrined in places like her former residence, the Harriet Tubman Home in Upstate New York, the National Park Service's Harriet

Tubman Underground Railroad National Historical Park, and the Harriet Tubman Underground Railroad Visitor Center and (Maryland) State Park.

Meticulously researched and visually powerful, *Harriet Tubman: Toward Freedom* chronicles Harriet's story through conversations with William Still, a Philadelphia abolitionist and a leader of the Underground Railroad. Her story begins around 1820 in Bucktown, Maryland, where she was born Araminta Ross, one of eleven children of Harriet Green and Benjamin Ross. As a child,

"Minty," as she was known, was hired out by her master. A nursemaid, she stayed awake nights so the baby would not wake the mother. If Minty nodded to sleep, the baby's mother whipped her.

From then on, Minty dreaded the lash and yearned to be free. She learned to layer clothing as padding—protection from the whip. When caught stealing a lump of sugar, Minty hid for days in a pigpen to avoid a beating. Years later, an overseer hurled an iron weight that missed its mark—an enslaved man—but hit Harriet instead. The blow crushed her

skull and knocked her unconscious for days, scarring her forehead and causing seizures for the rest of her life.

After her marriage to John Tubman, a free Black man, in 1844, Minty took his last name and her mother's first name, Harriet. The marriage was short-lived, though. In 1849, Harriet decided to run away for fear of being sold. When John refused to go with her, Harriet fled with her two brothers, who both turned back. Harriet pressed on alone all the way to Philadelphia. She worked as a household servant and a cook while saving money to return to the South to help others escape on the Underground Railroad.

The Underground Railroad was dangerous business. At great personal risk, Harriet made thirteen trips back to Maryland—intent on rescuing other family members. Beyond her own kin, her bands of runaways included other enslaved people. Harriet lost patience with fearful runaways who considered returning. Knowing they would imperil others, she pulled out a gun and threatened, "You'll be free or die a slave."

As this stunning graphic novel confirms, Harriet's suspenseful saga is particularly suited to a sequential narrative. This is evident as she leads runaways from the slave-holding states to northern free states and—after the 1850 Fugitive Slave Act threatened runaways with capture and re-enslavement—as far as Canada. With a $40,000 bounty (over $1.3 million today) on her head, she used her wit to elude the patrollers.

The same grit and ingenuity that earned her the moniker "the Moses of her people" made her vital to the Union Army. During the Civil War, she served as a nurse, a cook, and a spy. She enlisted formerly enslaved African Americans to scout Confederate camps and troop movements. Armed with inside information, she joined a gunboat raid by 150 Black soldiers in South Carolina. As a nurse, she used folk remedies to treat soldiers.

After the war, Harriet continued to serve humanity in her adopted hometown of Auburn, New York, where she founded a senior citizens' home. In her later years, she petitioned Congress to receive her military pension in addition to that of Nelson David's, her late husband, a Union veteran. In 1899, Congress passed, and the president signed, legislation to increase her pension to twenty dollars a month for her service as a nurse.

Harriet emerges from this action-packed epic—pitting freedom against slavery, good against evil—as a superhero of sorts. Her deeds were legendary, but her story is not a legend. Author Whit Taylor and illustrator Kazimir Lee vividly recreate Harriet's real-life adventure from the slavery era, the Civil War, and the Reconstruction to the women's suffrage movement.

Through authentic dialogue and expressive art, *Harriet Tubman: Toward Freedom* evokes Harriet's revolutionary spirit. This graphic novel will appeal to all who pursue liberty and who push back against injustice.

The struggle continues.

—C.B.W.

1850, PHILADELPHIA.

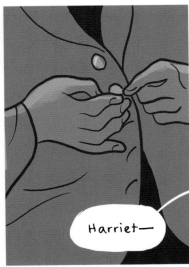

Harriet—

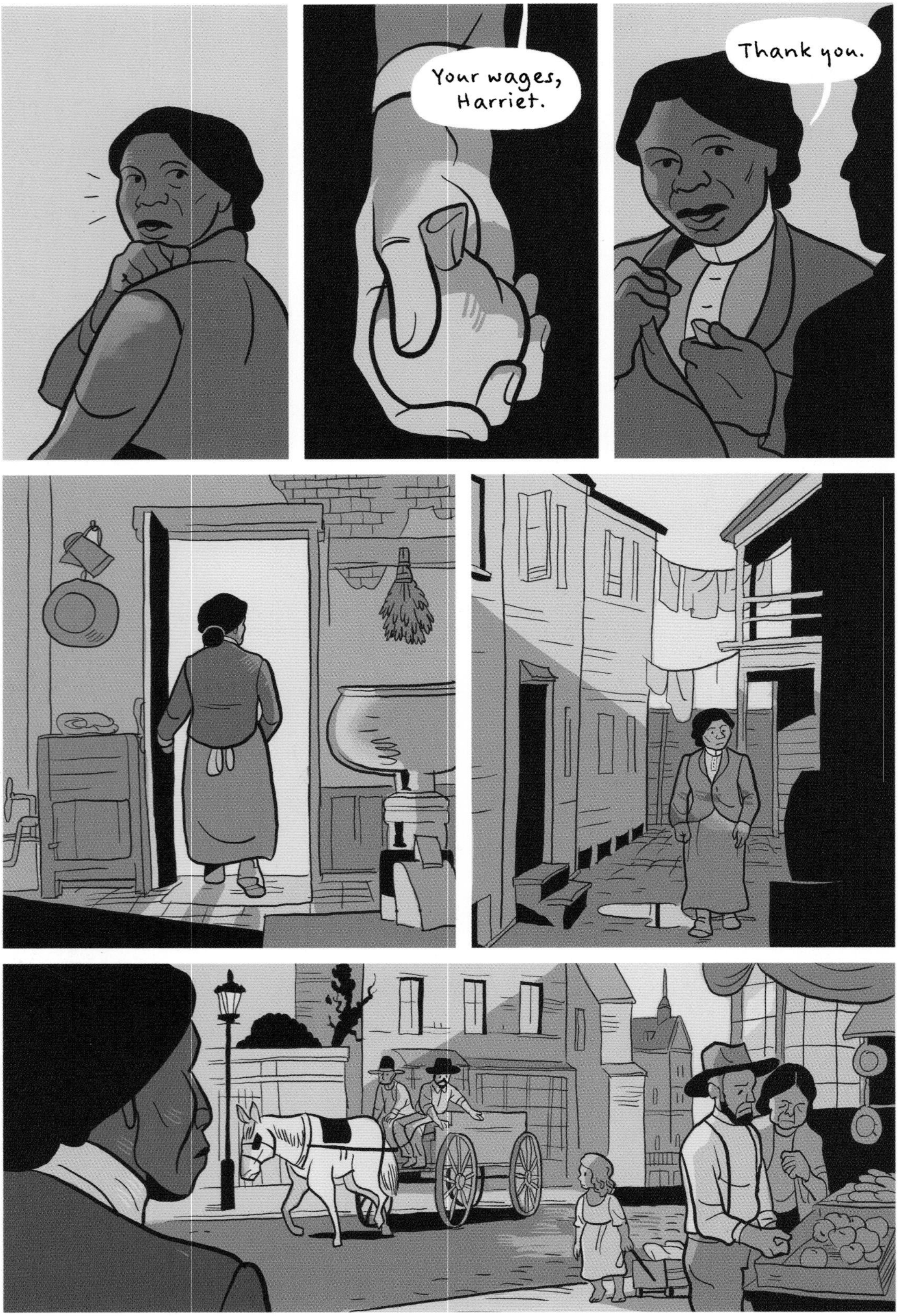
Your wages, Harriet.
Thank you.

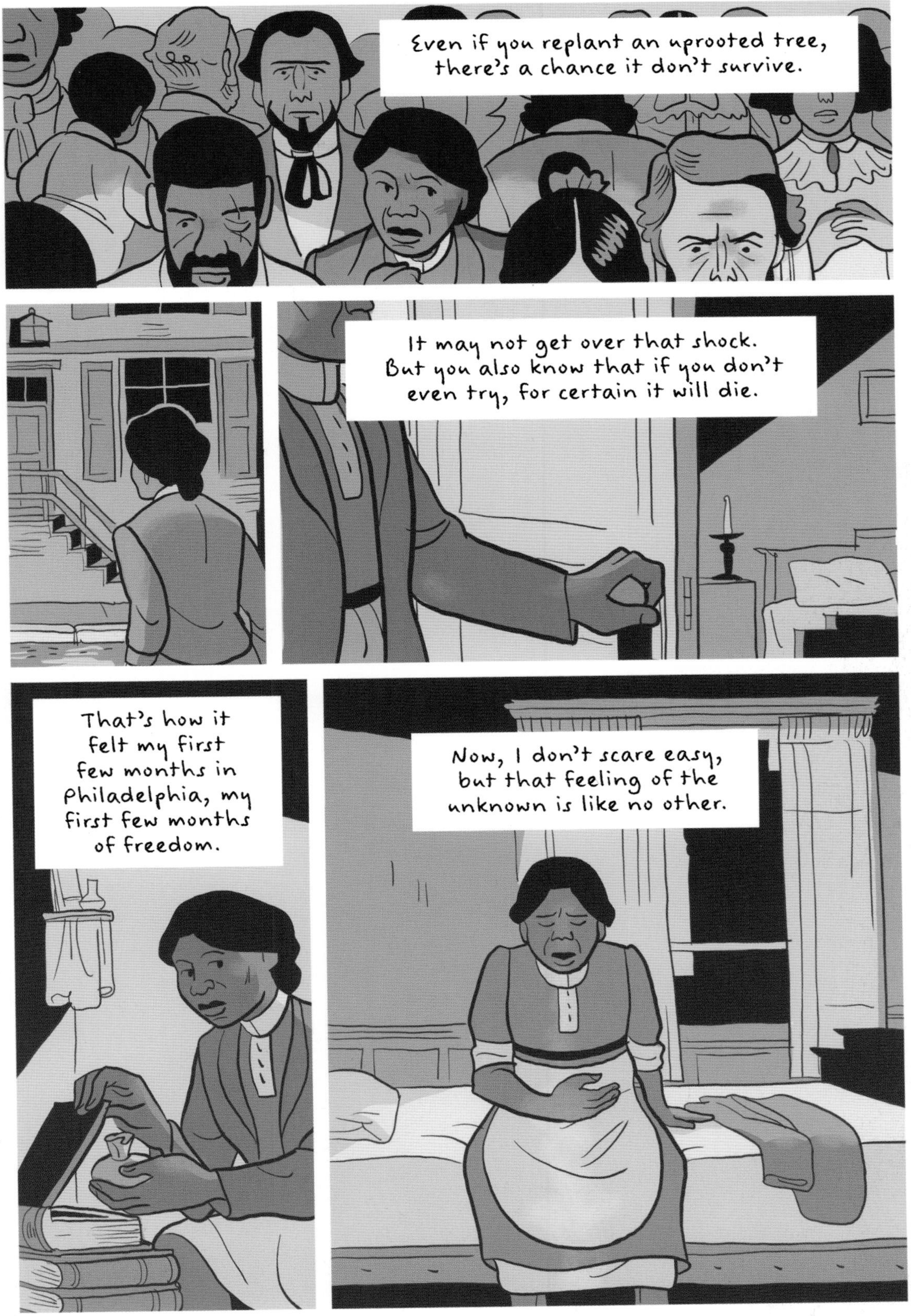
Even if you replant an uprooted tree, there's a chance it don't survive.
It may not get over that shock. But you also know that if you don't even try, for certain it will die.
That's how it felt my first few months in Philadelphia, my first few months of freedom.
Now, I don't scare easy, but that feeling of the unknown is like no other.

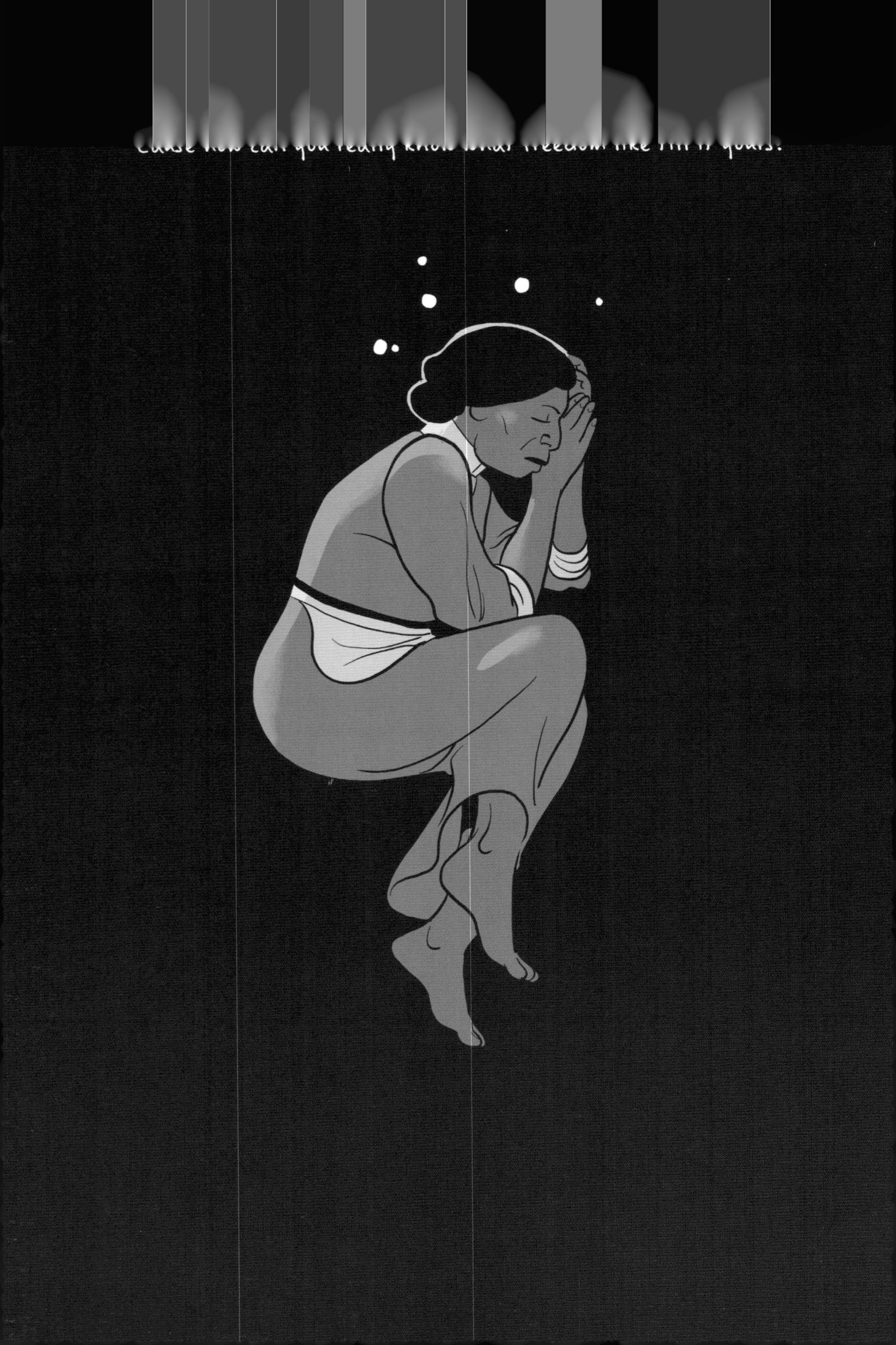
'Cause how can you really know what freedom like till it yours?

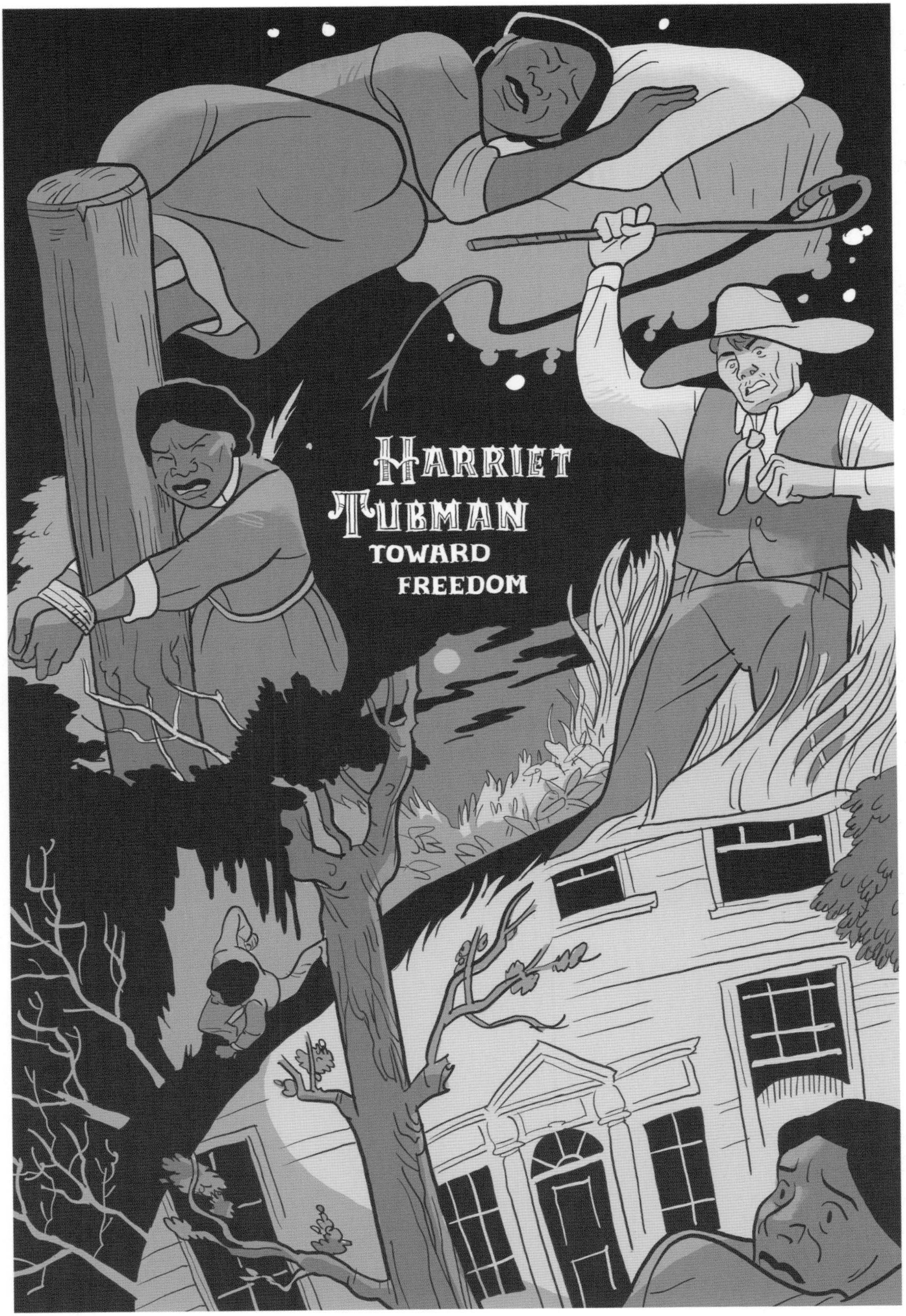
HARRIET
TUBMAN
TOWARD
FREEDOM

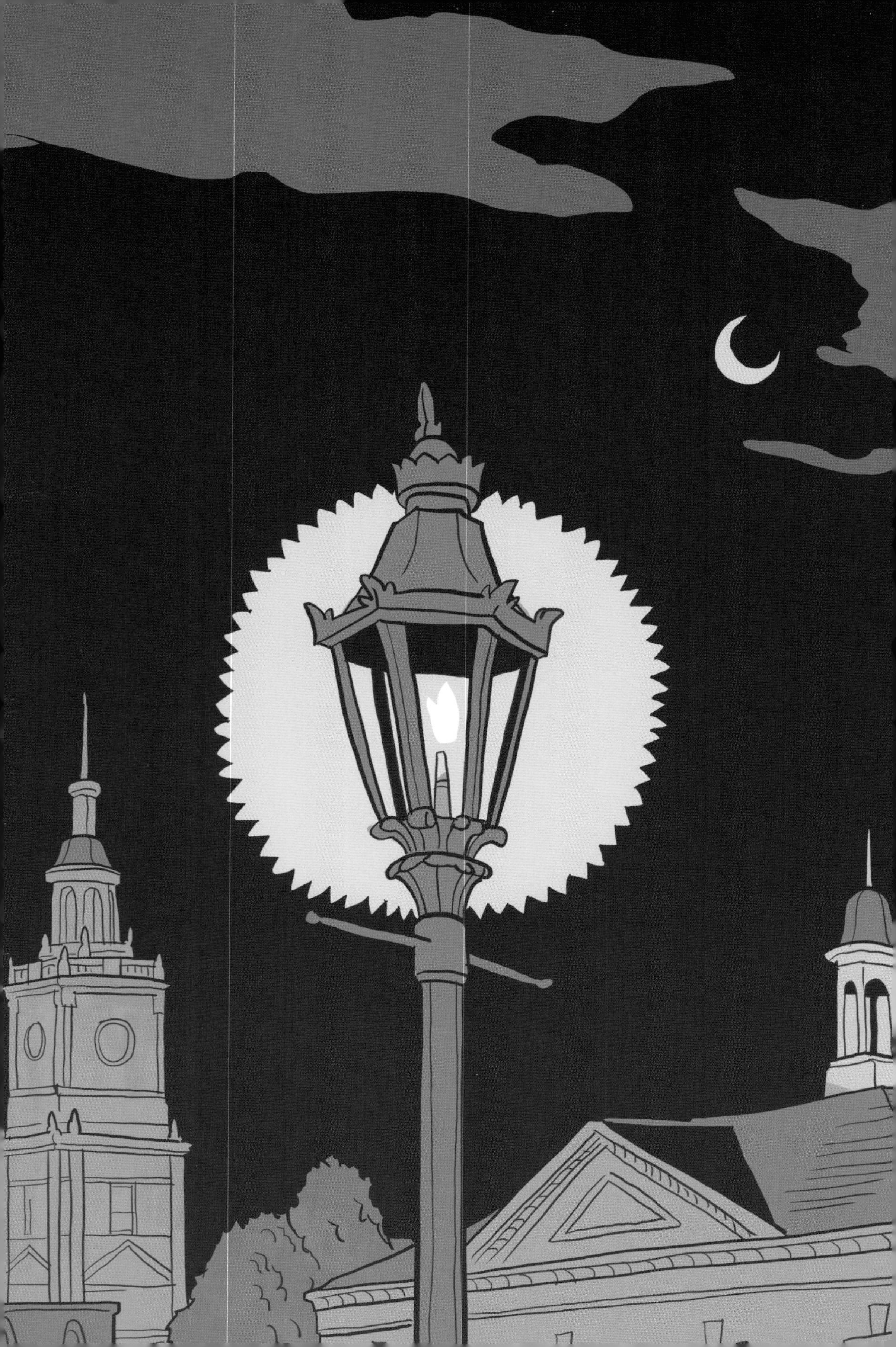

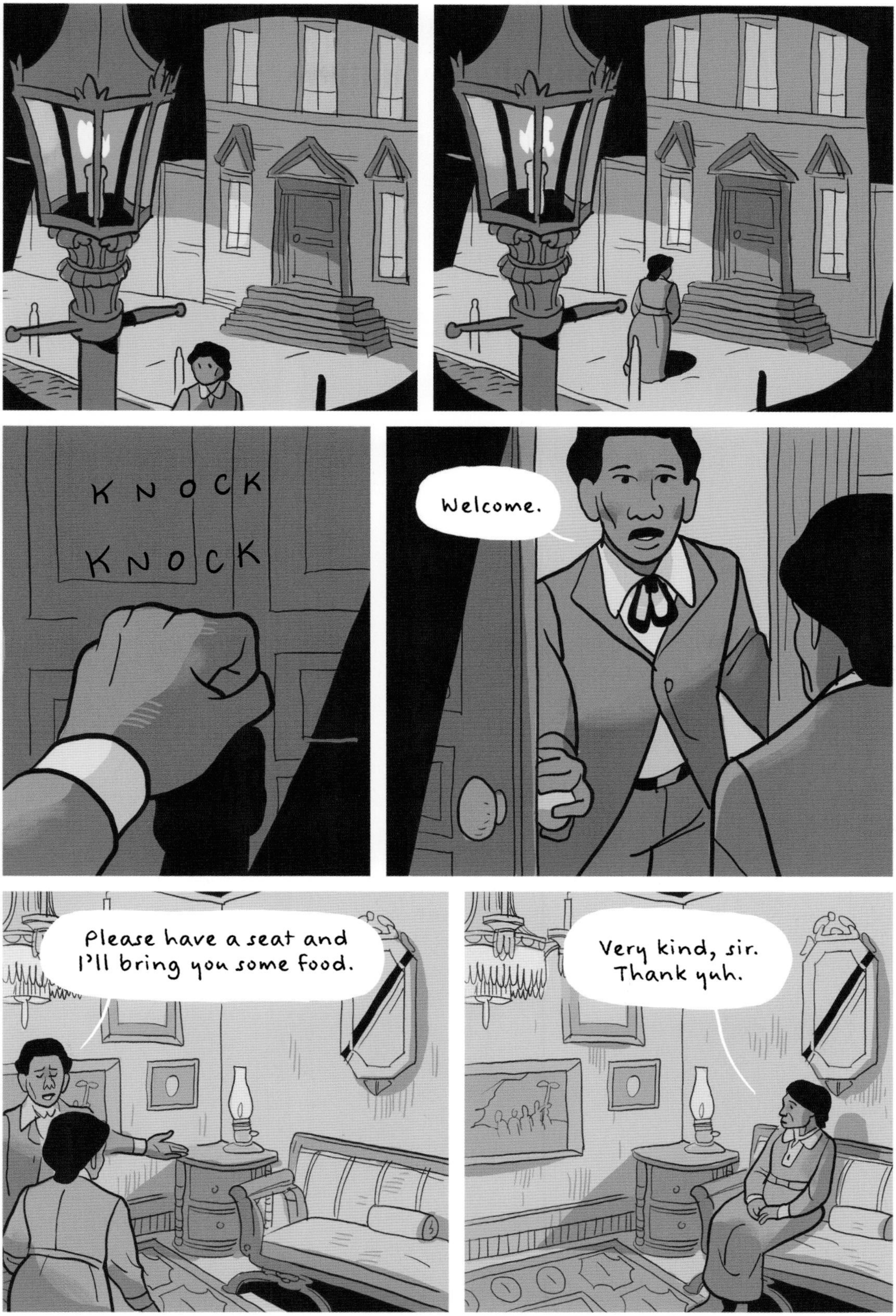
KNOCK
KNOCK
Welcome.
Please have a seat and I'll bring you some food.
Very kind, sir. Thank yuh.

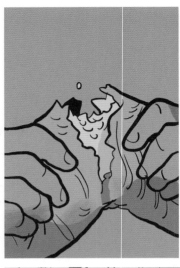

Take your time.

Harriet Tubman. Pleased to meet you, sir.

William Still, chairman of the Philadelphia Vigilance Committee.

Where are you coming from?

Dorchester County, Maryland, sir. But I been in Philadelphia a few months' time.

How did you hear about us?

You know... people talk.

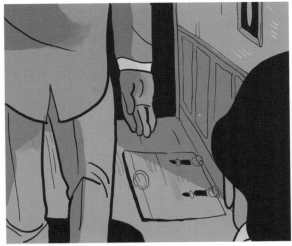

And I had a premonition. HE never steer me wrong.

Do you have a job?

Yes, Mr. Still. Laundry and house tending.

What do you all do?

Uh, well, we, the committee, are part of the Pennsylvania Anti-Slavery Society.

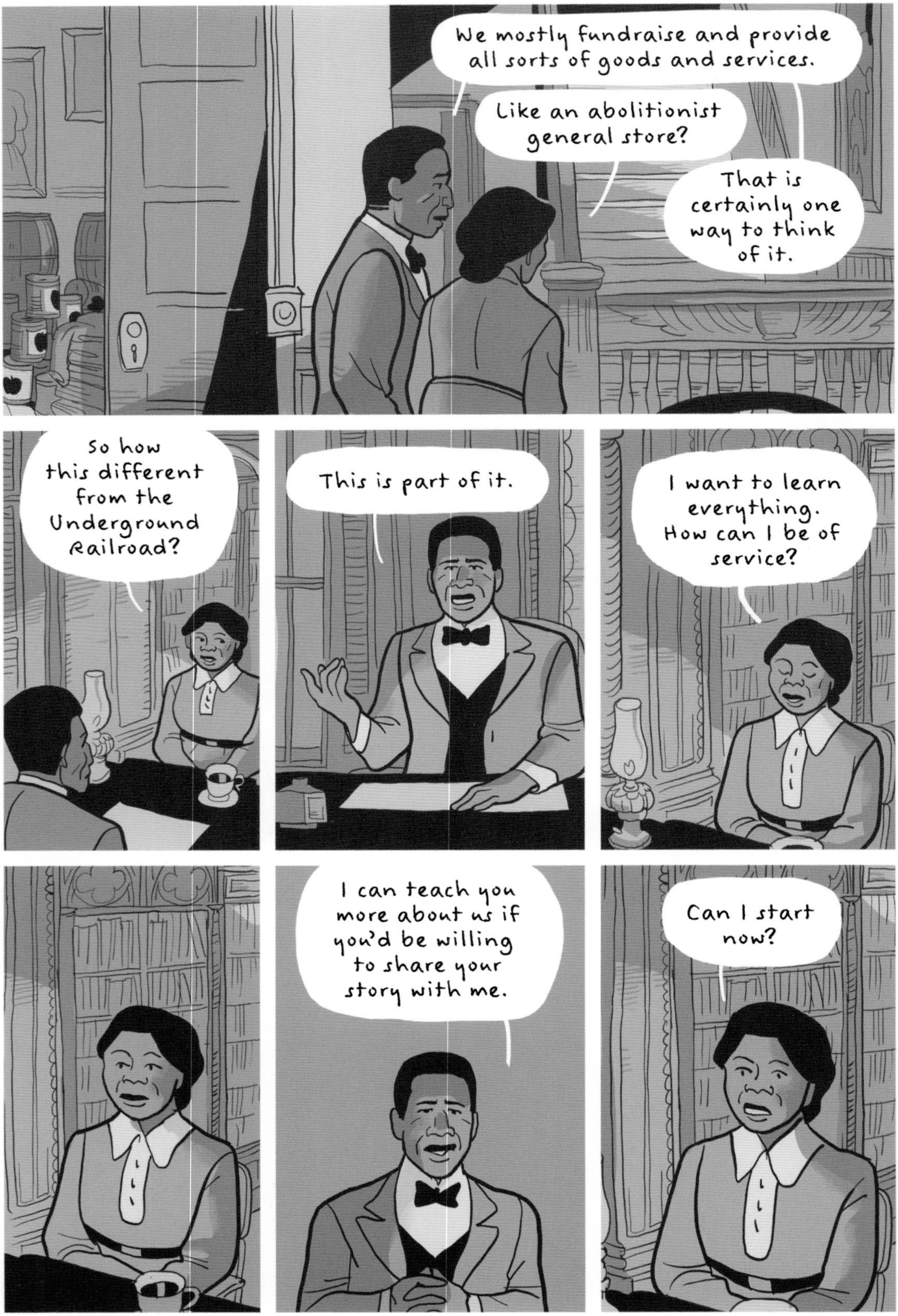
We mostly fundraise and provide all sorts of goods and services.
Like an abolitionist general store?
That is certainly one way to think of it.
So how this different from the Underground Railroad?
This is part of it.
I want to learn everything. How can I be of service?
I can teach you more about us if you'd be willing to share your story with me.
Can I start now?

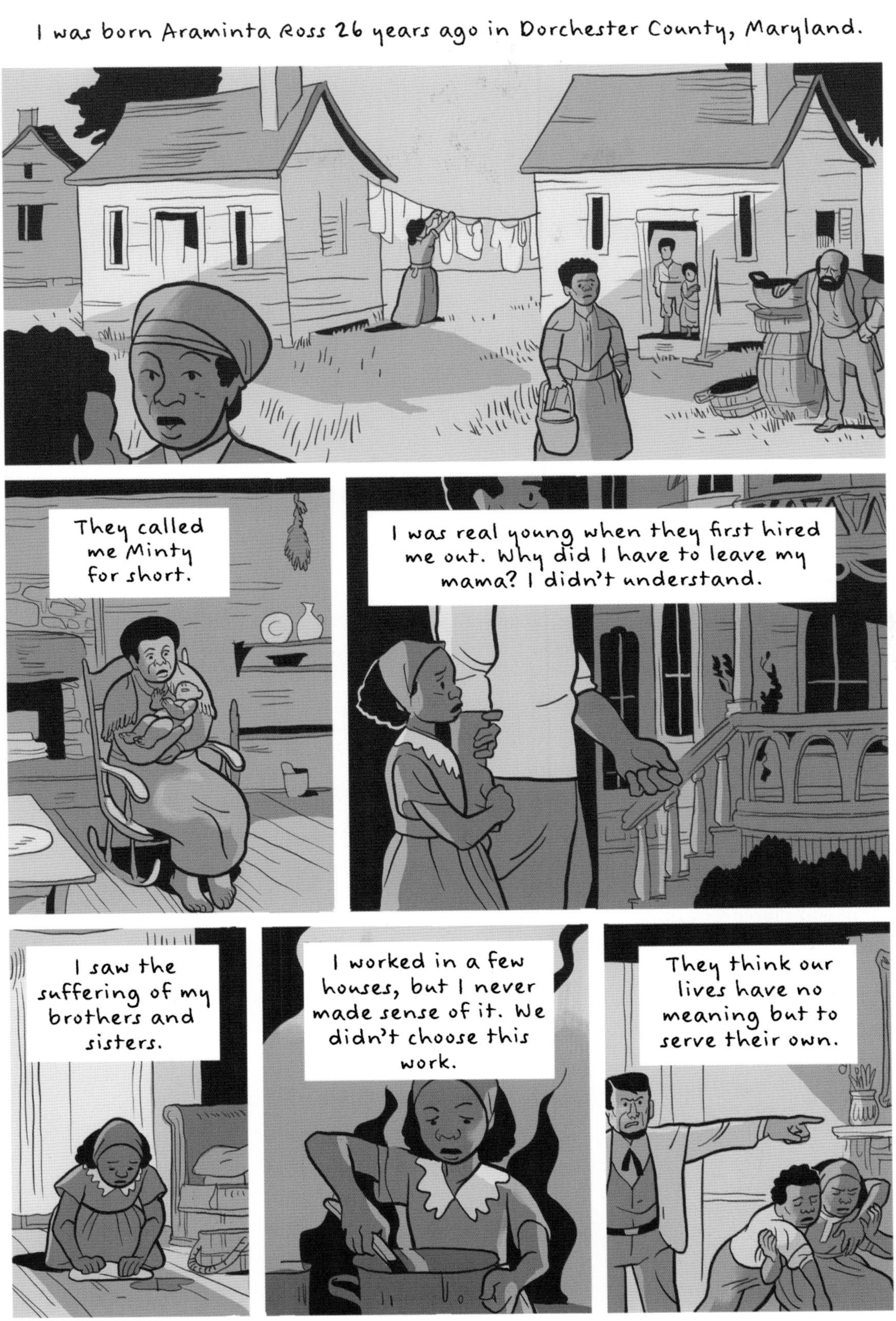
I was born Araminta Ross 26 years ago in Dorchester County, Maryland.
They called me Minty for short.
I was real young when they first hired me out. Why did I have to leave my mama? I didn't understand.
I saw the suffering of my brothers and sisters.
I worked in a few houses, but I never made sense of it. We didn't choose this work.
They think our lives have no meaning but to serve their own.

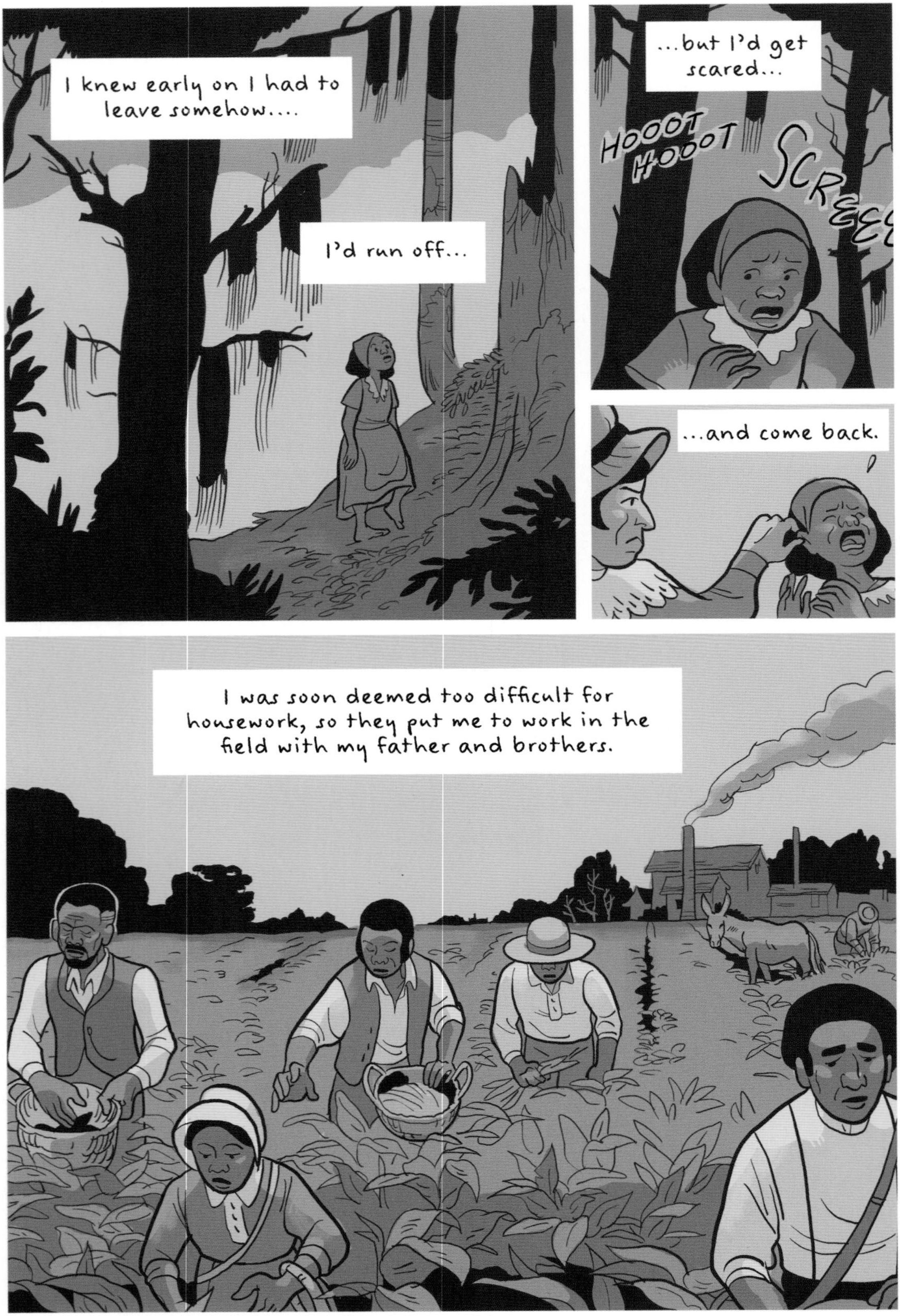
I knew early on I had to leave somehow....
I'd run off...
...but I'd get scared...
HOOOT HOOOT
SCREE
...and come back.
I was soon deemed too difficult for housework, so they put me to work in the field with my father and brothers.

Let me see, Minty.

R IIIIp

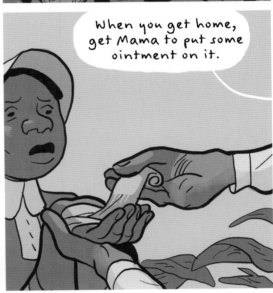

When you get home, get Mama to put some ointment on it.

A couple more weeks in these fields and you'll soon have hands like me, rough and thick like leather!

Don't be scared.

It'll be your armor.

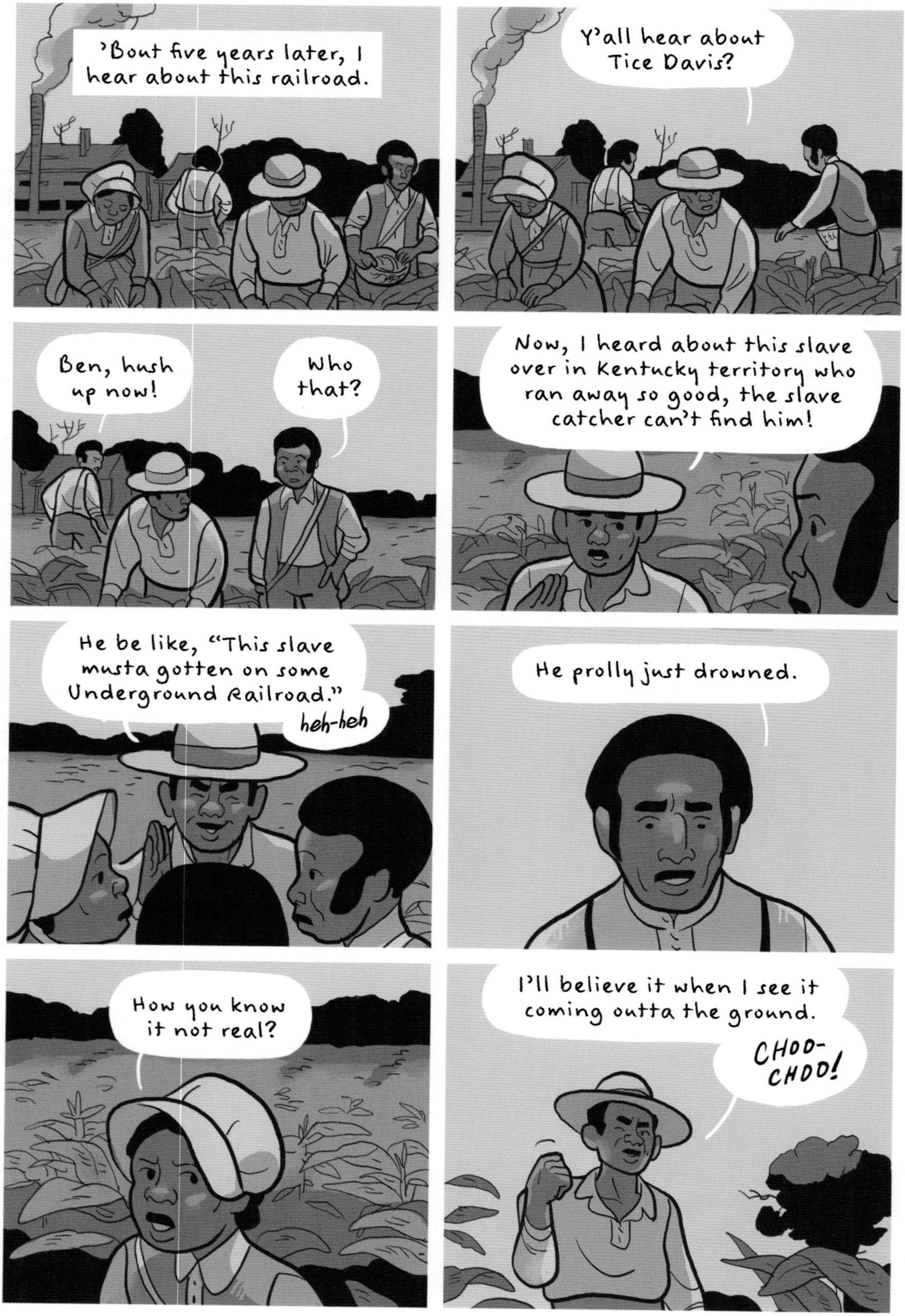
'Bout five years later, I hear about this railroad.
Y'all hear about Tice Davis?
Ben, hush up now!
Who that?
Now, I heard about this slave over in Kentucky territory who ran away so good, the slave catcher can't find him!
He be like, "This slave musta gotten on some Underground Railroad."
heh-heh
He prolly just drowned.
How you know it not real?
I'll believe it when I see it coming outta the ground.
CHOO-CHOO!

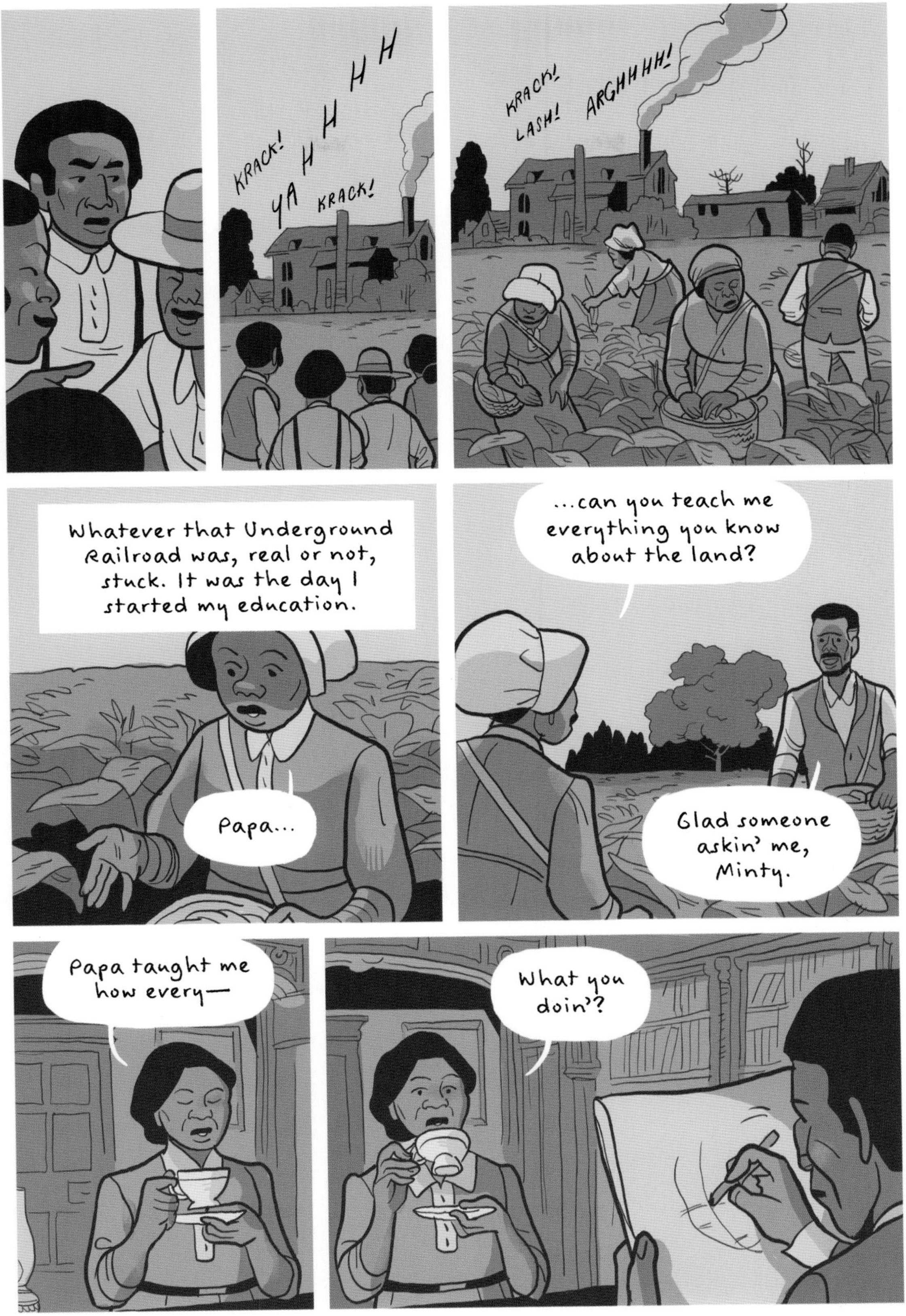
KRACK!
YA H H H H
KRACK!
KRACK!
LASH!
ARGHHHH!
Whatever that Underground Railroad was, real or not, stuck. It was the day I started my education.
Papa...
...can you teach me everything you know about the land?
Glad someone askin' me, Minty.
Papa taught me how every—
What you doin'?

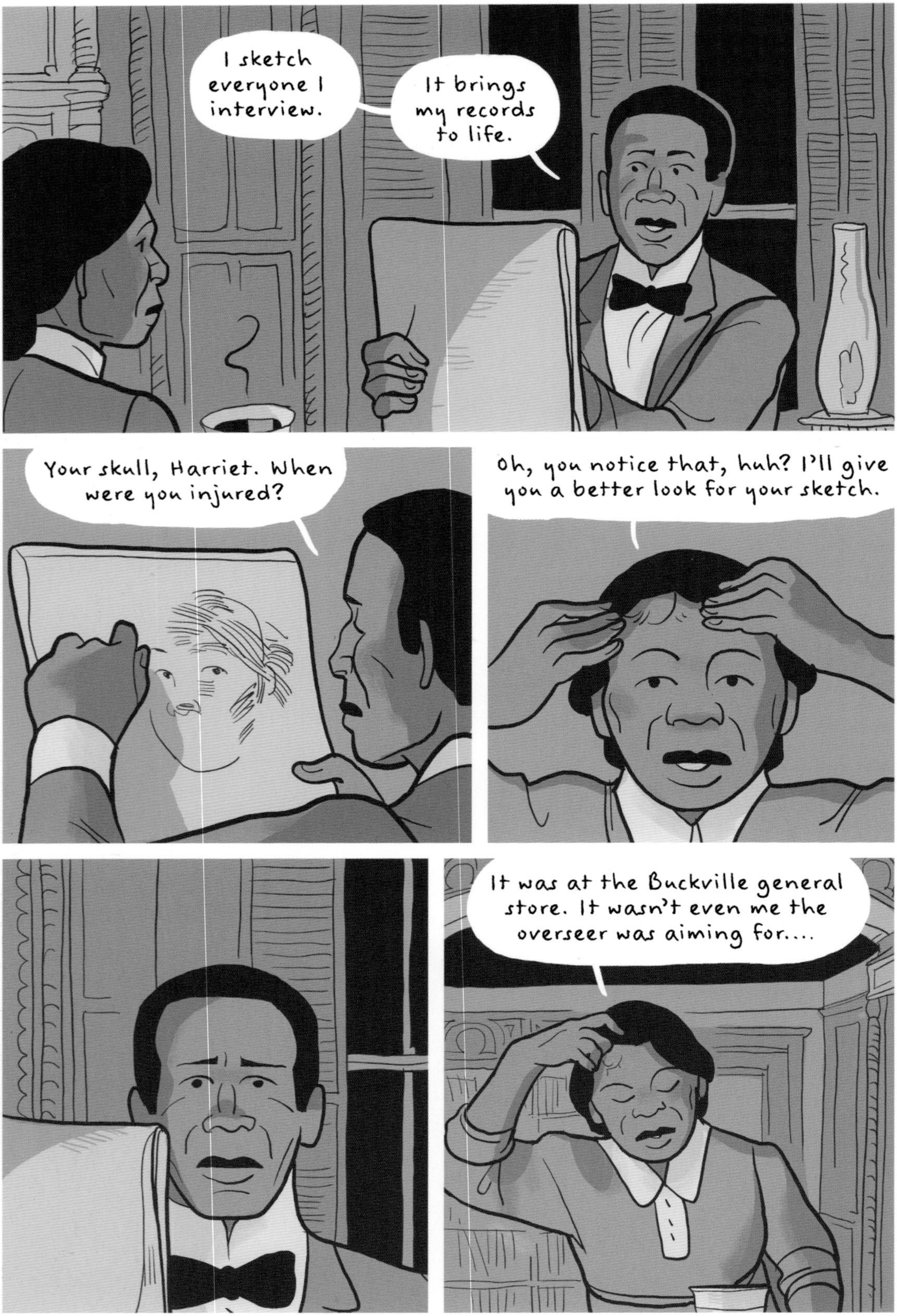
I sketch everyone I interview.
It brings my records to life.
Your skull, Harriet. When were you injured?
Oh, you notice that, huh? I'll give you a better look for your sketch.
It was at the Buckville general store. It wasn't even me the overseer was aiming for....

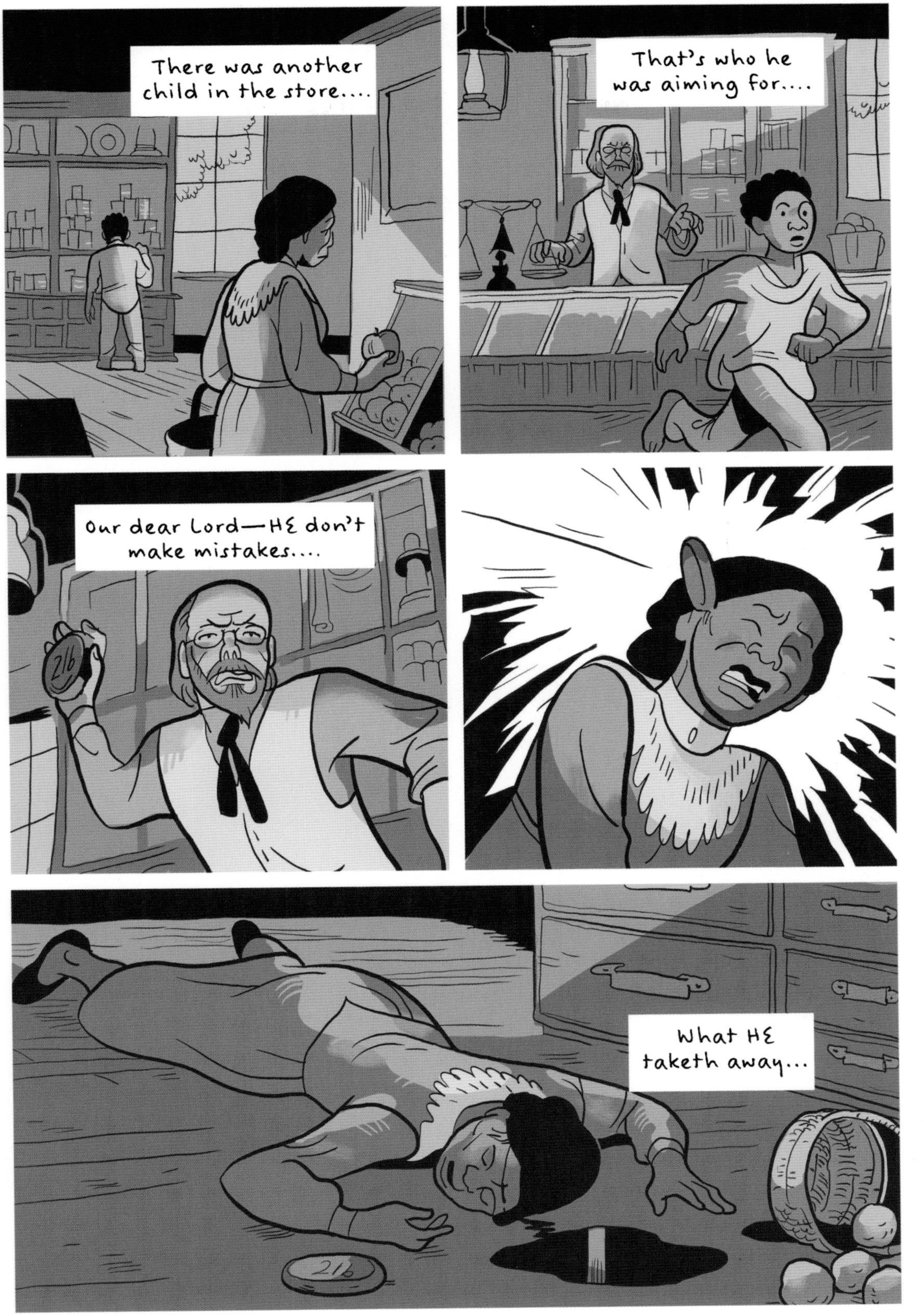
There was another child in the store....
That's who he was aiming for....
Our dear Lord—HE don't make mistakes....
2lb
What HE taketh away...
2lb

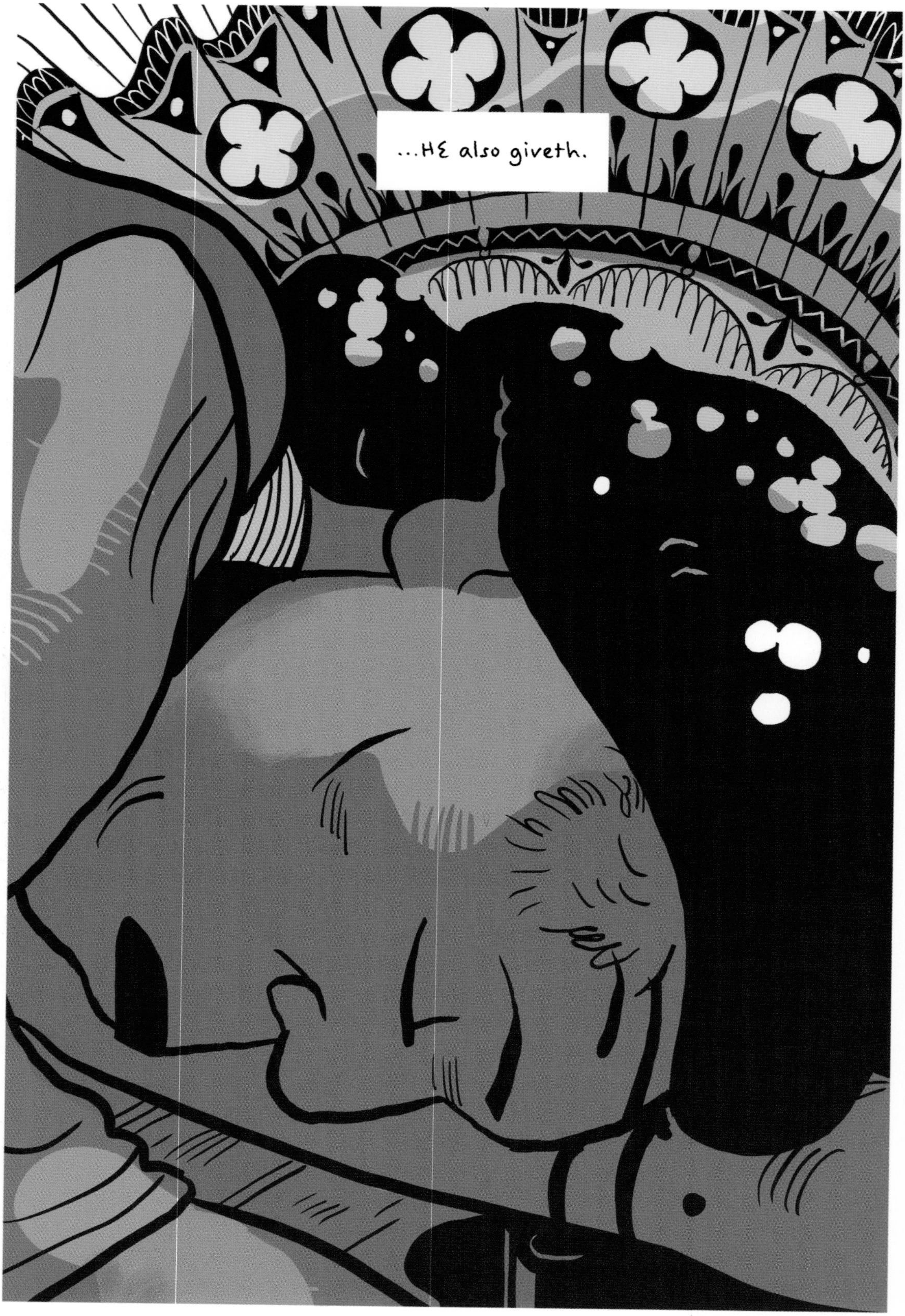
...HE also giveth.

HE told me what I need to do now, set me on this path. Mainly...

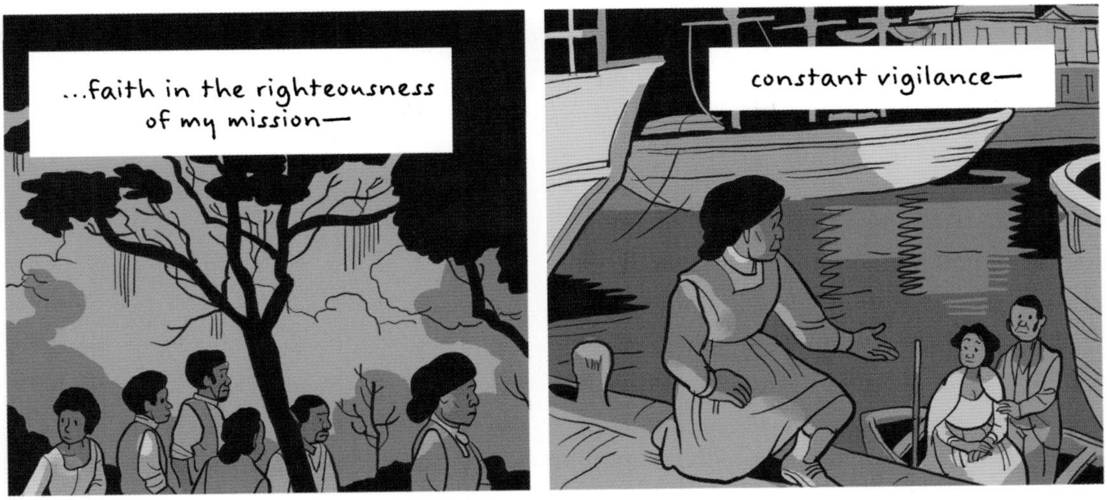
...faith in the righteousness of my mission—
constant vigilance—

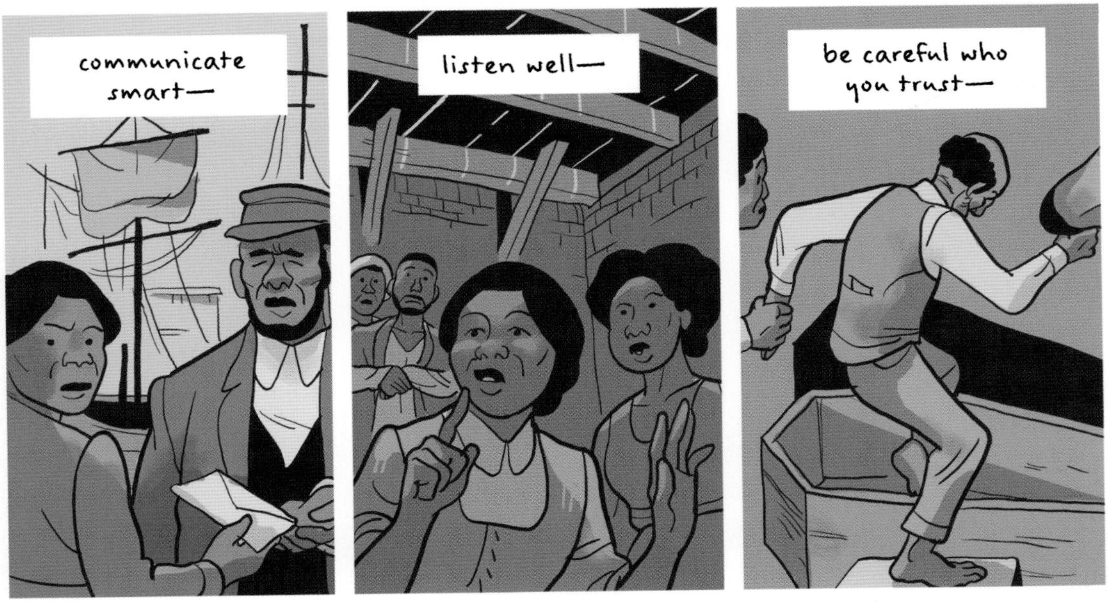
communicate smart—
listen well—
be careful who you trust—

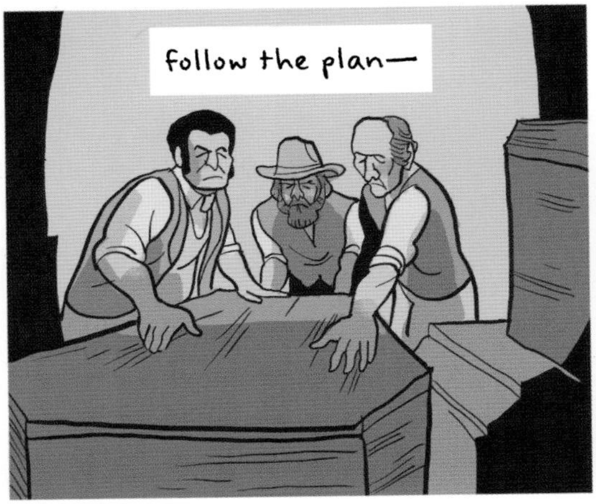
follow the plan—

and pray that it gone be all right.

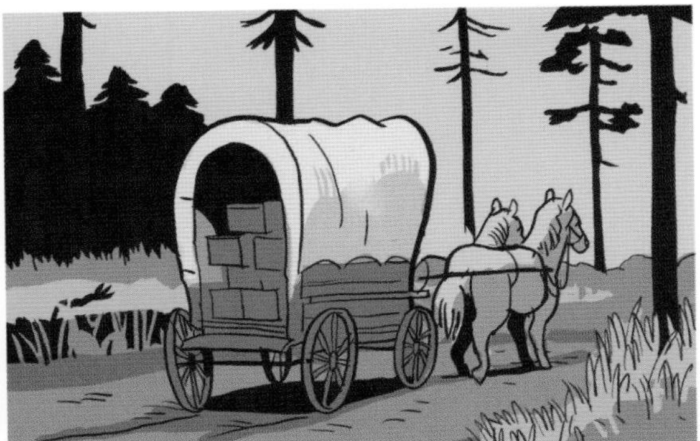

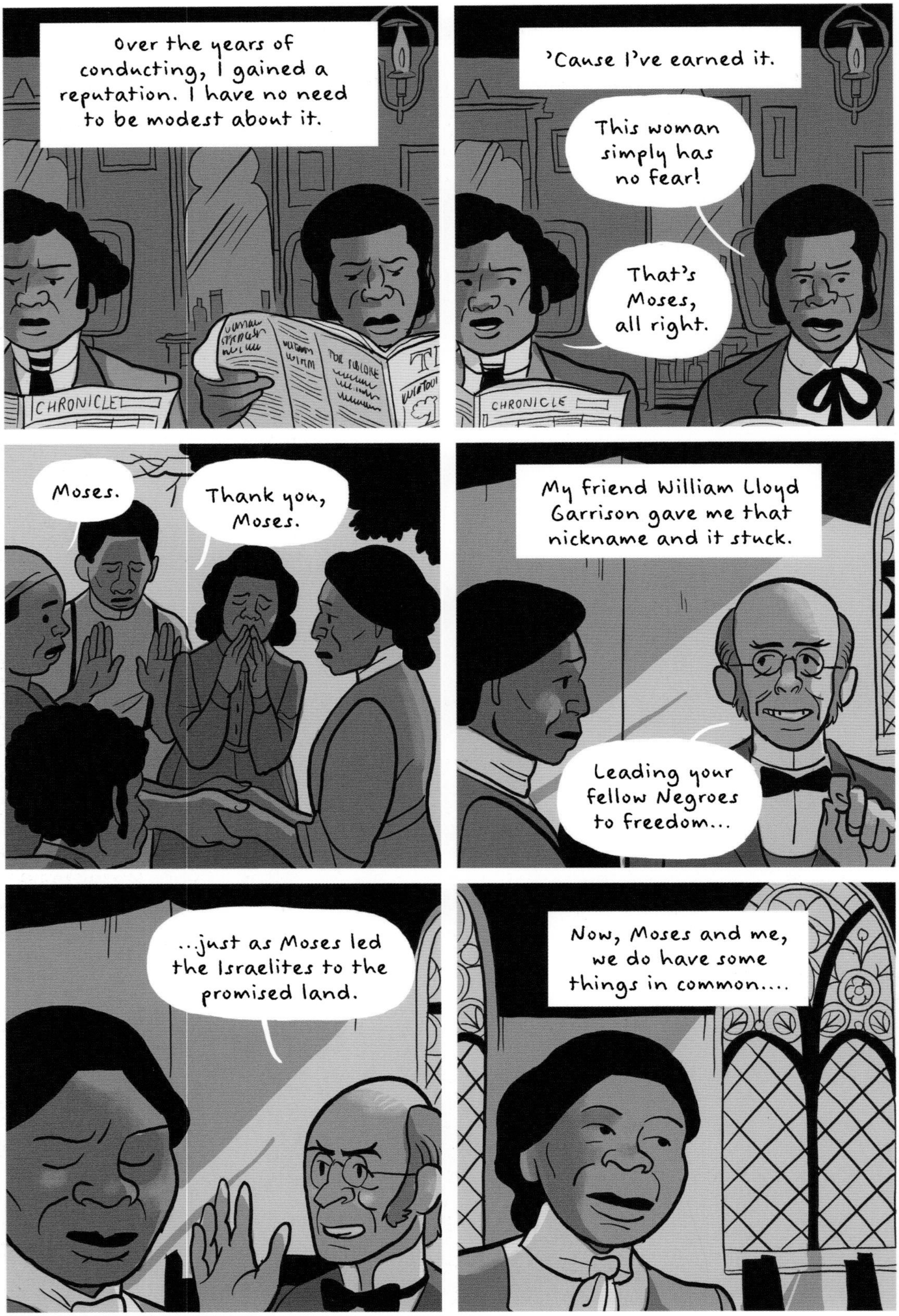
Over the years of conducting, I gained a reputation. I have no need to be modest about it.
CHRONICLE
'Cause I've earned it.
This woman simply has no fear!
That's Moses, all right.
CHRONICLE
Moses.
Thank you, Moses.
My friend William Lloyd Garrison gave me that nickname and it stuck.
Leading your fellow Negroes to freedom...
...just as Moses led the Israelites to the promised land.
Now, Moses and me, we do have some things in common....

We take our orders directly from God.

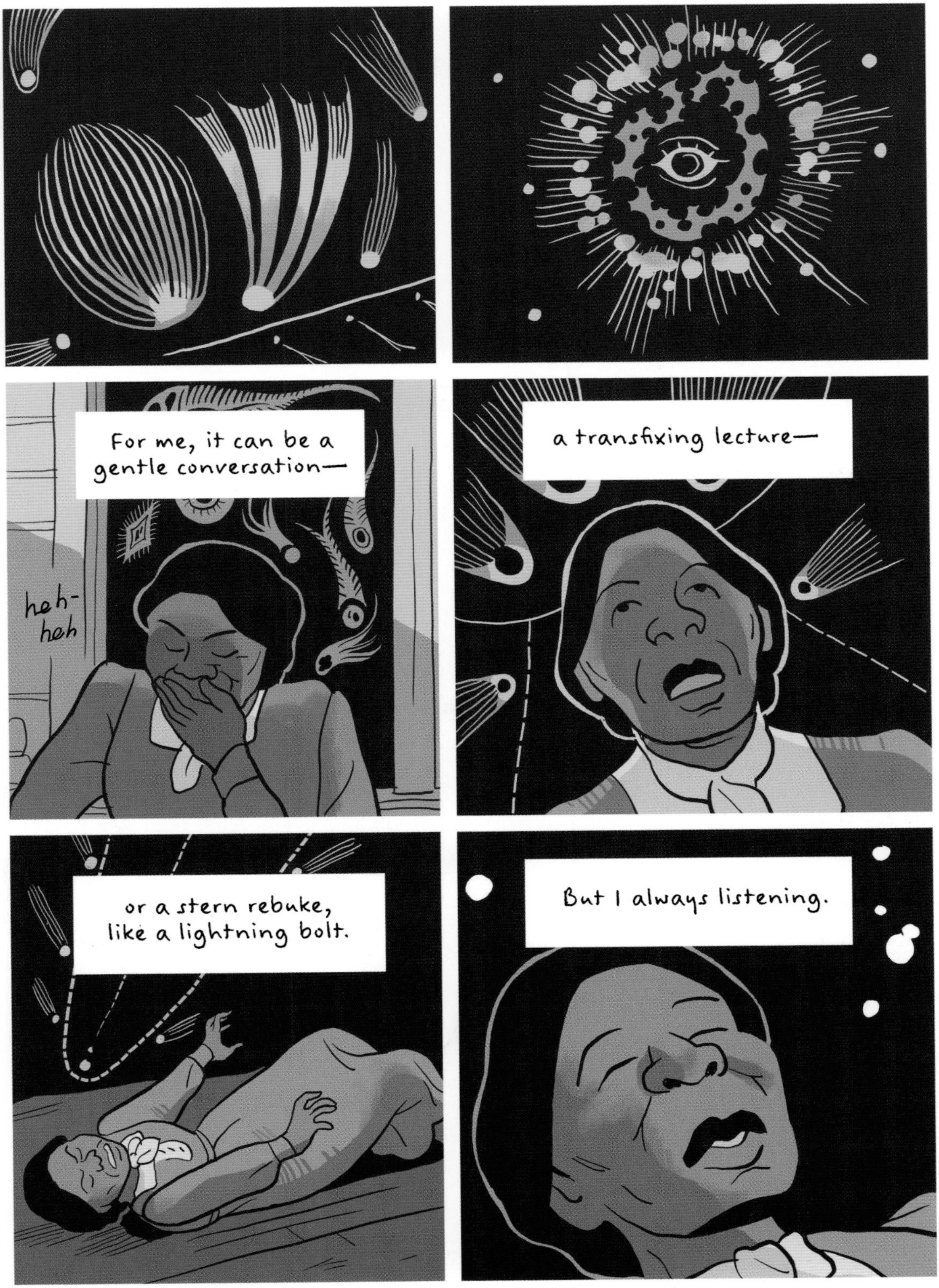
For me, it can be a gentle conversation—
heh-heh
a transfixing lecture—
or a stern rebuke, like a lightning bolt.
But I always listening.

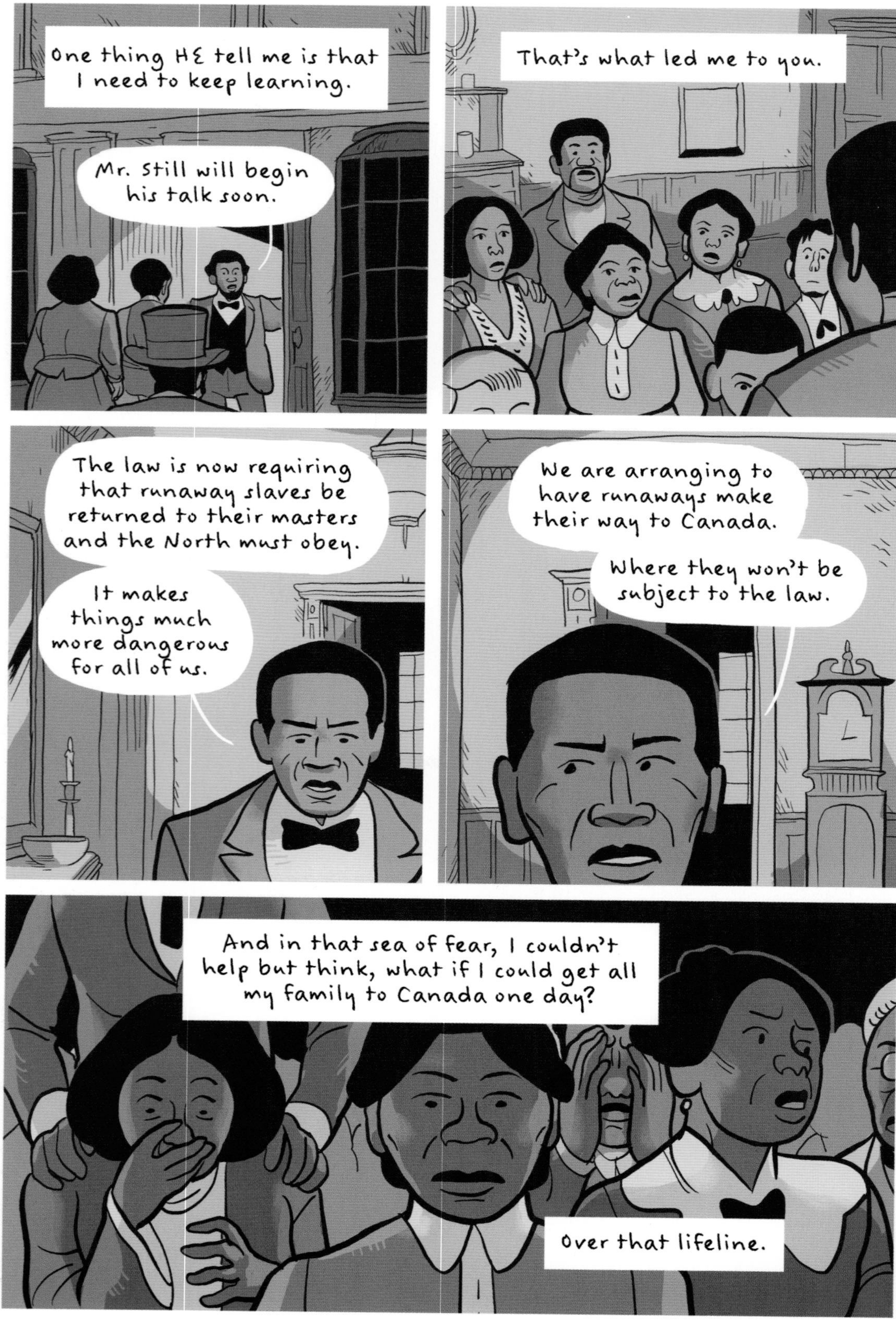
One thing HE tell me is that I need to keep learning.
Mr. Still will begin his talk soon.
That's what led me to you.
The law is now requiring that runaway slaves be returned to their masters and the North must obey.
It makes things much more dangerous for all of us.
We are arranging to have runaways make their way to Canada.
Where they won't be subject to the law.
And in that sea of fear, I couldn't help but think, what if I could get all my family to Canada one day?
Over that lifeline.

1854, PHILADELPHIA.

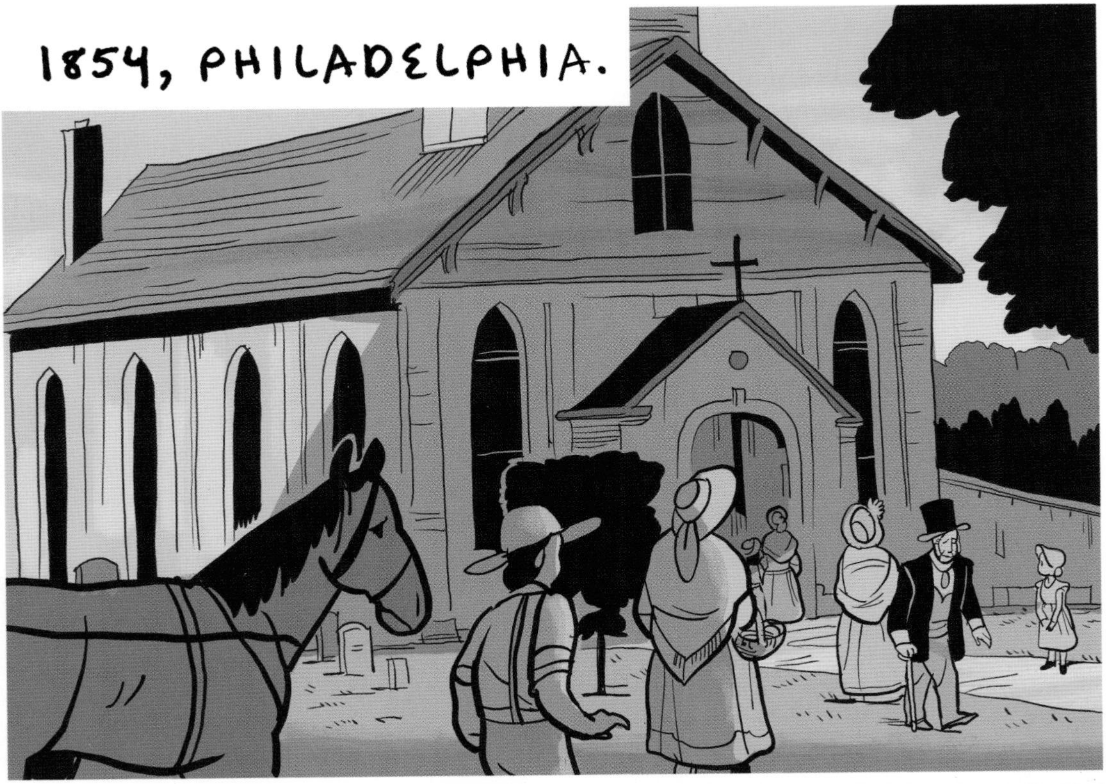

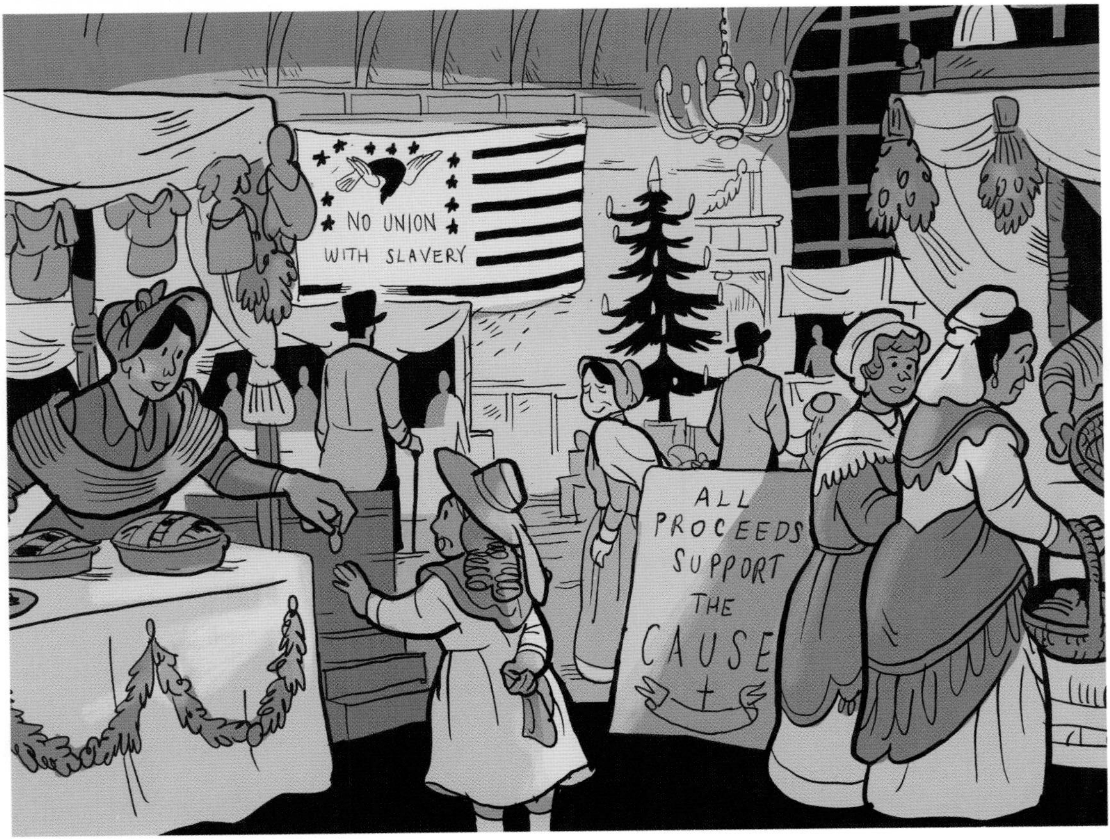
NO UNION WITH SLAVERY
ALL PROCEEDS SUPPORT THE CAUSE

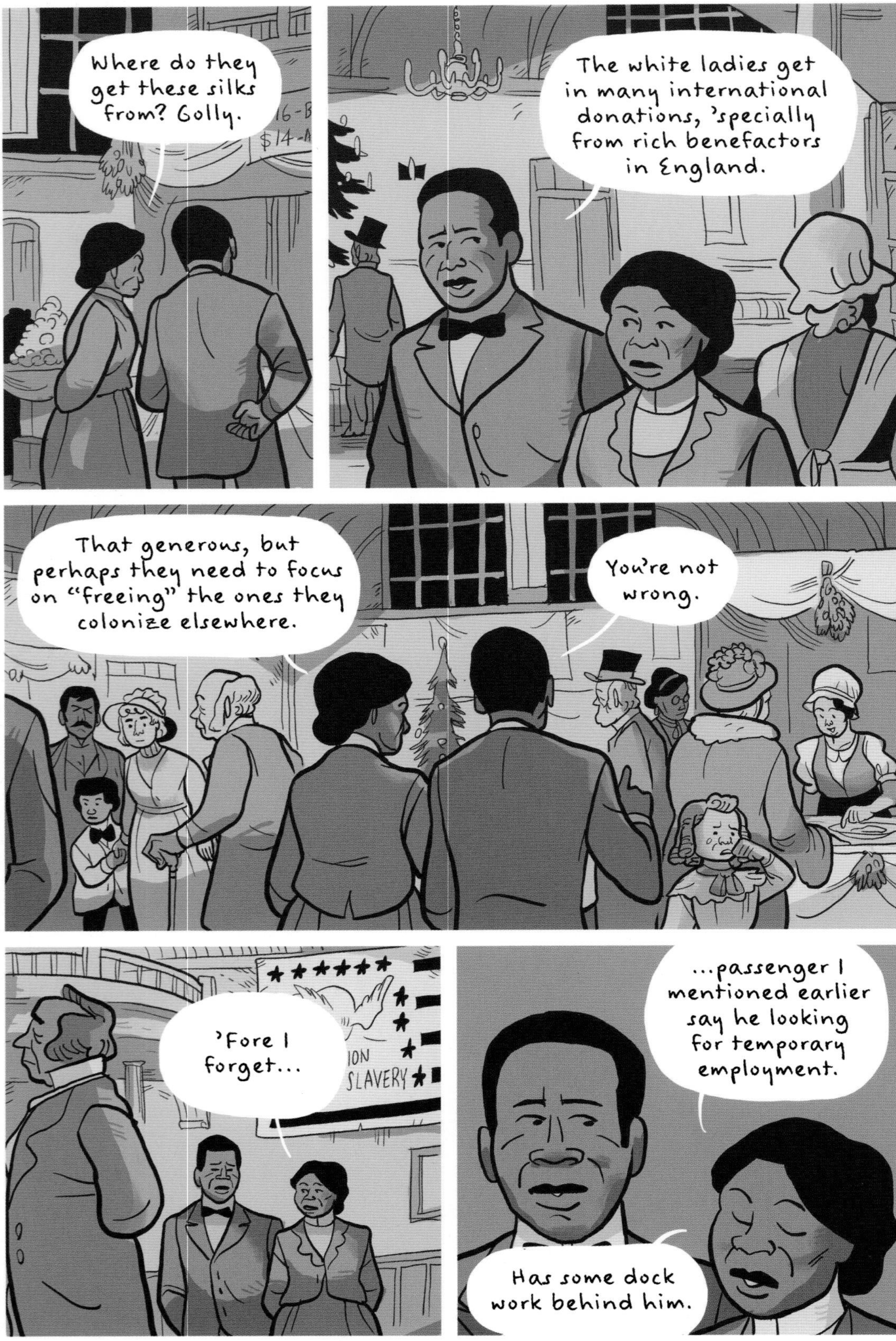
Where do they get these silks from? Golly.
The white ladies get in many international donations, 'specially from rich benefactors in England.
That generous, but perhaps they need to focus on "freeing" the ones they colonize elsewhere.
You're not wrong.
'Fore I forget...
SLAVERY
...passenger I mentioned earlier say he looking for temporary employment.
Has some dock work behind him.

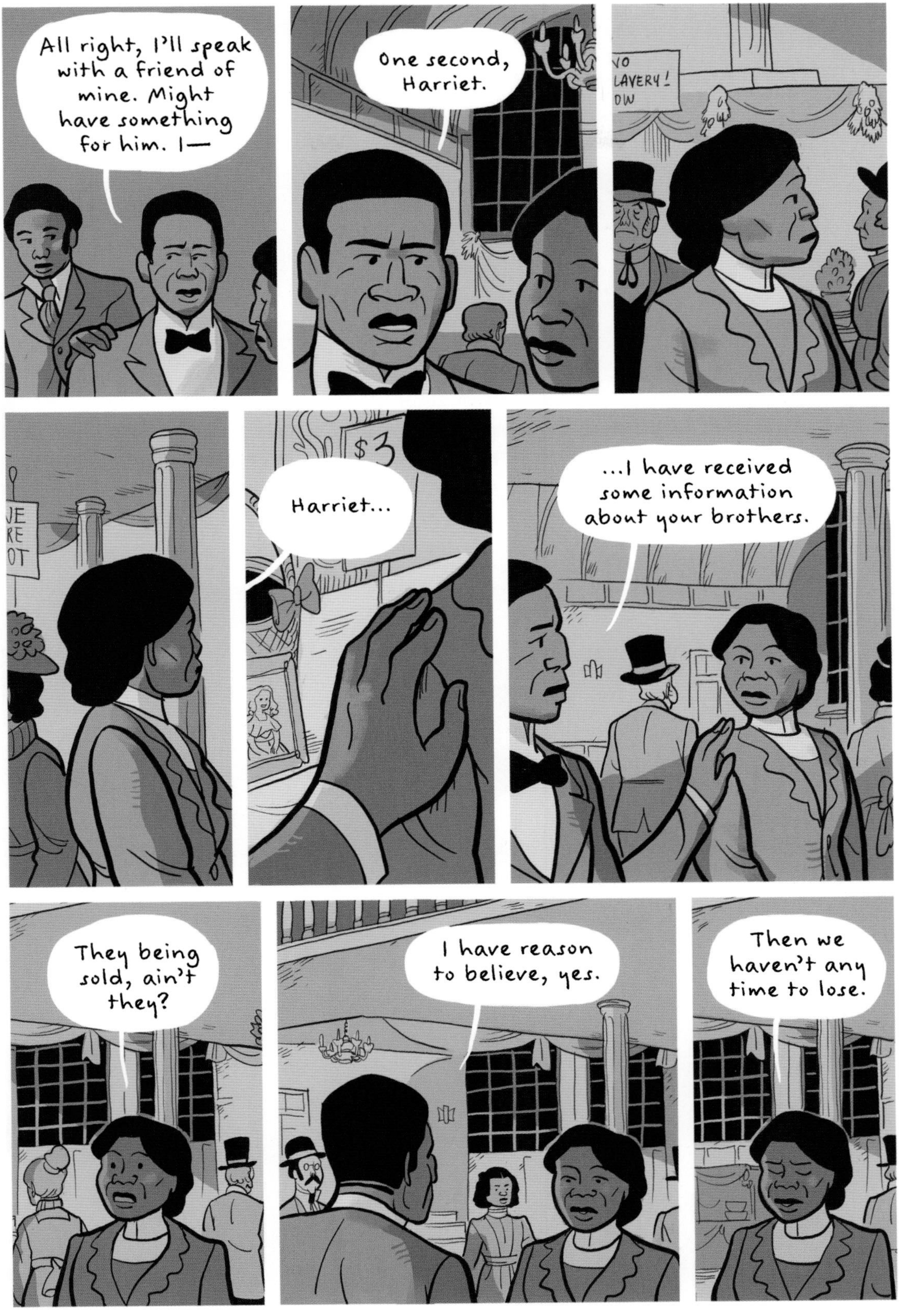
All right, I'll speak with a friend of mine. Might have something for him. I—
One second, Harriet.
NO SLAVERY! NOW
Harriet...
$3
...I have received some information about your brothers.
They being sold, ain't they?
I have reason to believe, yes.
Then we haven't any time to lose.

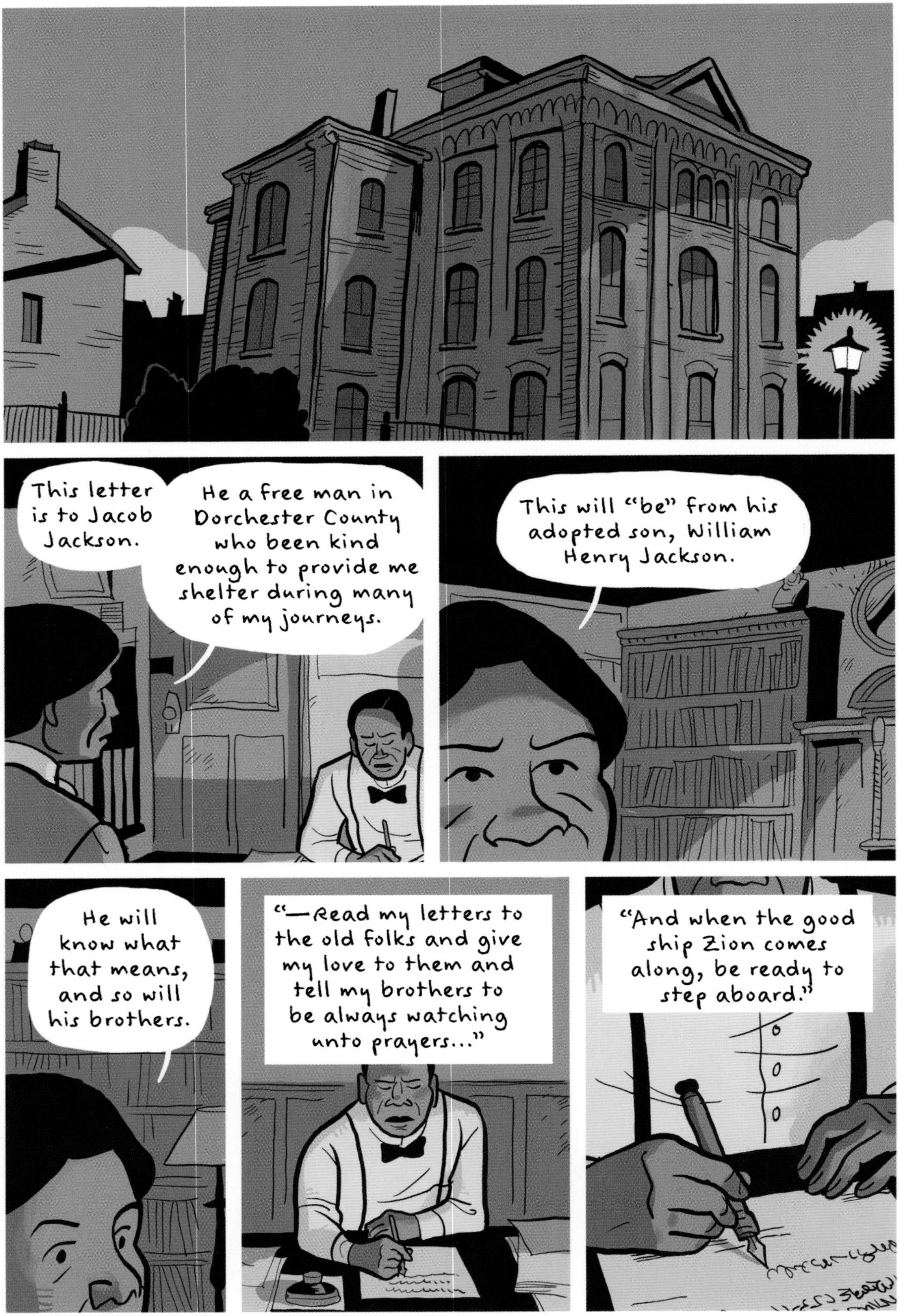
This letter is to Jacob Jackson.
He a free man in Dorchester County who been kind enough to provide me shelter during many of my journeys.
This will "be" from his adopted son, William Henry Jackson.
He will know what that means, and so will his brothers.
"—Read my letters to the old folks and give my love to them and tell my brothers to be always watching unto prayers..."
"And when the good ship Zion comes along, be ready to step aboard."

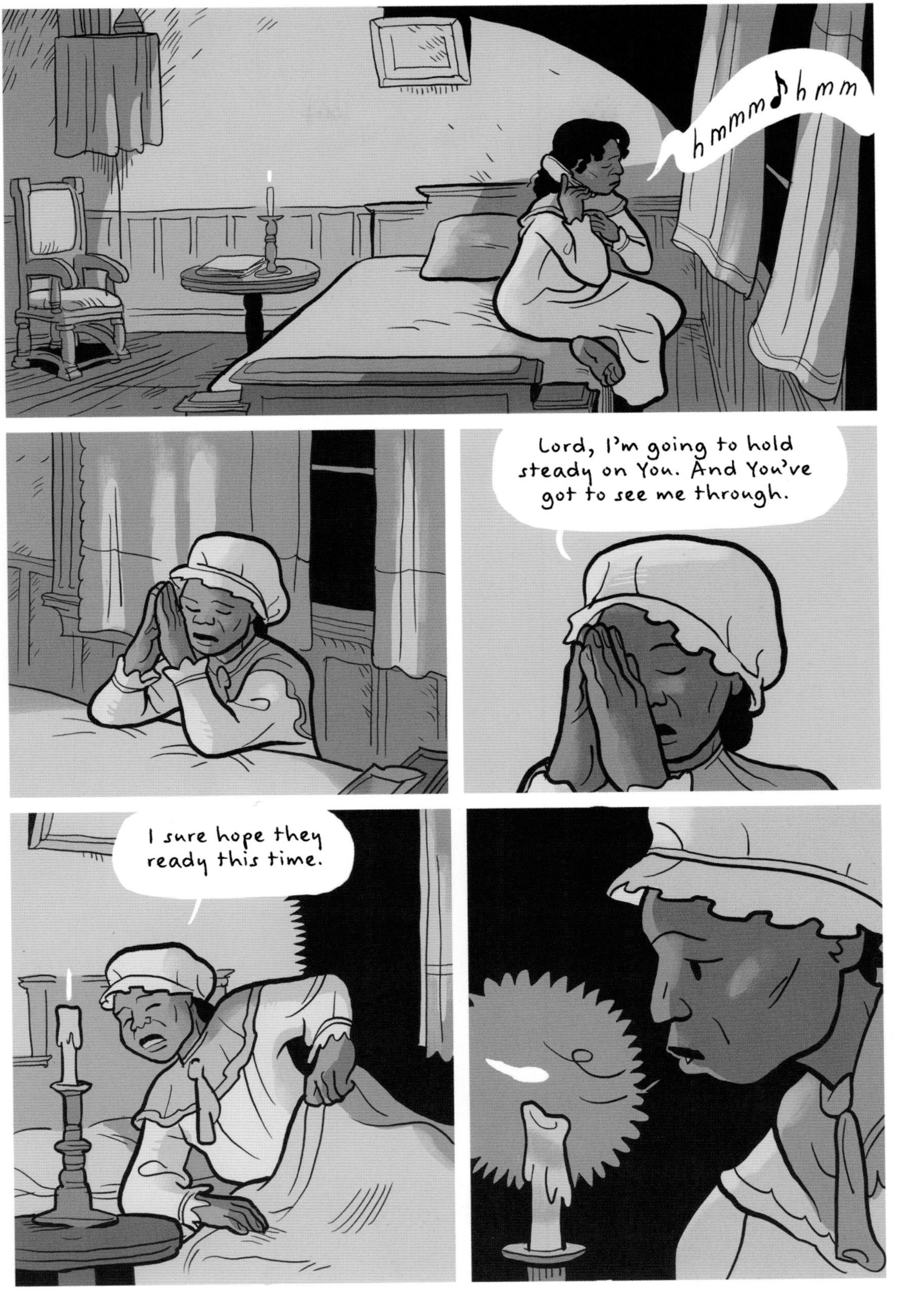
hmmm♪hmm
Lord, I'm going to hold steady on You. And You've got to see me through.
I sure hope they ready this time.

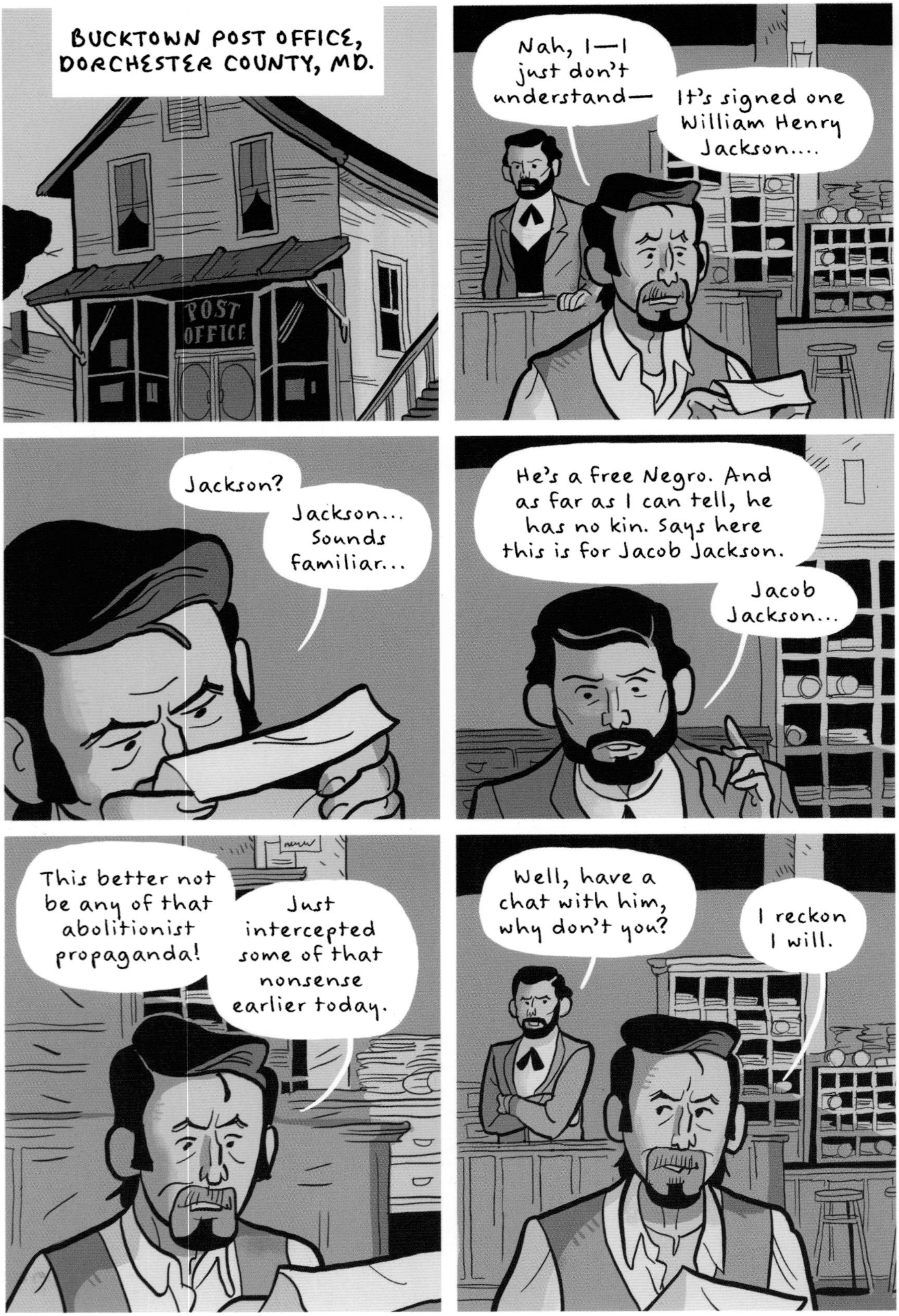
BUCKTOWN POST OFFICE, DORCHESTER COUNTY, MD.
POST OFFICE
Nah, I—I just don't understand—
It's signed one William Henry Jackson....
Jackson?
Jackson... Sounds familiar...
He's a free Negro. And as far as I can tell, he has no kin. Says here this is for Jacob Jackson.
Jacob Jackson...
This better not be any of that abolitionist propaganda!
Just intercepted some of that nonsense earlier today.
Well, have a chat with him, why don't you?
I reckon I will.

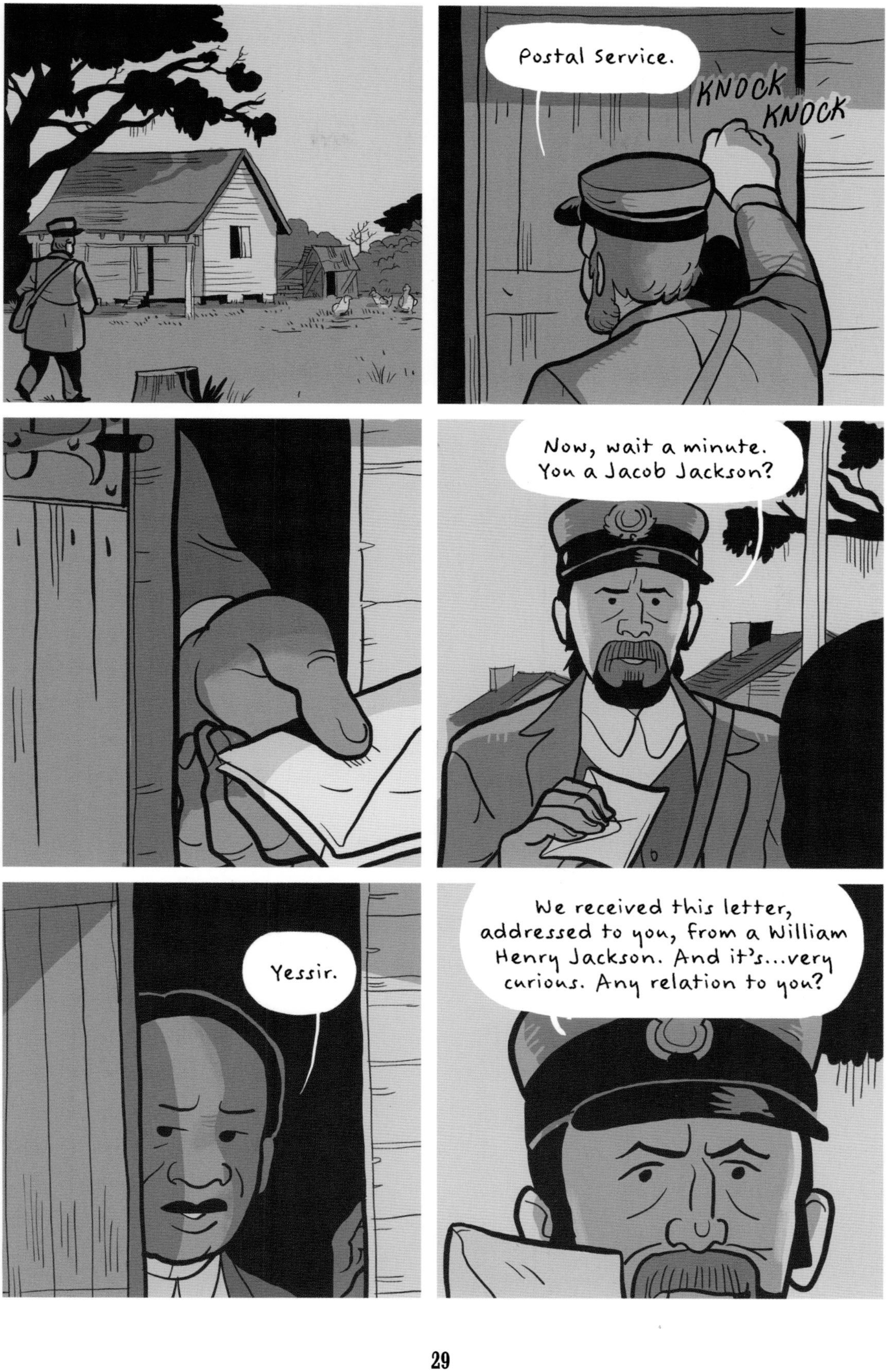
Postal Service.
KNOCK KNOCK
Now, wait a minute. You a Jacob Jackson?
Yessir.
We received this letter, addressed to you, from a William Henry Jackson. And it's...very curious. Any relation to you?

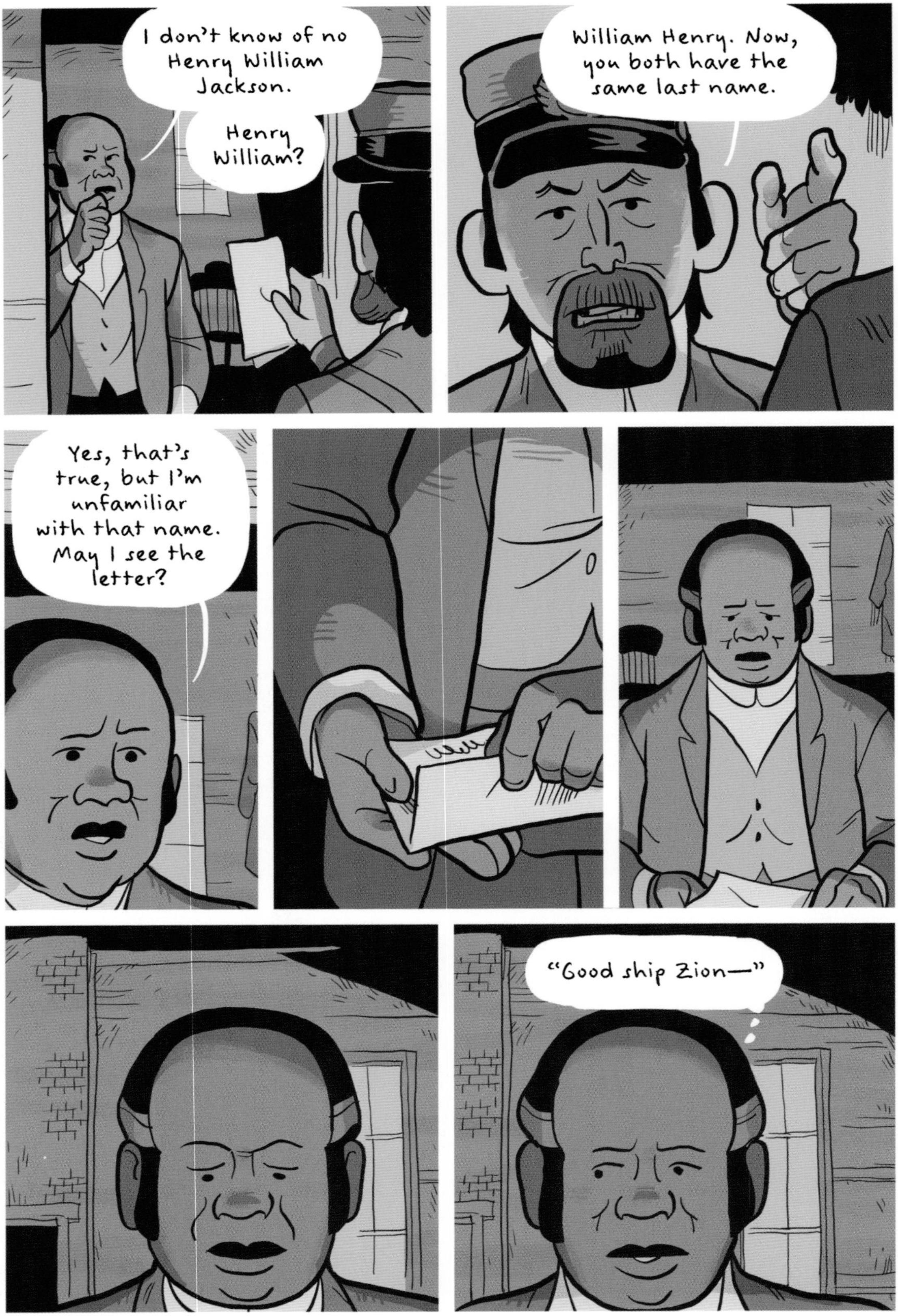
I don't know of no Henry William Jackson.
Henry William?
William Henry. Now, you both have the same last name.
Yes, that's true, but I'm unfamiliar with that name. May I see the letter?
"Good ship Zion—"

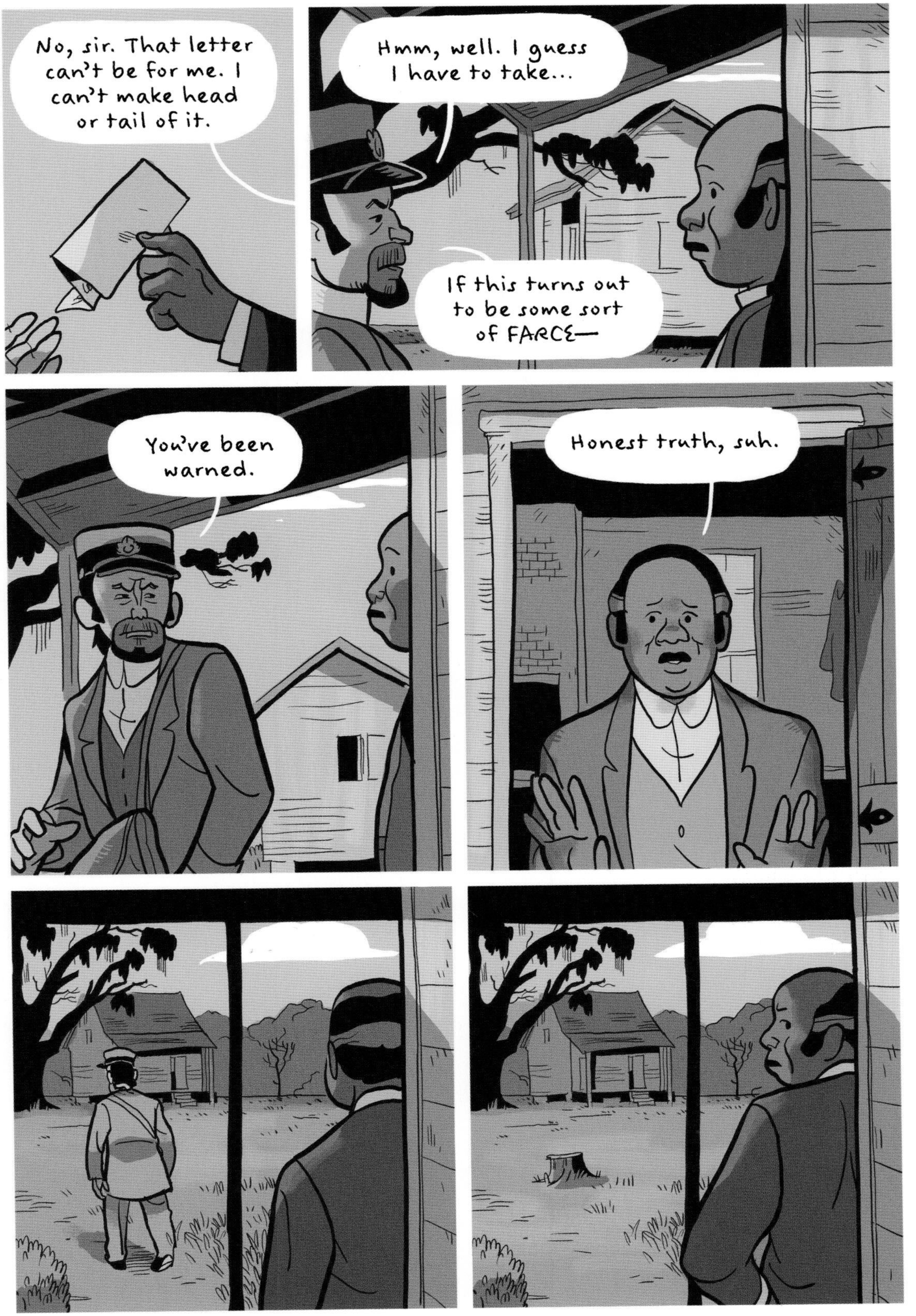
No, sir. That letter can't be for me. I can't make head or tail of it.
Hmm, well. I guess I have to take...
If this turns out to be some sort of FARCE—
You've been warned.
Honest truth, suh.

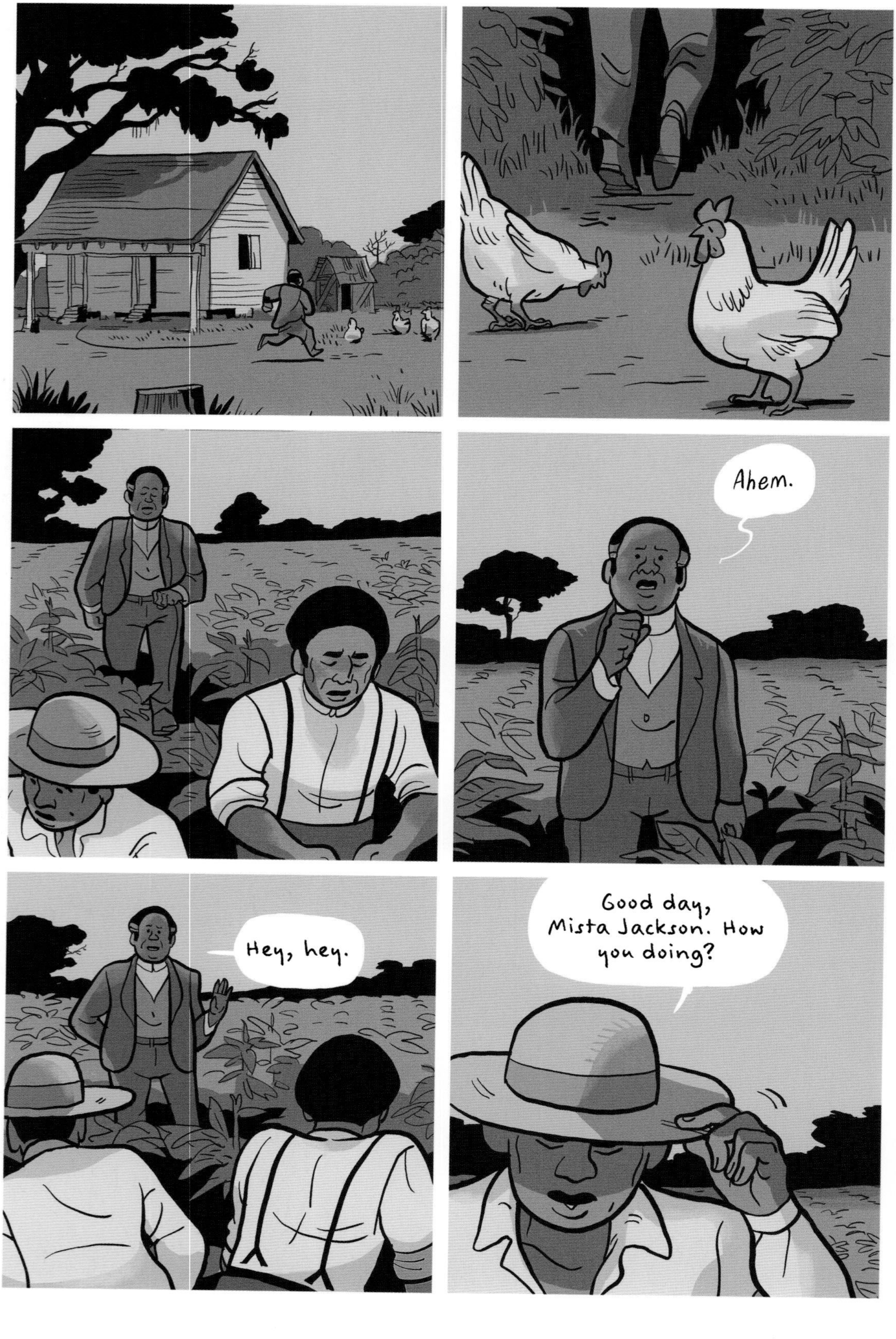
Ahem.
Hey, hey.
Good day, Mista Jackson. How you doing?

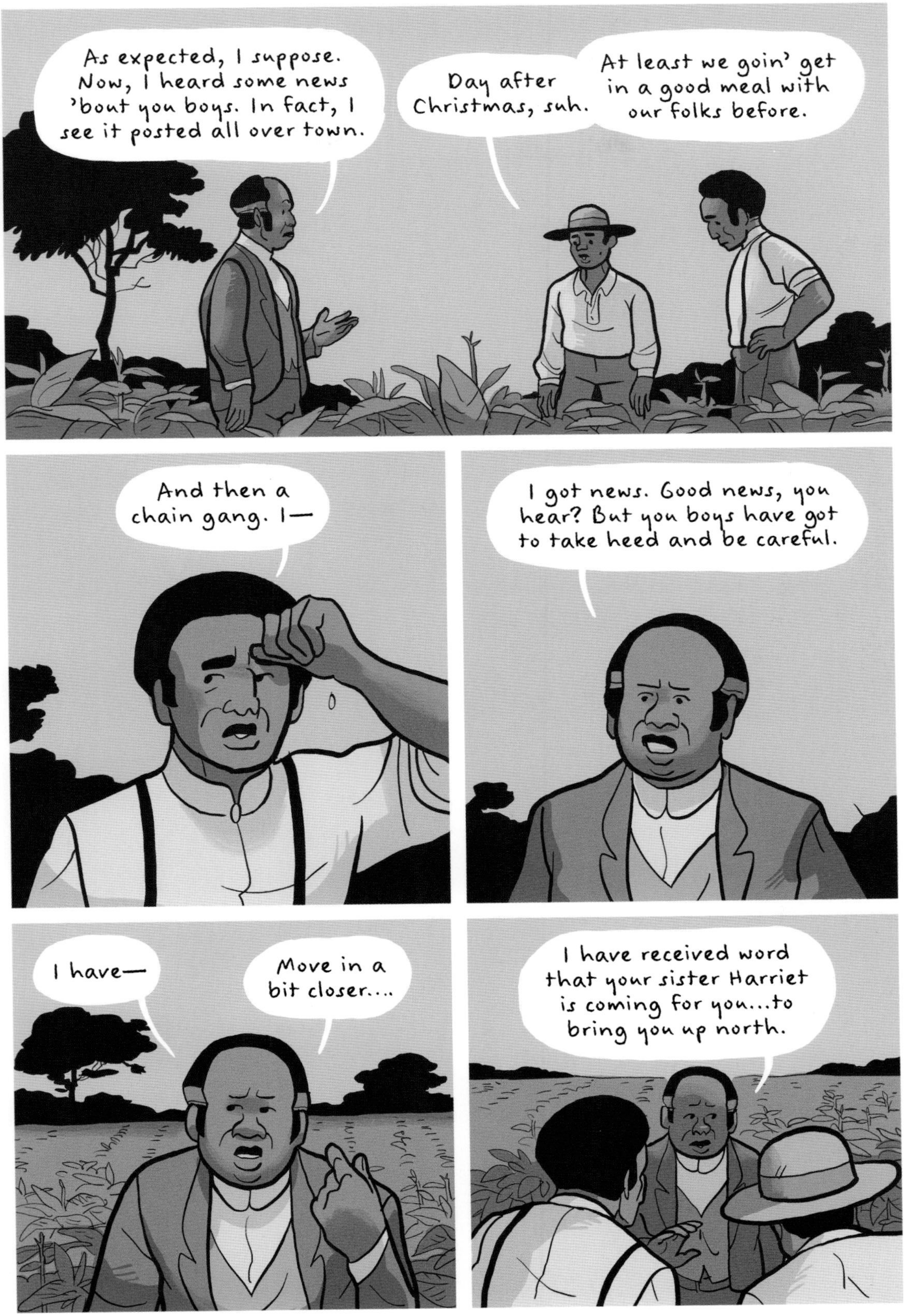
As expected, I suppose. Now, I heard some news 'bout you boys. In fact, I see it posted all over town.
Day after Christmas, suh.
At least we goin' get in a good meal with our folks before.
And then a chain gang. I—
I got news. Good news, you hear? But you boys have got to take heed and be careful.
I have—
Move in a bit closer....
I have received word that your sister Harriet is coming for you...to bring you up north.

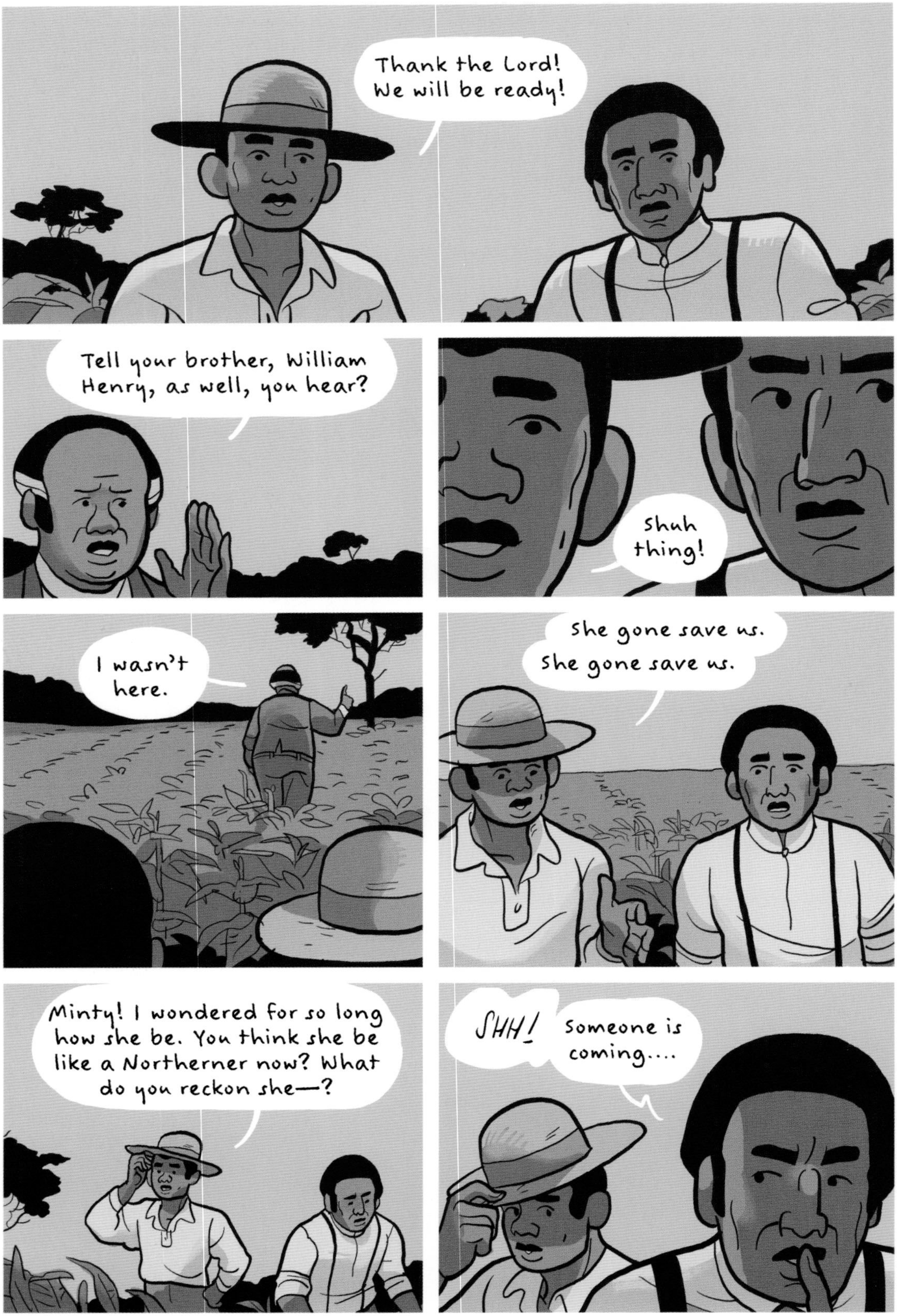
Thank the Lord! We will be ready!
Tell your brother, William Henry, as well, you hear?
Shuh thing!
I wasn't here.
She gone save us. She gone save us.
Minty! I wondered for so long how she be. You think she be like a Northerner now? What do you reckon she—?
SHH!
Someone is coming....

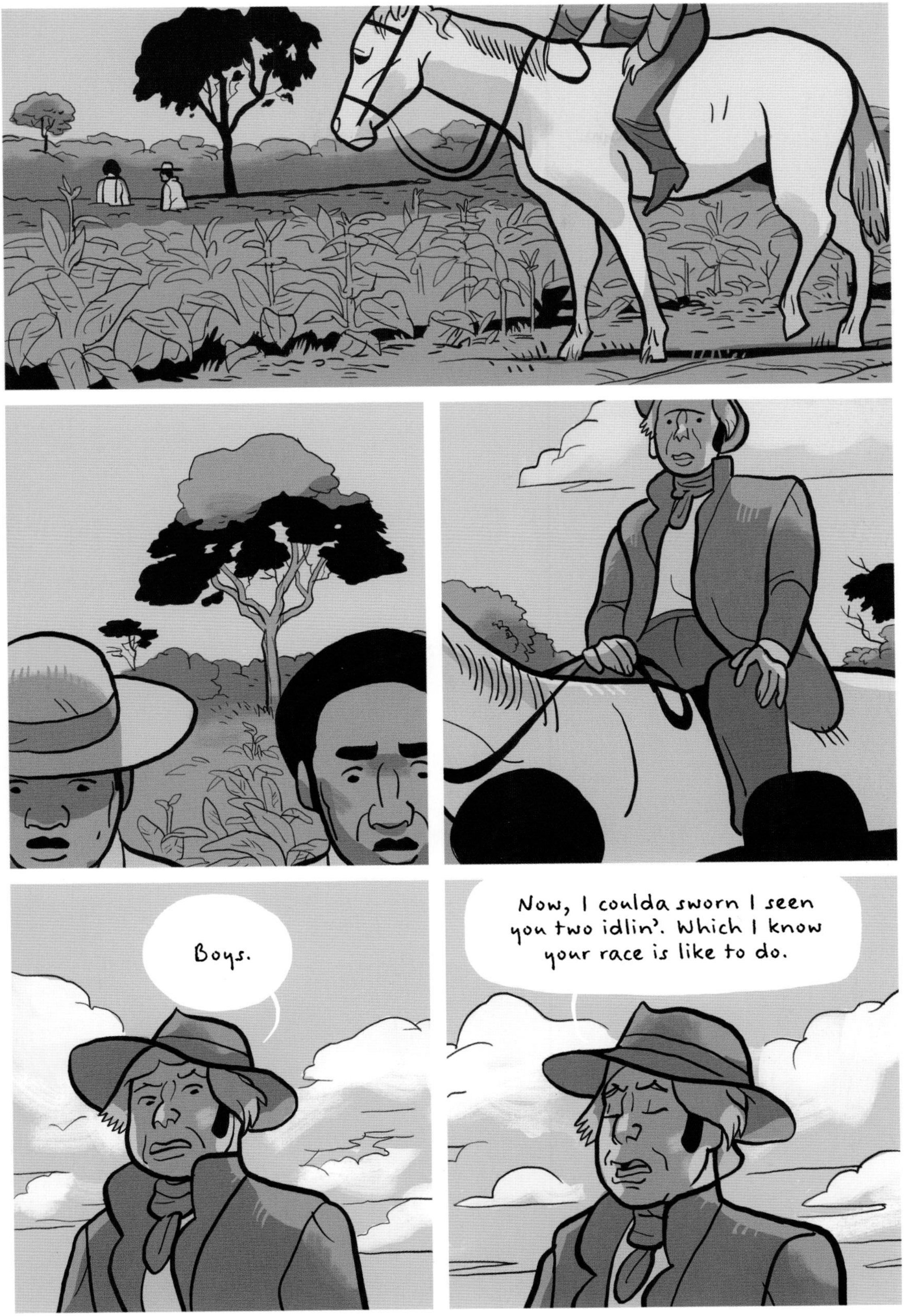
Boys.
Now, I coulda sworn I seen you two idlin'. Which I know your race is like to do.

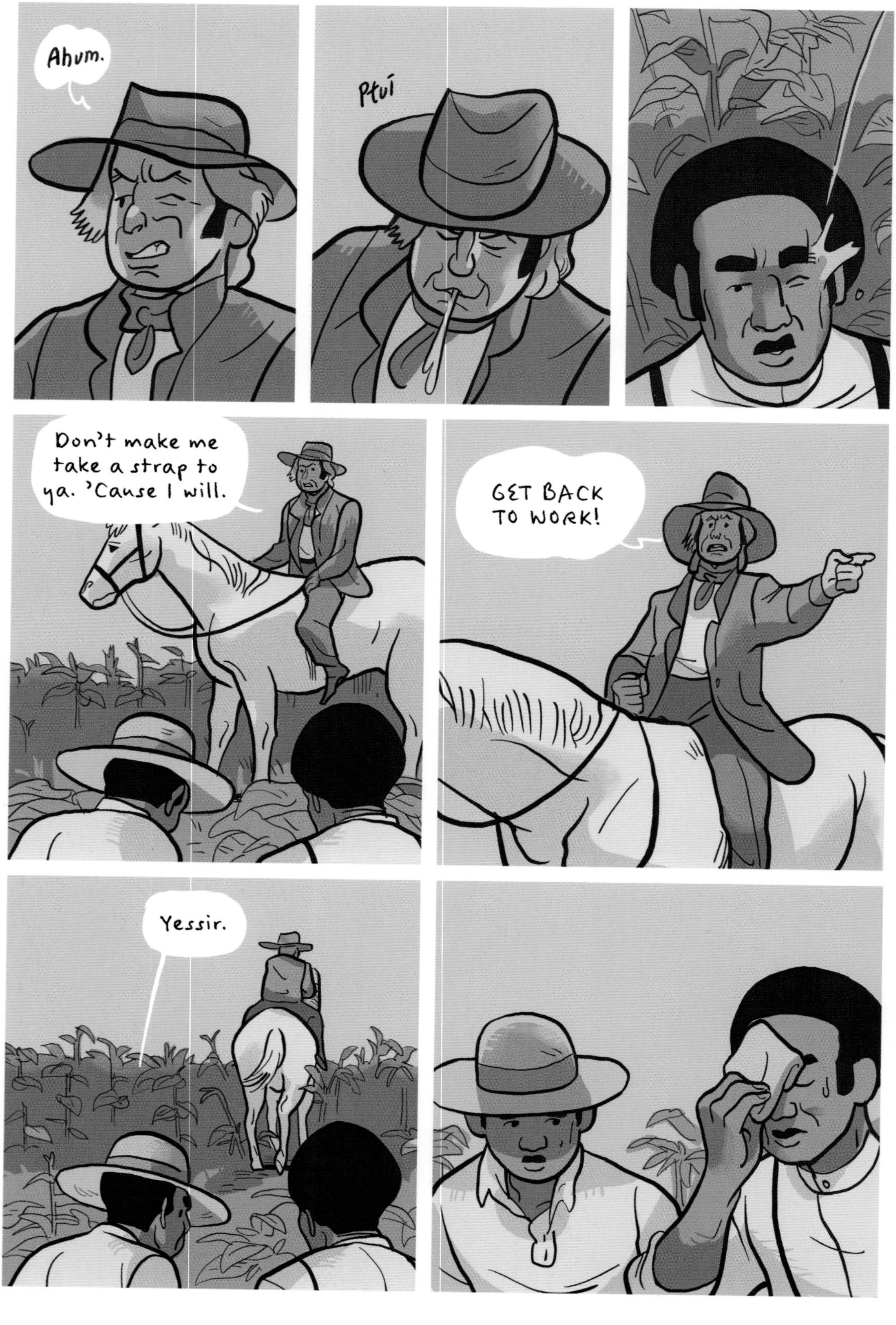
Ahum.
Ptui
Don't make me take a strap to ya. 'Cause I will.
GET BACK TO WORK!
Yessir.

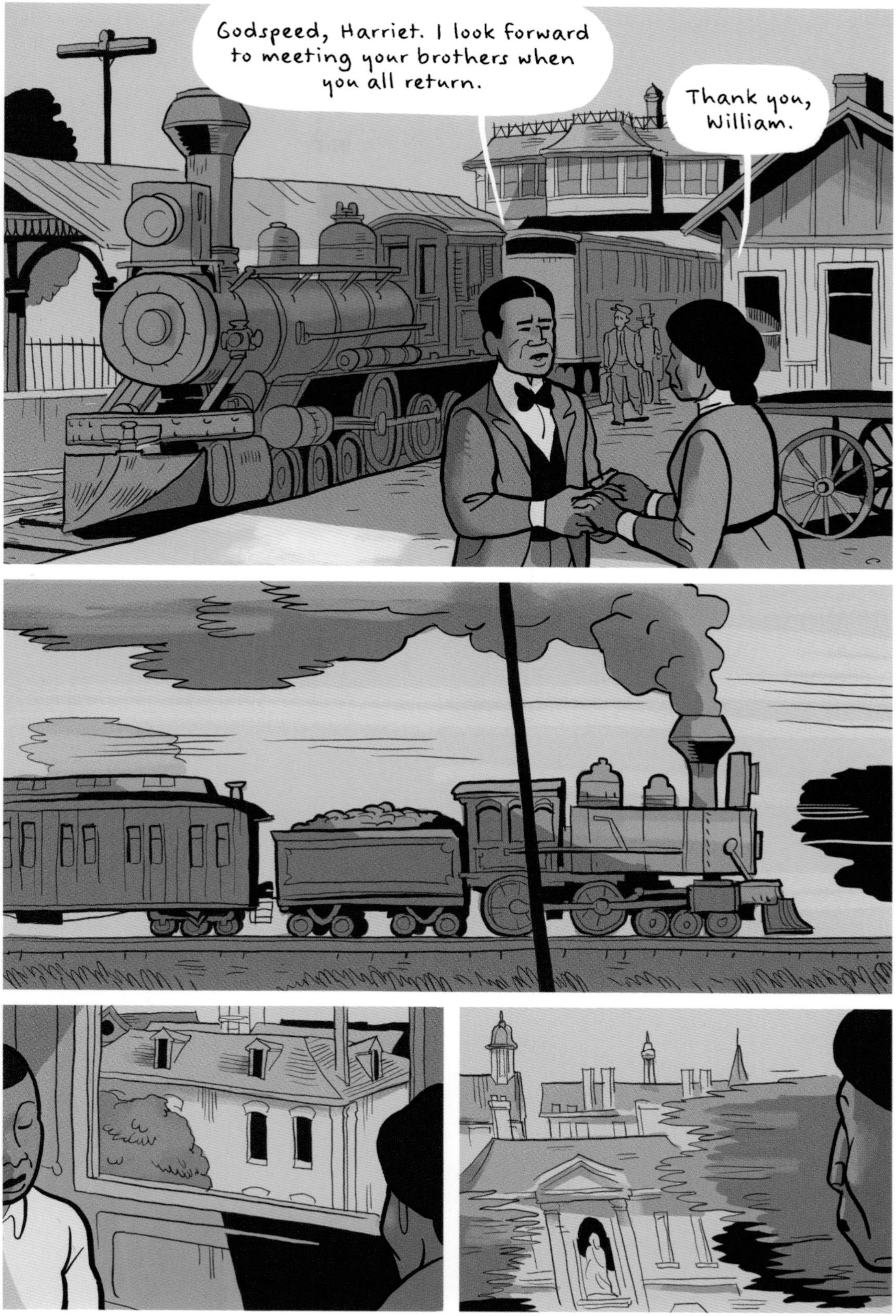
Godspeed, Harriet. I look forward to meeting your brothers when you all return.
Thank you, William.

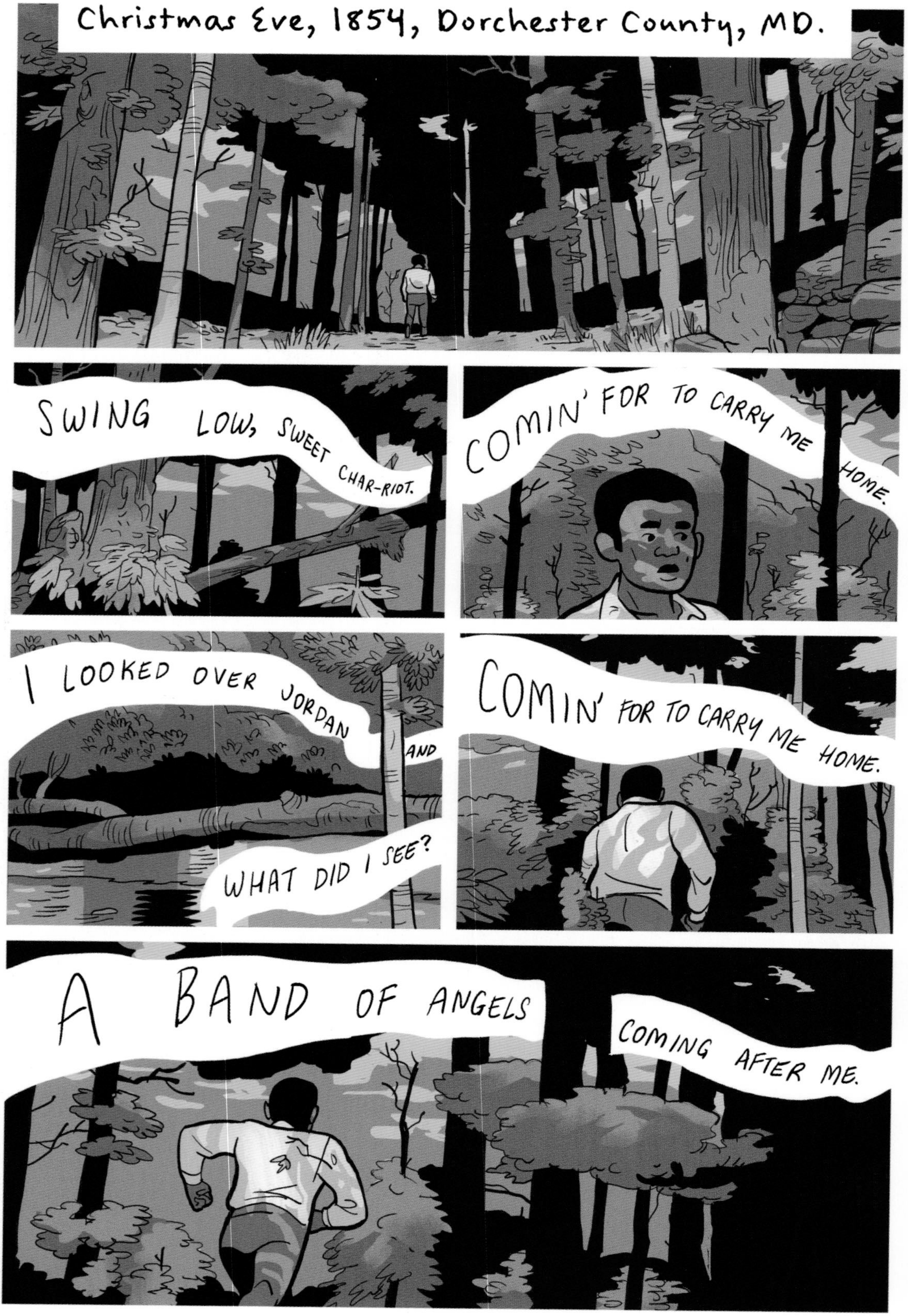
Christmas Eve, 1854, Dorchester County, MD.
SWING LOW, SWEET CHAR-RIOT.
COMIN' FOR TO CARRY ME HOME.
I LOOKED OVER JORDAN AND WHAT DID I SEE?
COMIN' FOR TO CARRY ME HOME.
A BAND OF ANGELS
COMING AFTER ME.

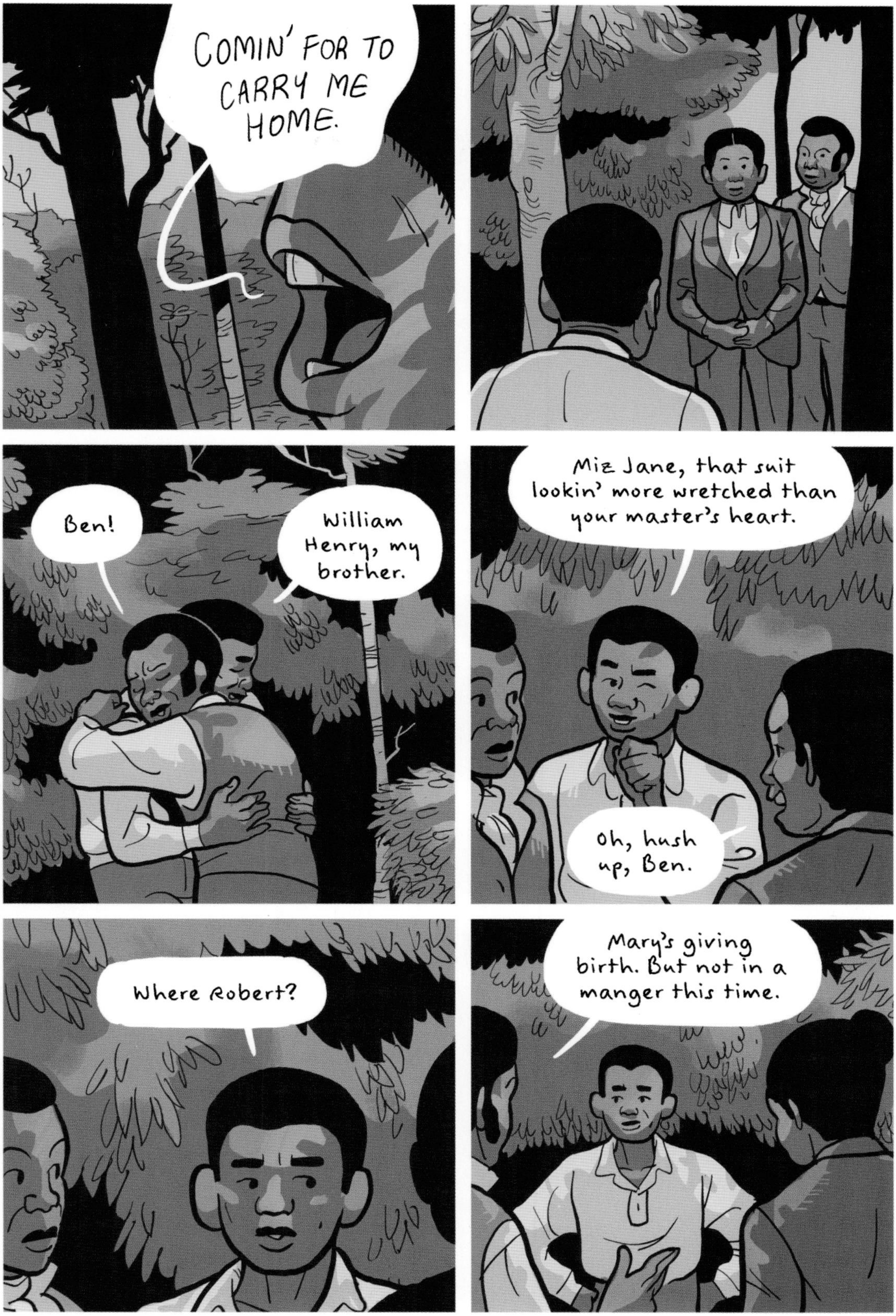
COMIN' FOR TO CARRY ME HOME.
Ben!
William Henry, my brother.
Miz Jane, that suit lookin' more wretched than your master's heart.
Oh, hush up, Ben.
Where Robert?
Mary's giving birth. But not in a manger this time.

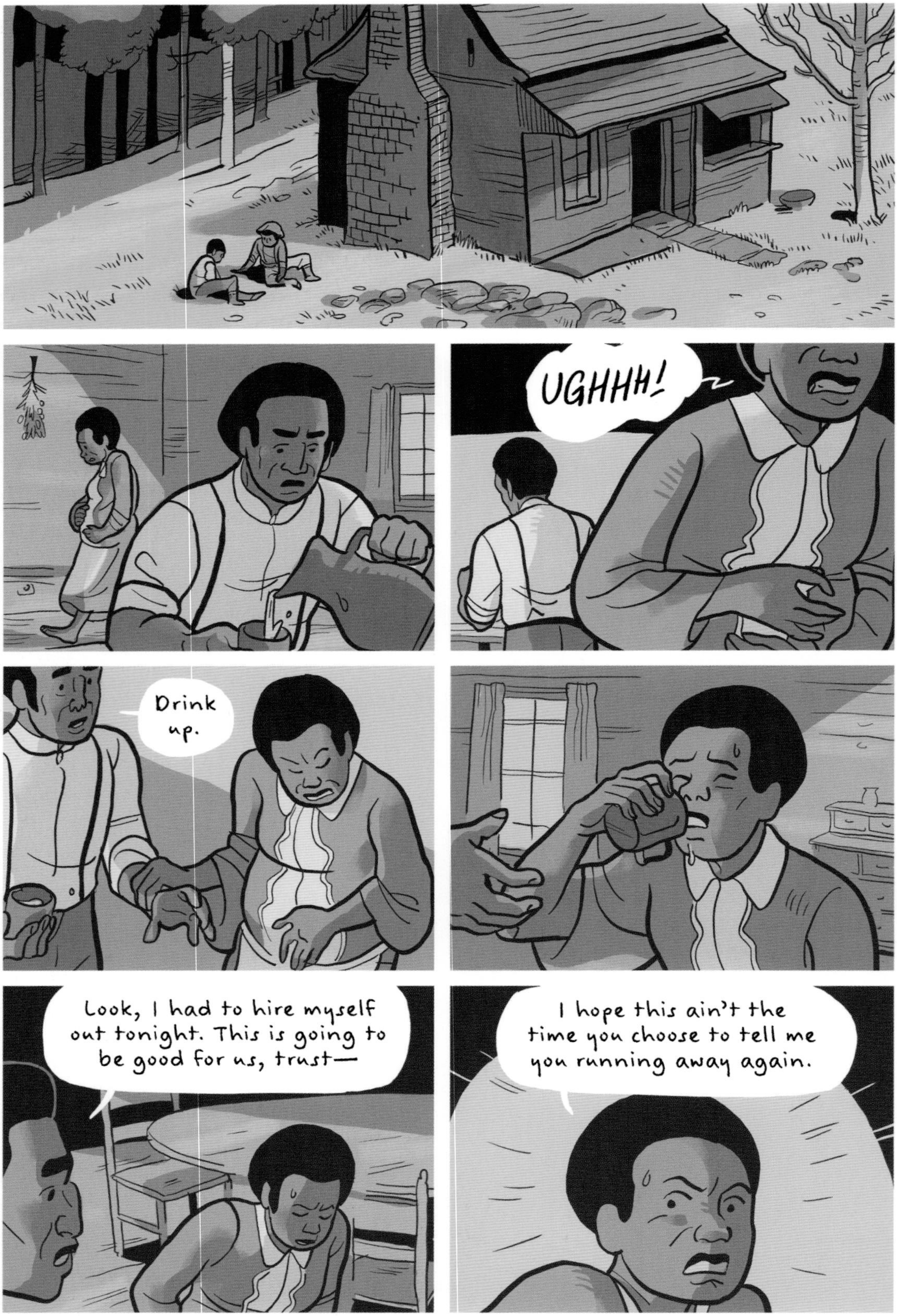
UGHHH!
Drink up.
Look, I had to hire myself out tonight. This is going to be good for us, trust—
I hope this ain't the time you choose to tell me you running away again.

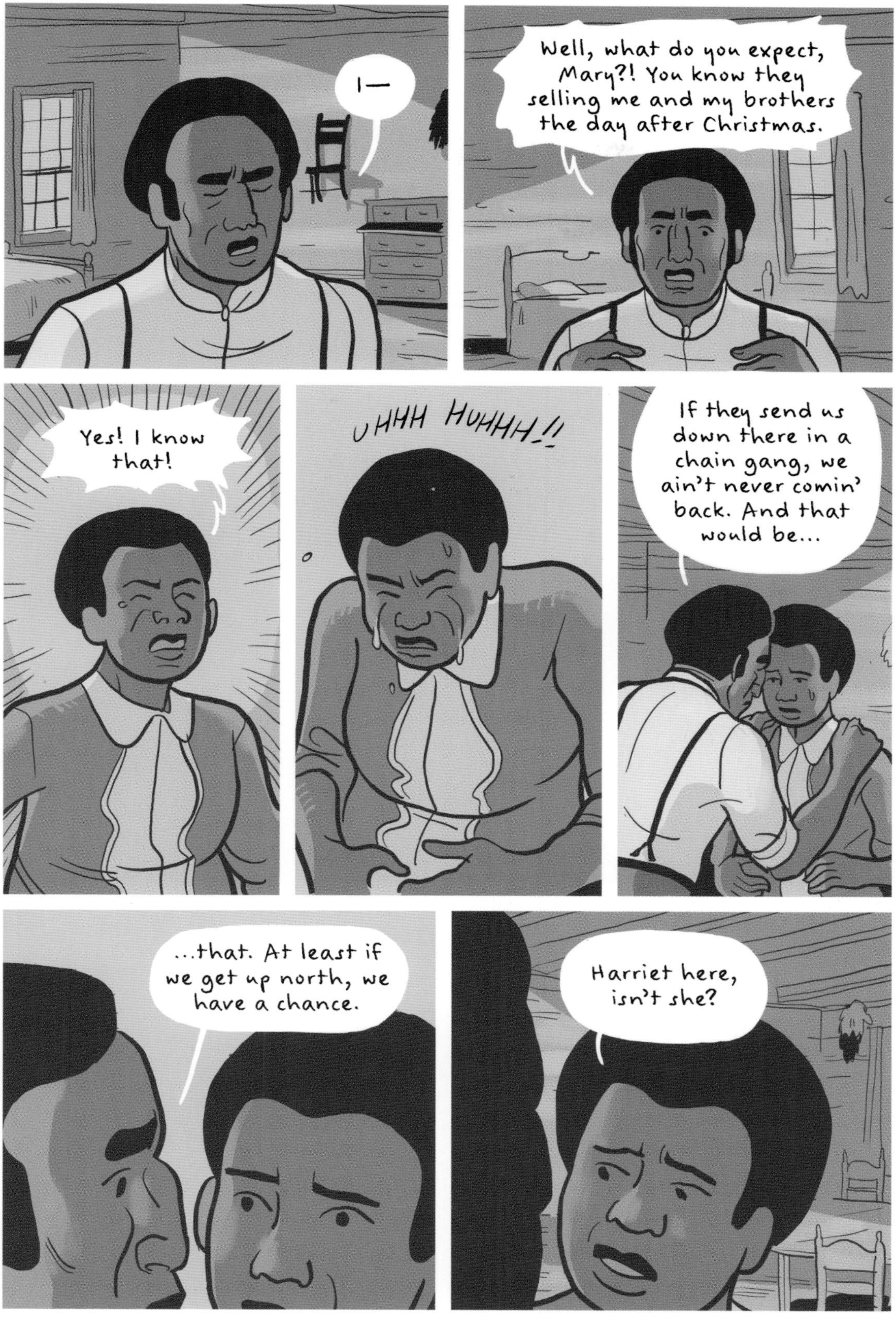
I—
Well, what do you expect, Mary?! You know they selling me and my brothers the day after Christmas.
Yes! I know that!
UHHH HUHHH!!
If they send us down there in a chain gang, we ain't never comin' back. And that would be...
...that. At least if we get up north, we have a chance.
Harriet here, isn't she?

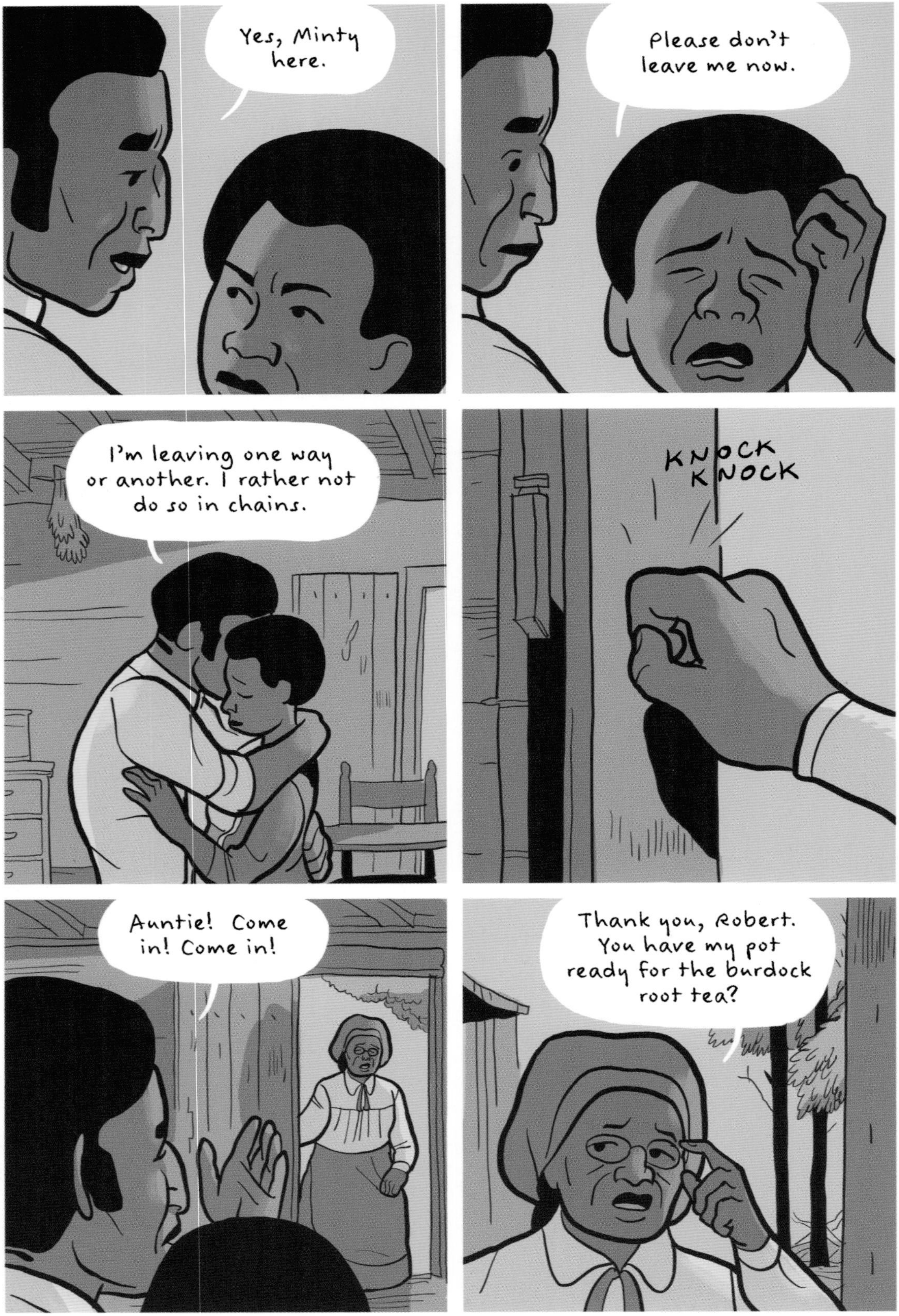
Yes, Minty here.
Please don't leave me now.
I'm leaving one way or another. I rather not do so in chains.
KNOCK KNOCK
Auntie! Come in! Come in!
Thank you, Robert. You have my pot ready for the burdock root tea?

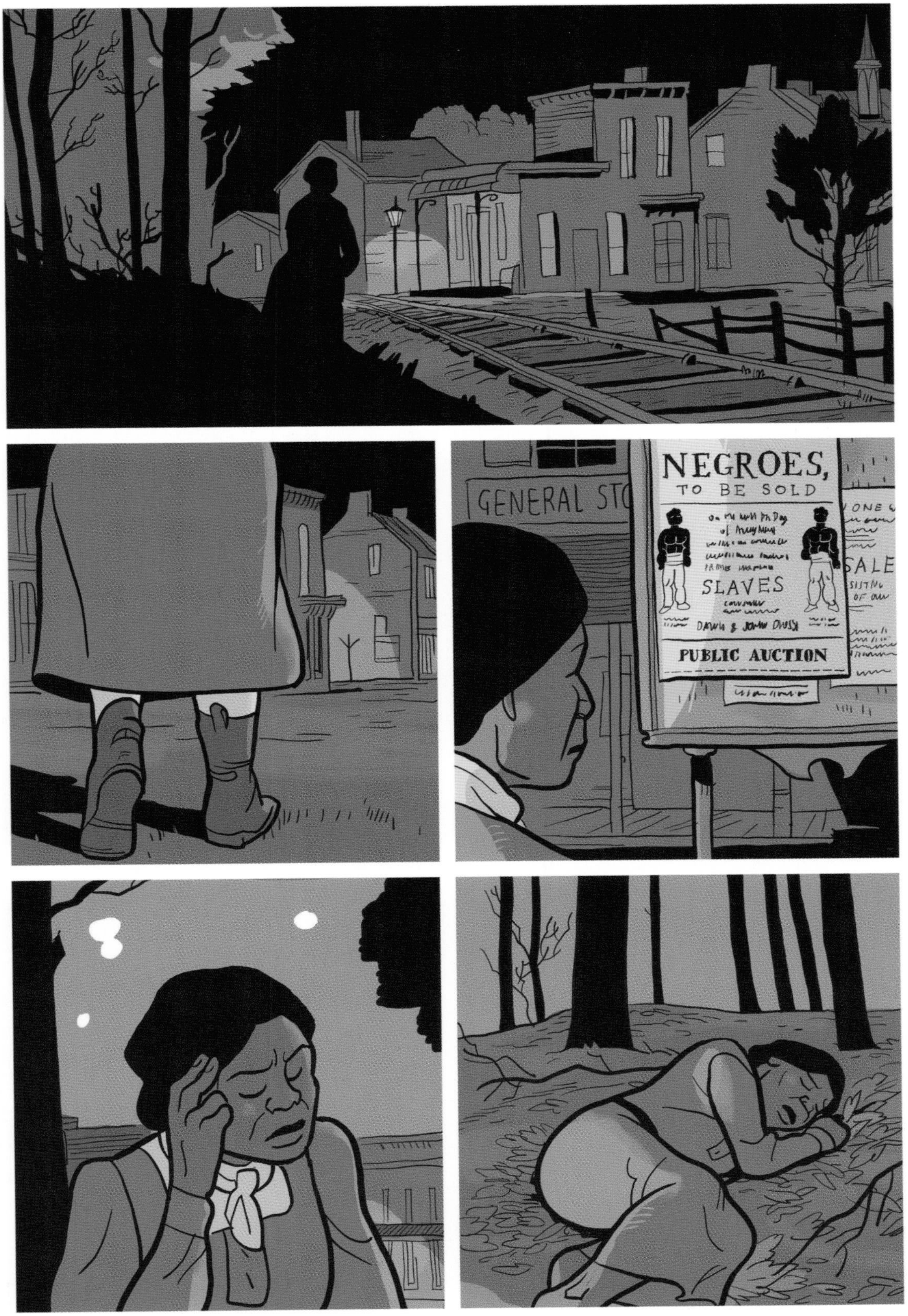
GENERAL STO
NEGROES,
TO BE SOLD
SLAVES
PUBLIC AUCTION
SALE

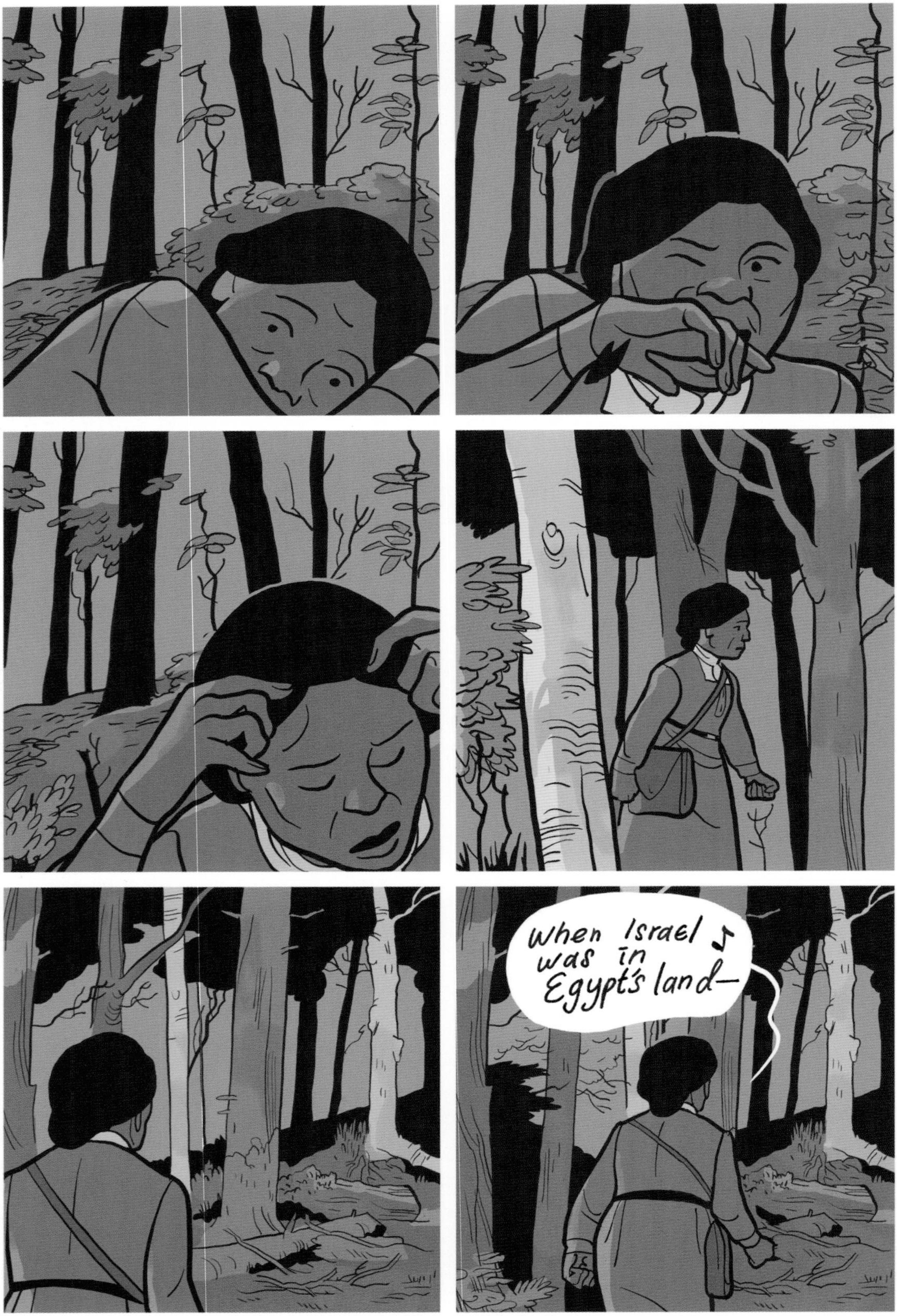
When Israel was in Egypt's land—

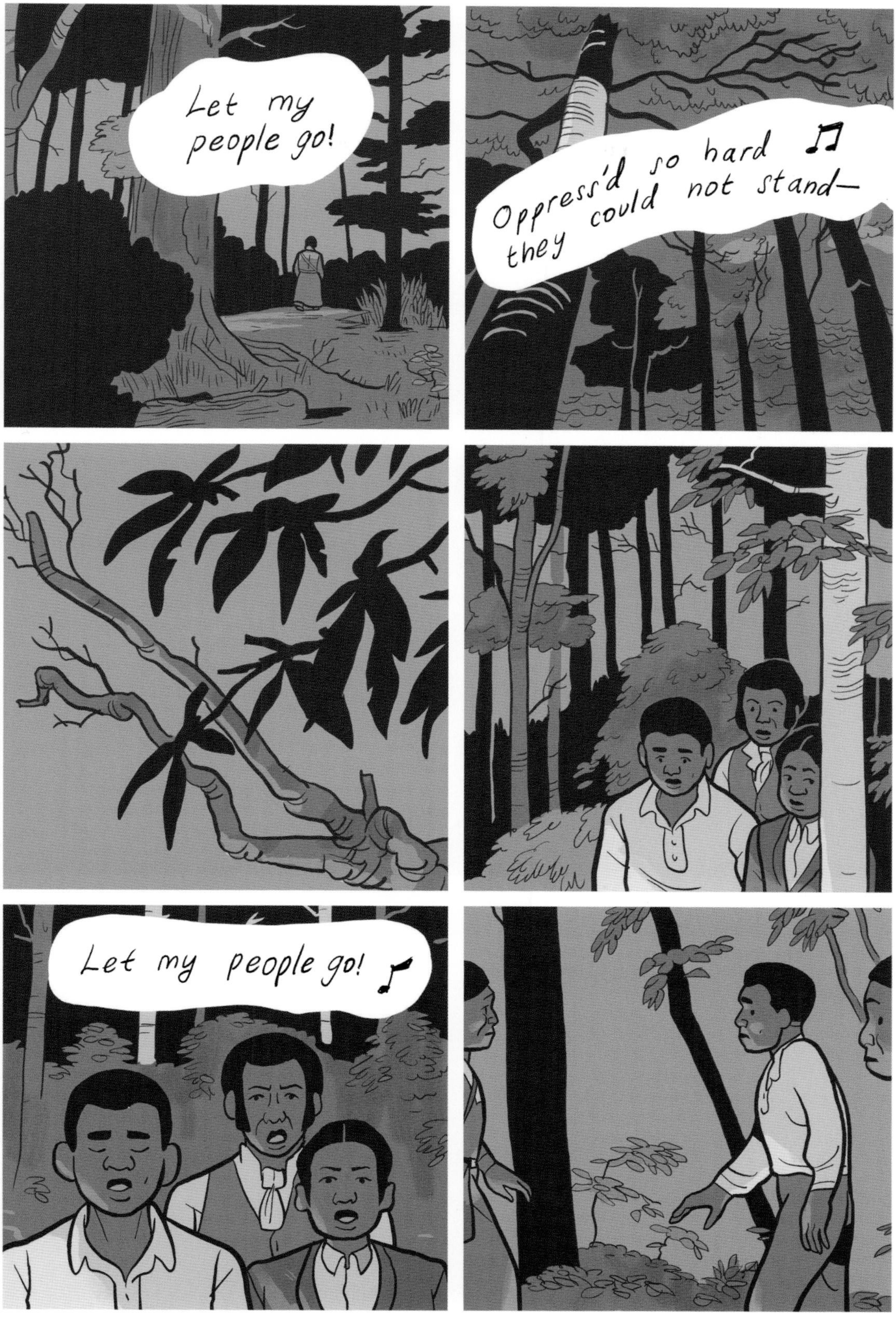
Let my people go!
Oppress'd so hard ♫ they could not stand—
Let my people go! ♪

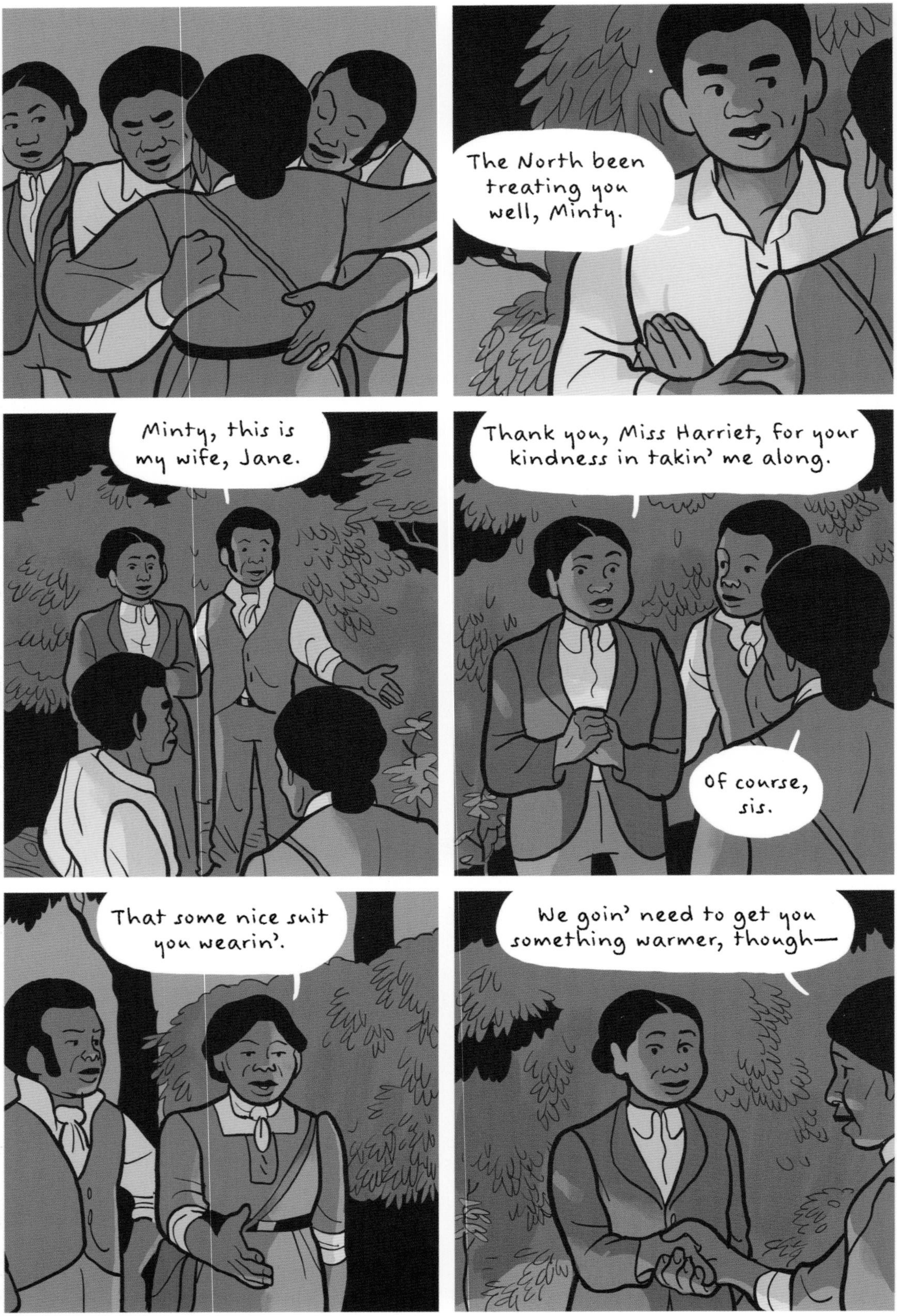
The North been treating you well, Minty.
Minty, this is my wife, Jane.
Thank you, Miss Harriet, for your kindness in takin' me along.
Of course, sis.
That some nice suit you wearin'.
We goin' need to get you something warmer, though—

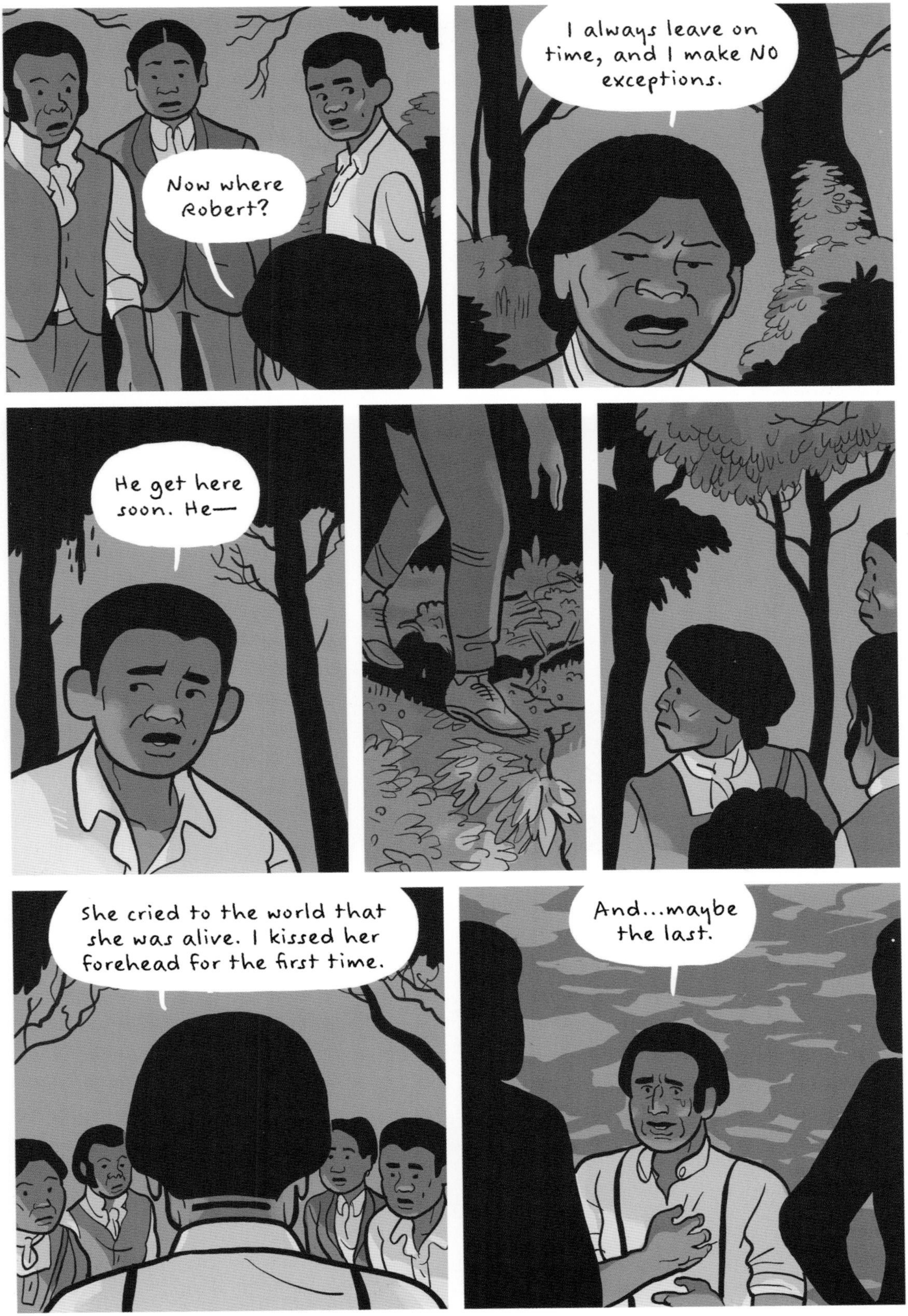
Now where Robert?
I always leave on time, and I make NO exceptions.
He get here soon. He—
She cried to the world that she was alive. I kissed her forehead for the first time.
And...maybe the last.

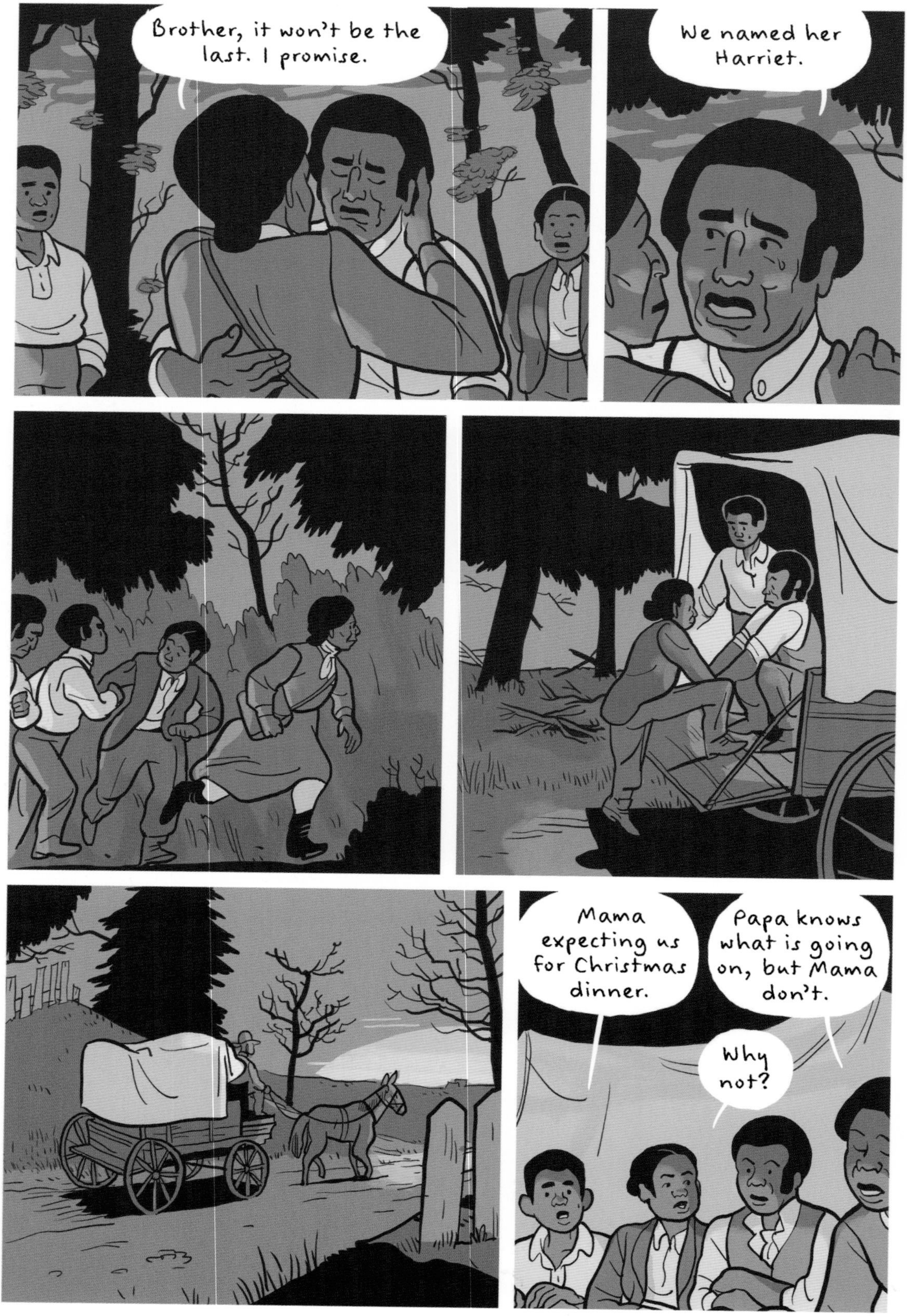
Brother, it won't be the last. I promise.
We named her Harriet.
Mama expecting us for Christmas dinner.
Papa knows what is going on, but Mama don't.
Why not?

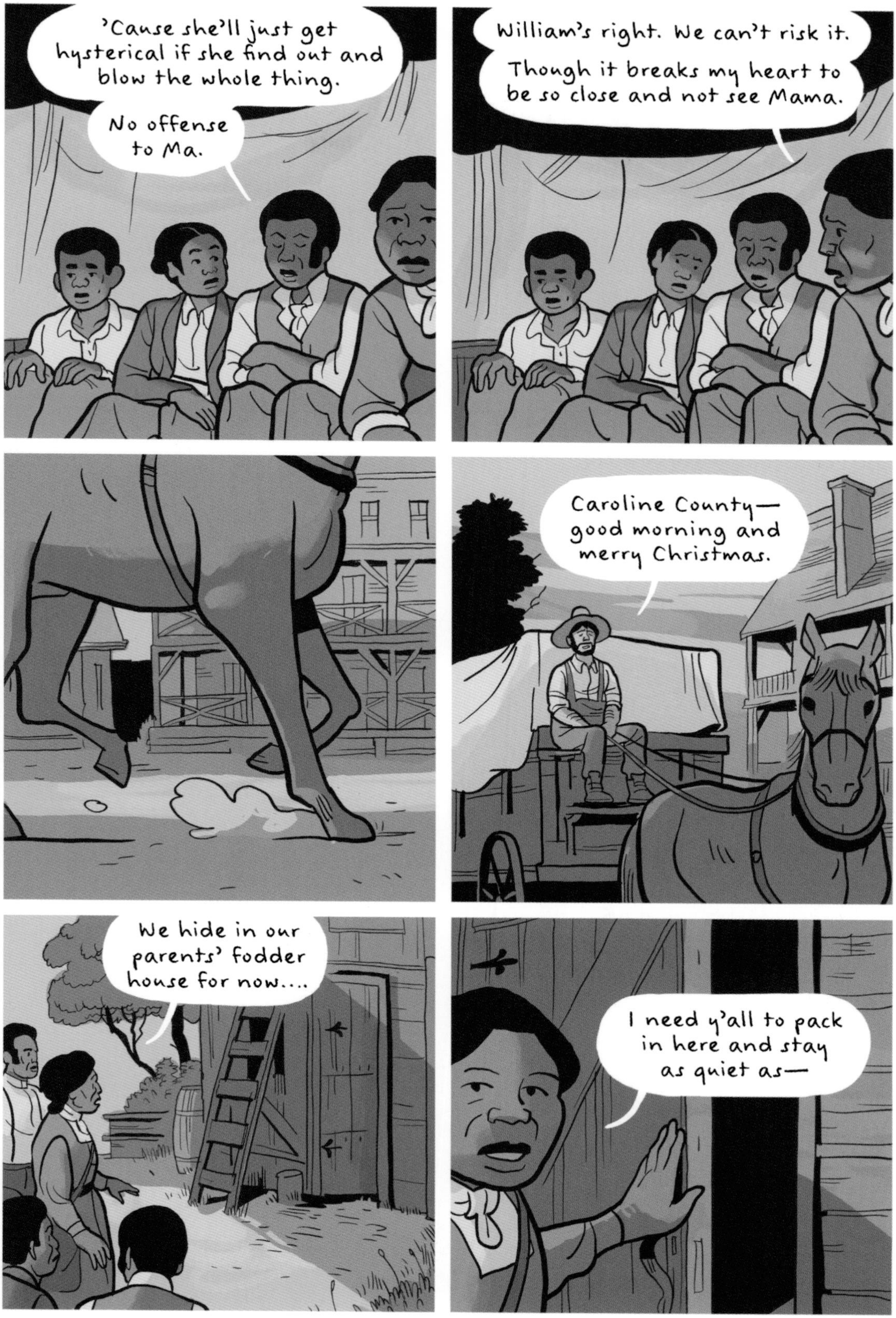
'Cause she'll just get hysterical if she find out and blow the whole thing.
No offense to Ma.
William's right. We can't risk it.
Though it breaks my heart to be so close and not see Mama.
Caroline County—good morning and merry Christmas.
We hide in our parents' fodder house for now....
I need y'all to pack in here and stay as quiet as—

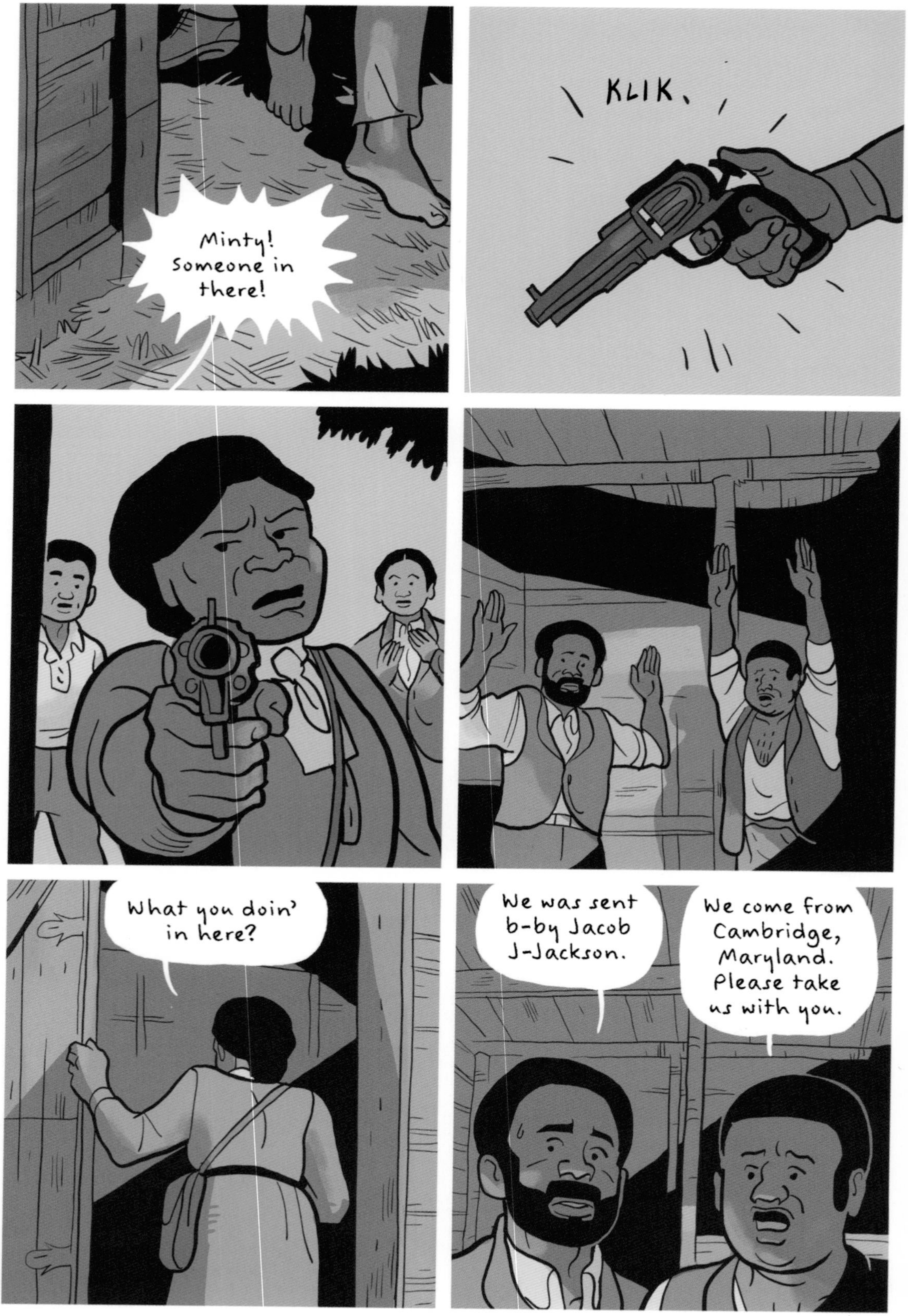
Minty! Someone in there!
KLIK.
What you doin' in here?
We was sent b-by Jacob J-Jackson.
We come from Cambridge, Maryland. Please take us with you.

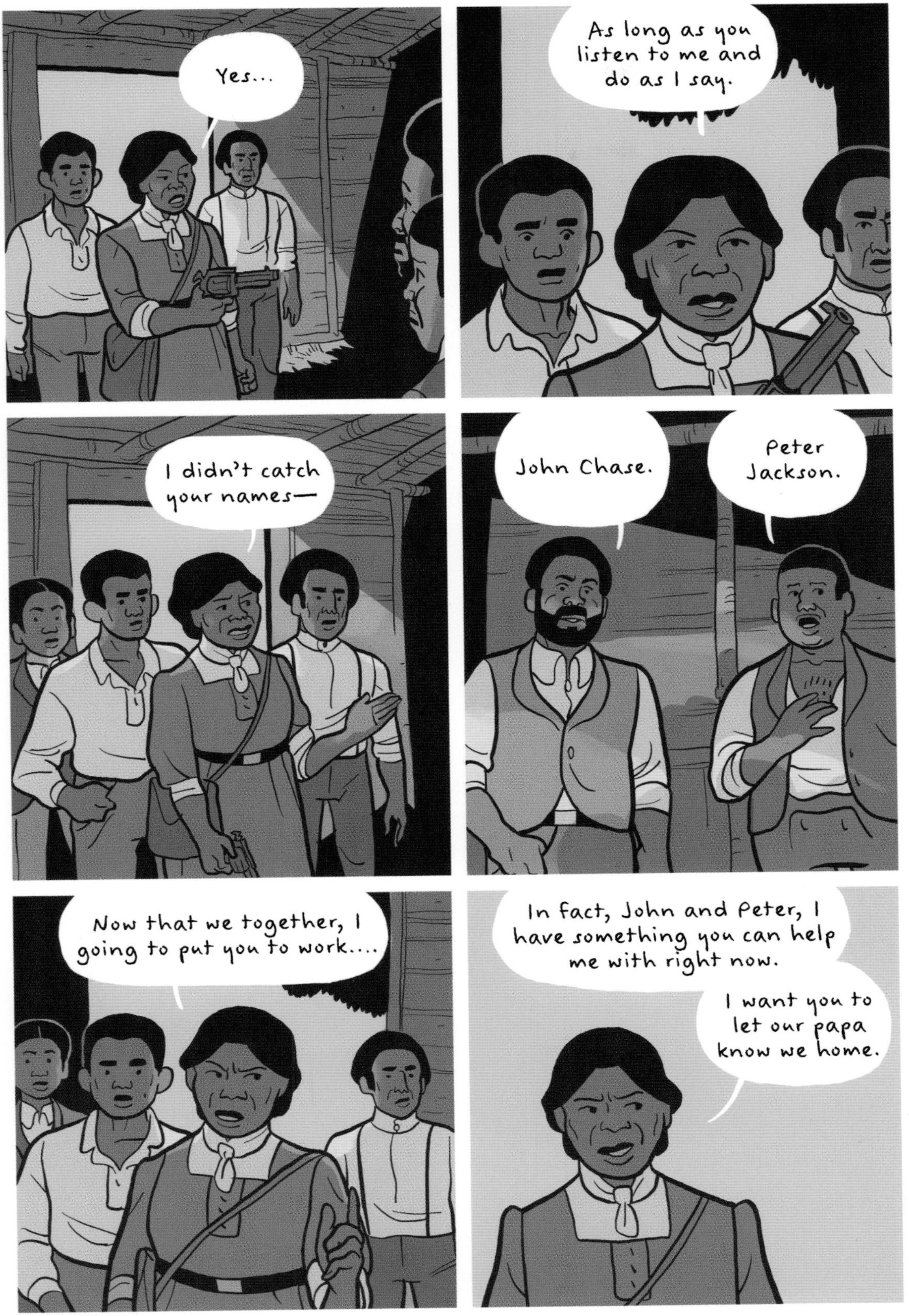
Yes...
As long as you listen to me and do as I say.
I didn't catch your names—
John Chase.
Peter Jackson.
Now that we together, I going to put you to work....
In fact, John and Peter, I have something you can help me with right now.
I want you to let our papa know we home.

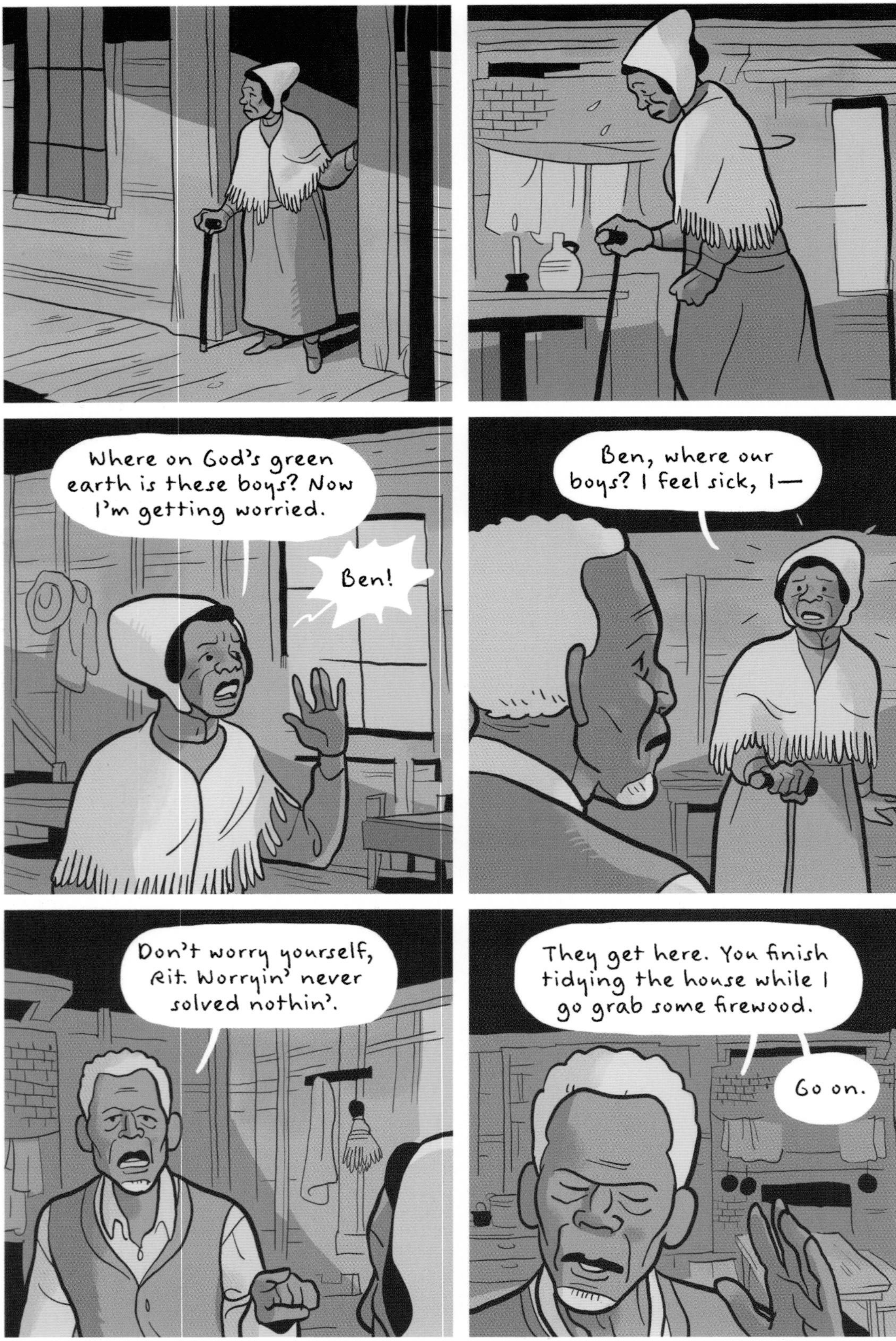

Where on God's green earth is these boys? Now I'm getting worried.
Ben!
Ben, where our boys? I feel sick, I—
Don't worry yourself, Rit. Worryin' never solved nothin'.
They get here. You finish tidying the house while I go grab some firewood.
Go on.

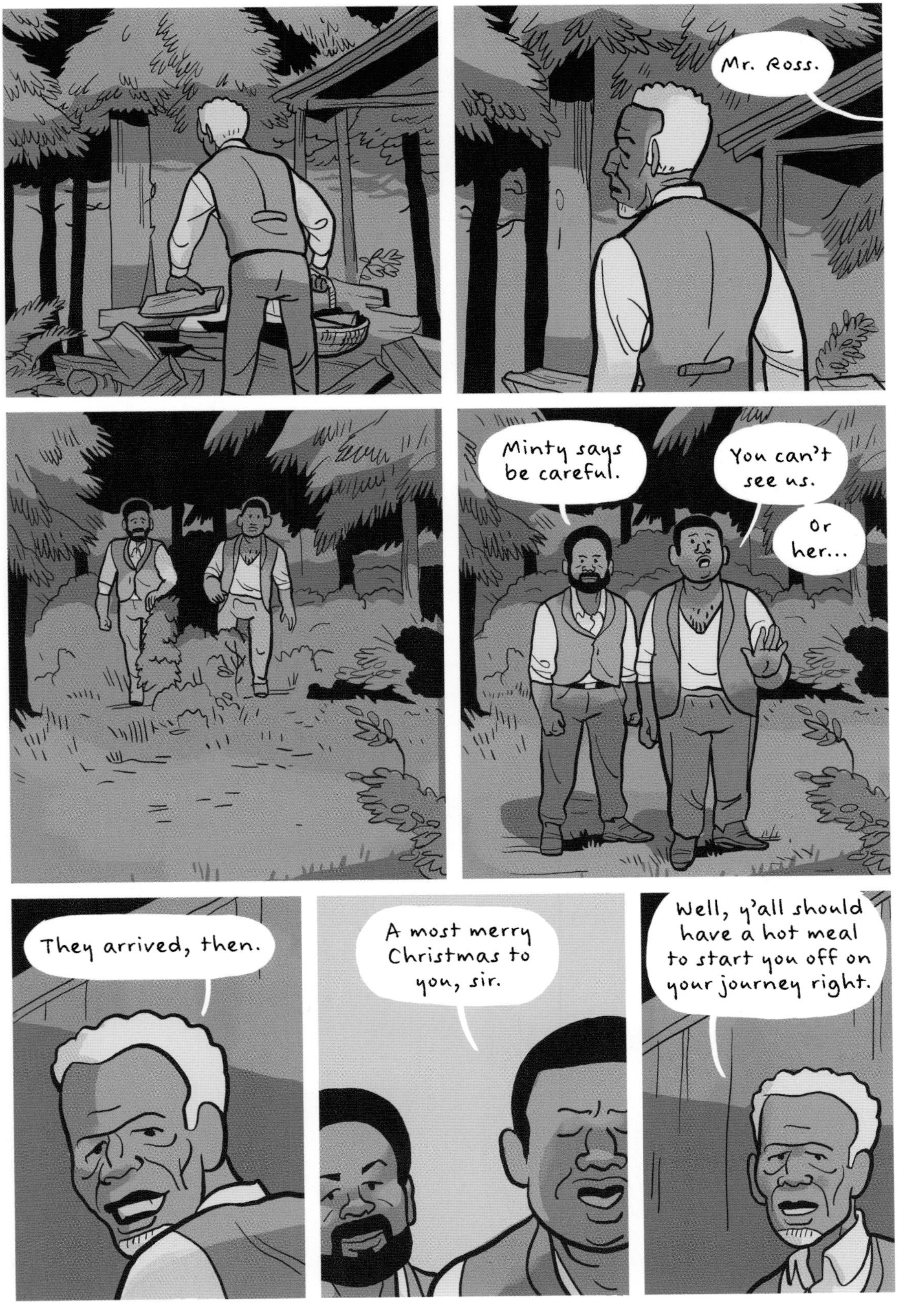
Mr. Ross.
Minty says be careful.
You can't see us.
Or her...
They arrived, then.
A most merry Christmas to you, sir.
Well, y'all should have a hot meal to start you off on your journey right.

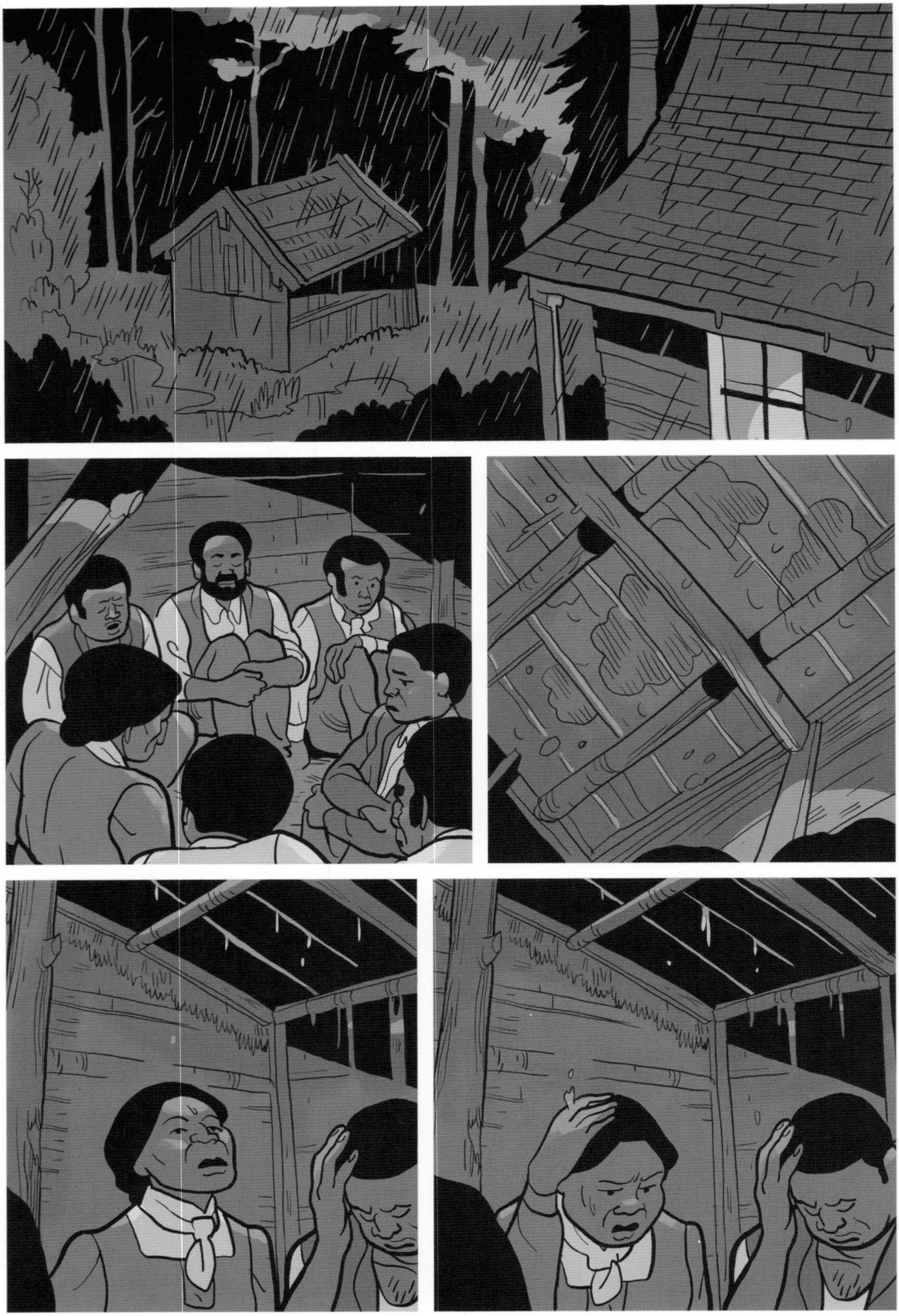

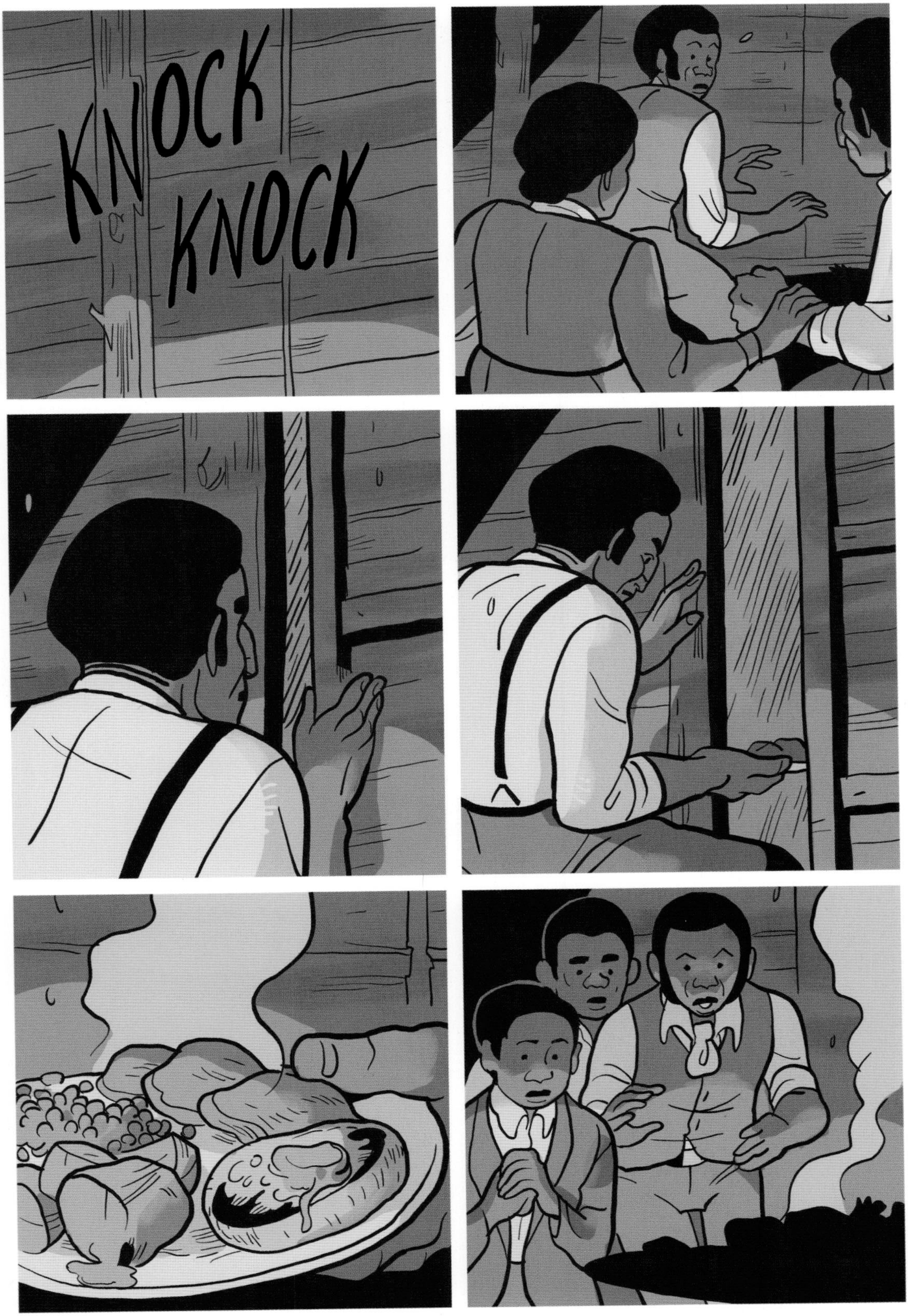
KNOCK
KNOCK

SLOW DOWN!

Now, I know we all hungry, but this ain't no way to eat.

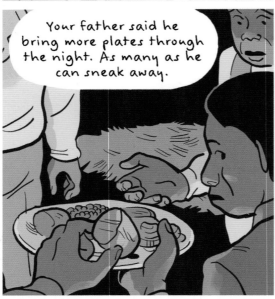

Your father said he bring more plates through the night. As many as he can sneak away.

sniff

As many as he can sneak away.

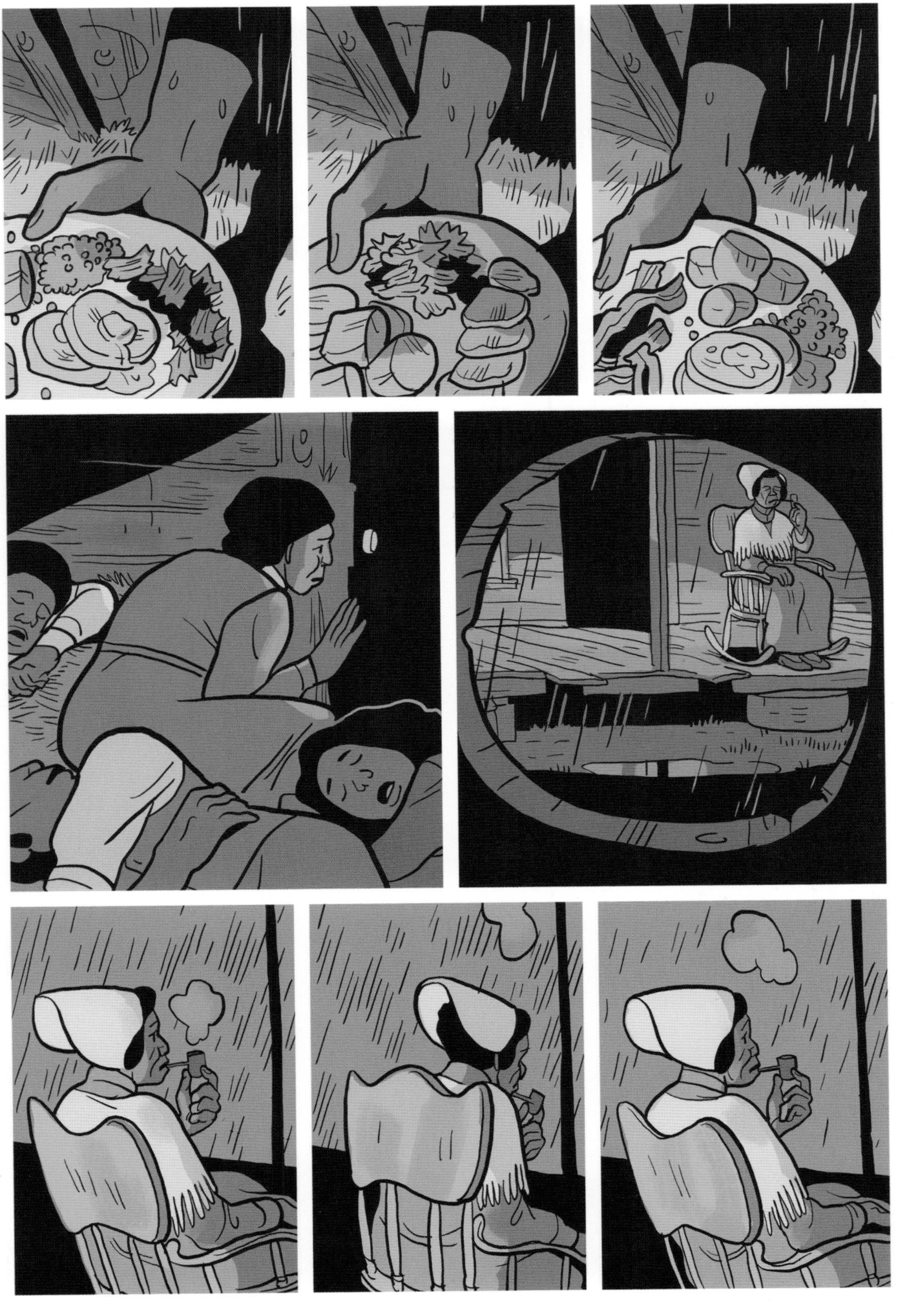

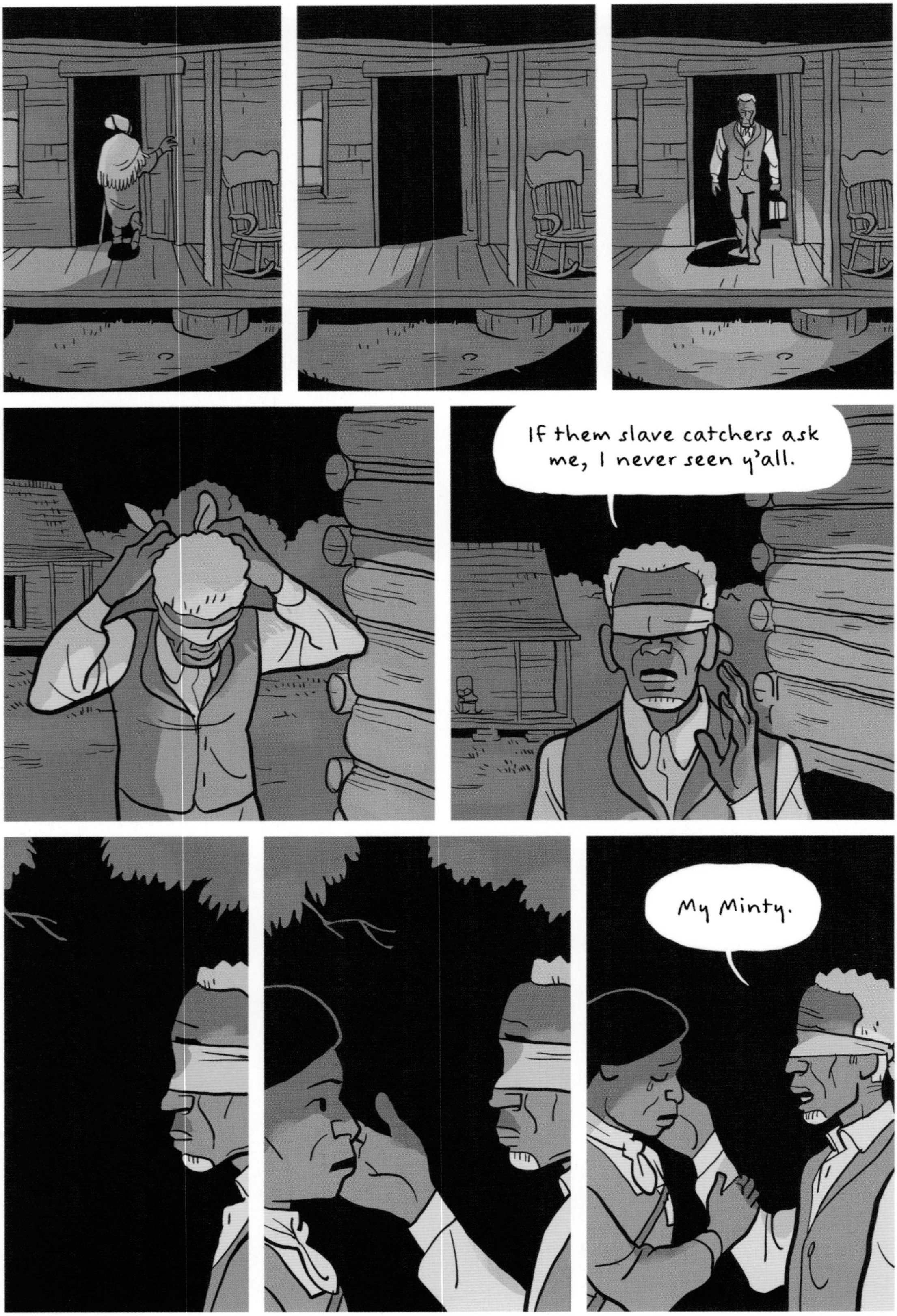
If them slave catchers ask me, I never seen y'all.
My Minty.

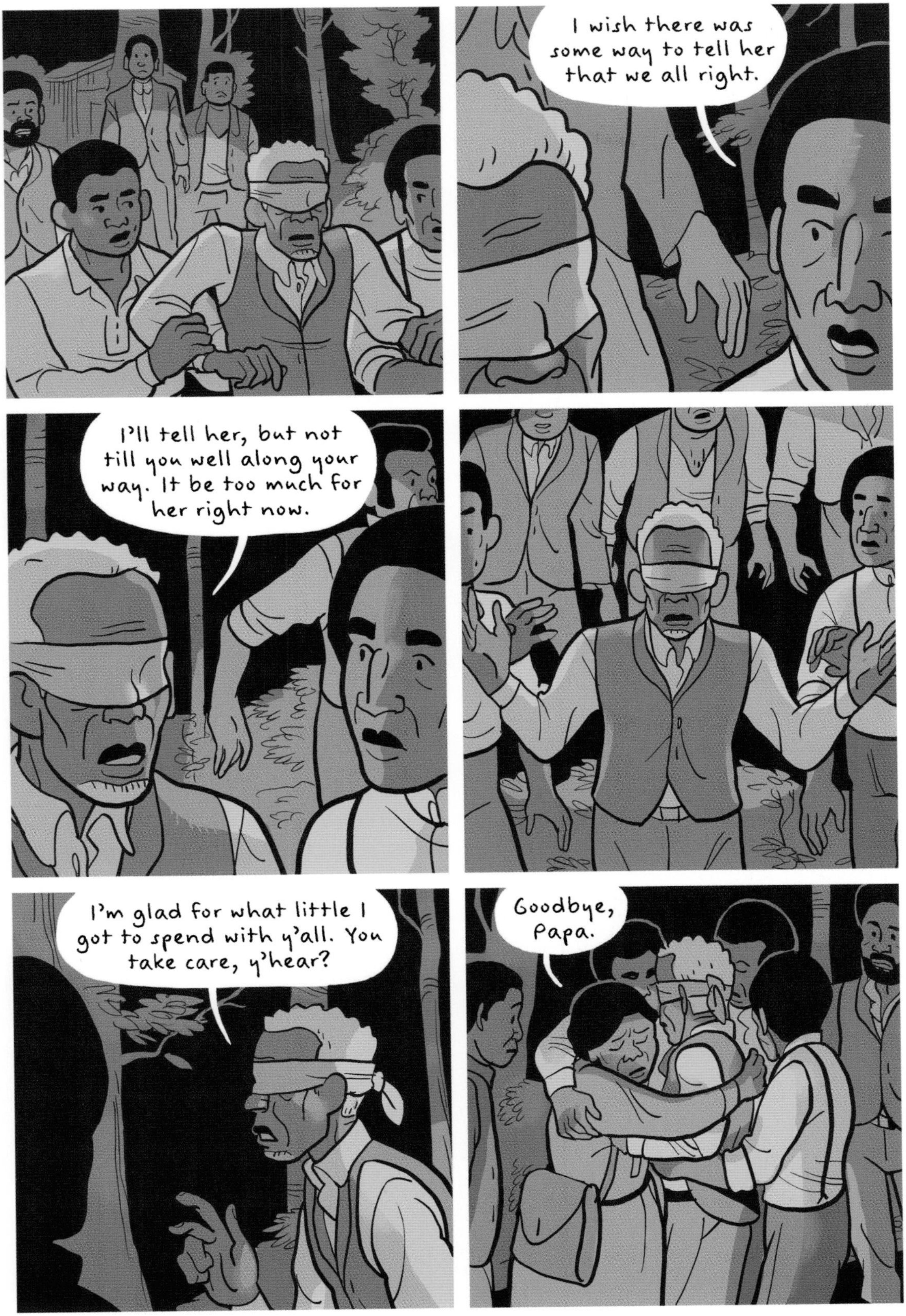

I wish there was some way to tell her that we all right.
I'll tell her, but not till you well along your way. It be too much for her right now.
I'm glad for what little I got to spend with y'all. You take care, y'hear?
Goodbye, Papa.

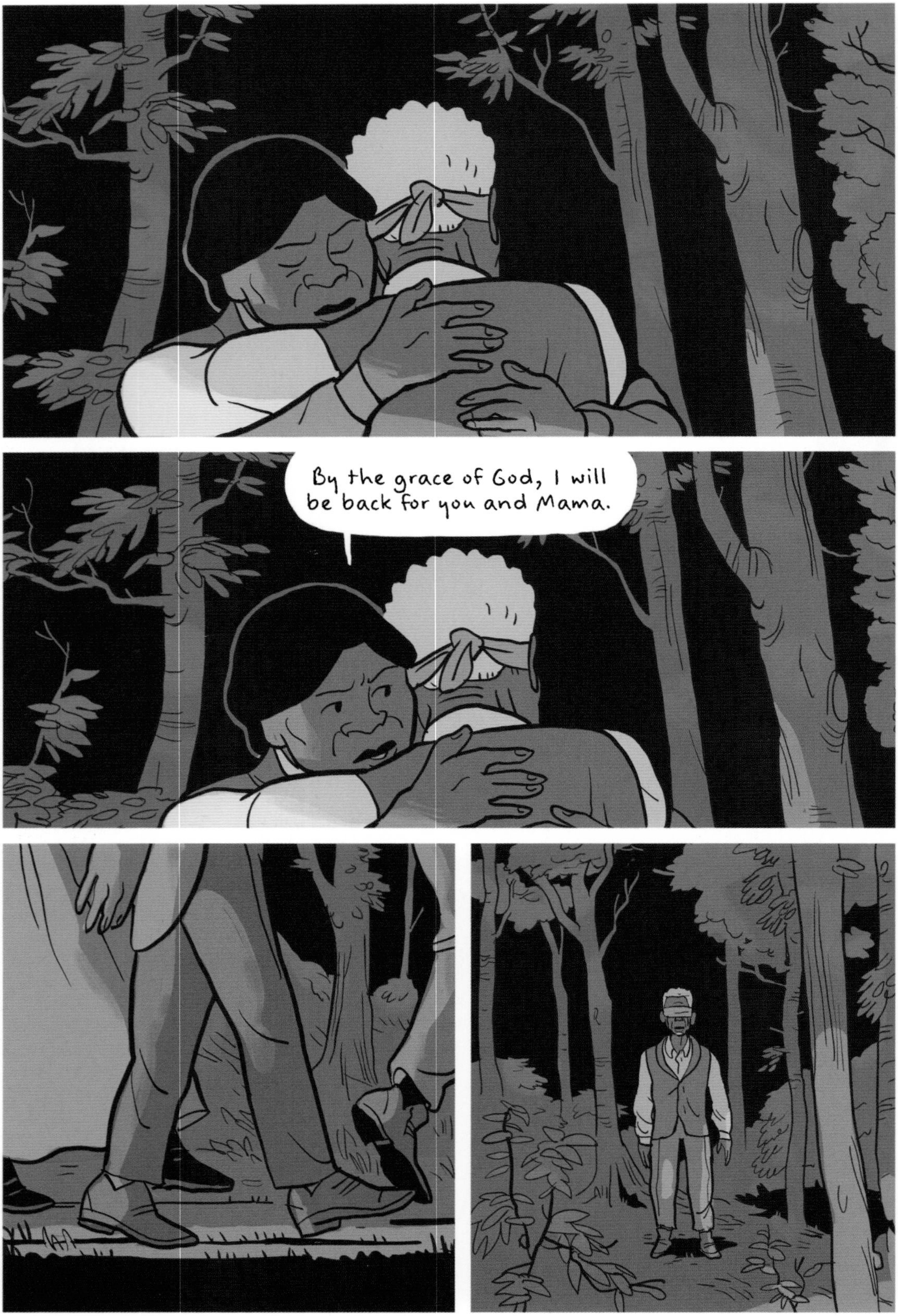
By the grace of God, I will be back for you and Mama.

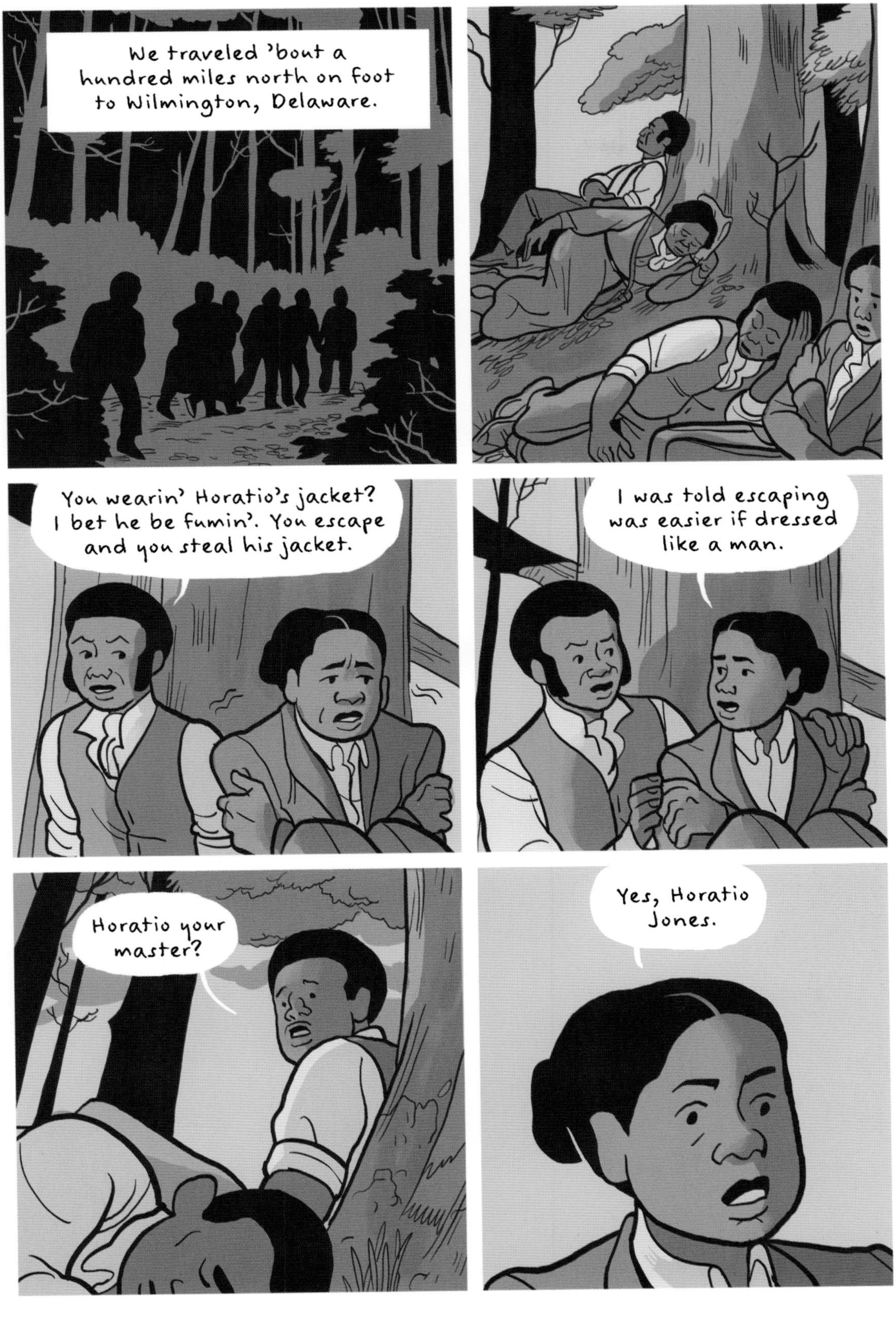
We traveled 'bout a hundred miles north on foot to Wilmington, Delaware.
You wearin' Horatio's jacket? I bet he be fumin'. You escape and you steal his jacket.
I was told escaping was easier if dressed like a man.
Horatio your master?
Yes, Horatio Jones.

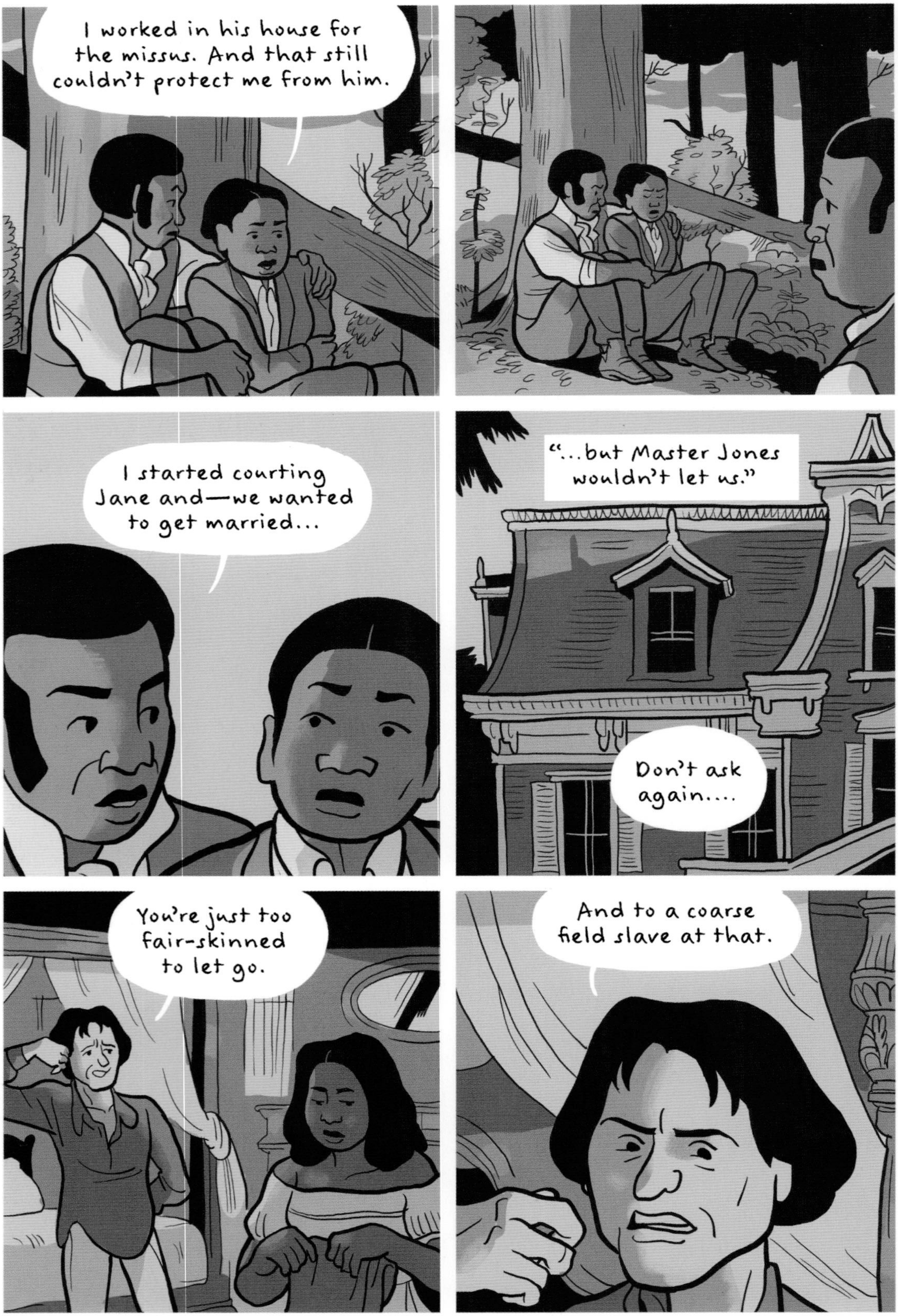
I worked in his house for the missus. And that still couldn't protect me from him.
I started courting Jane and—we wanted to get married...
"...but Master Jones wouldn't let us."
Don't ask again....
You're just too fair-skinned to let go.
And to a coarse field slave at that.

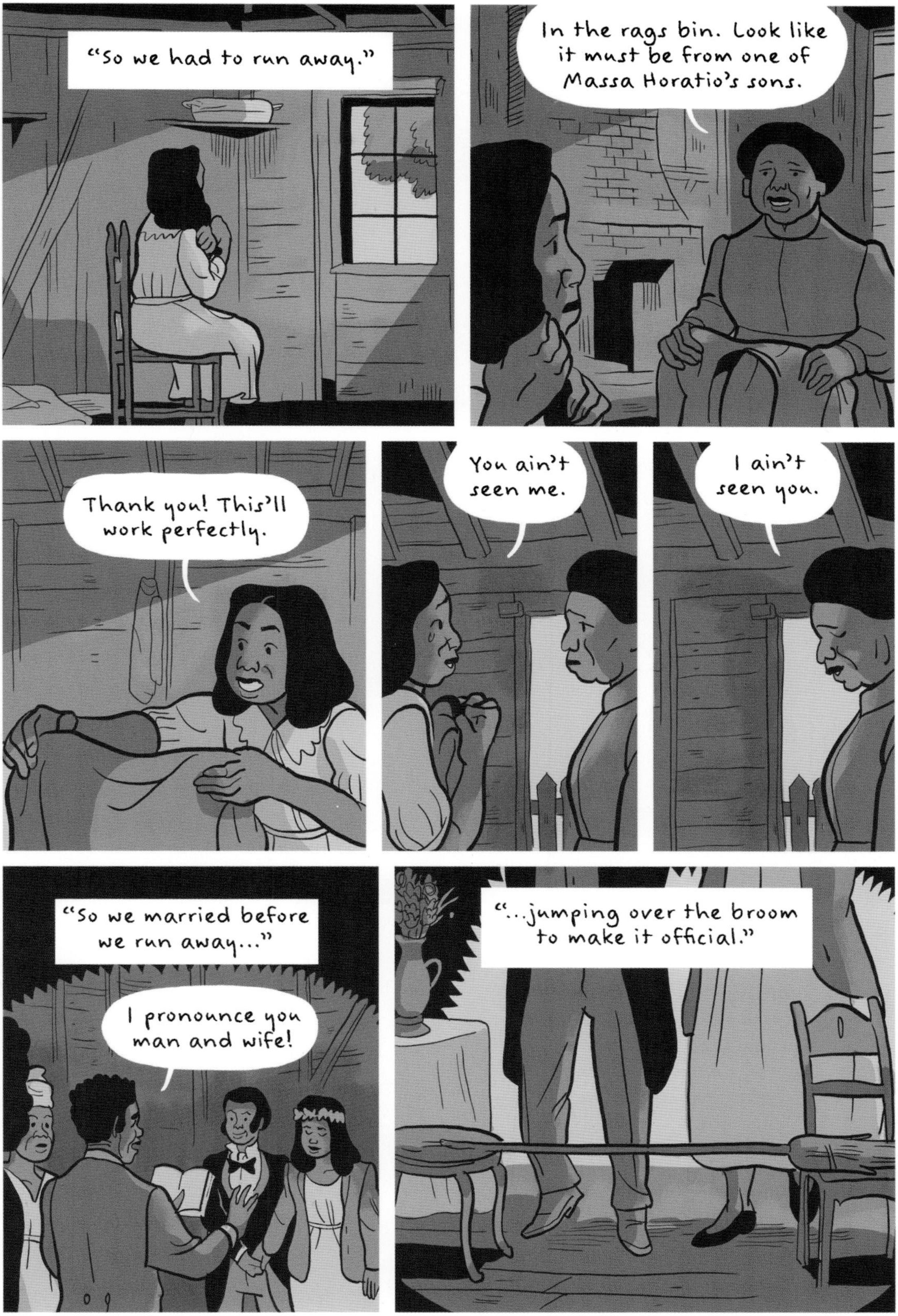

"So we had to run away."
In the rags bin. Look like it must be from one of Massa Horatio's sons.
Thank you! This'll work perfectly.
You ain't seen me.
I ain't seen you.
"So we married before we run away..."
I pronounce you man and wife!
"...jumping over the broom to make it official."

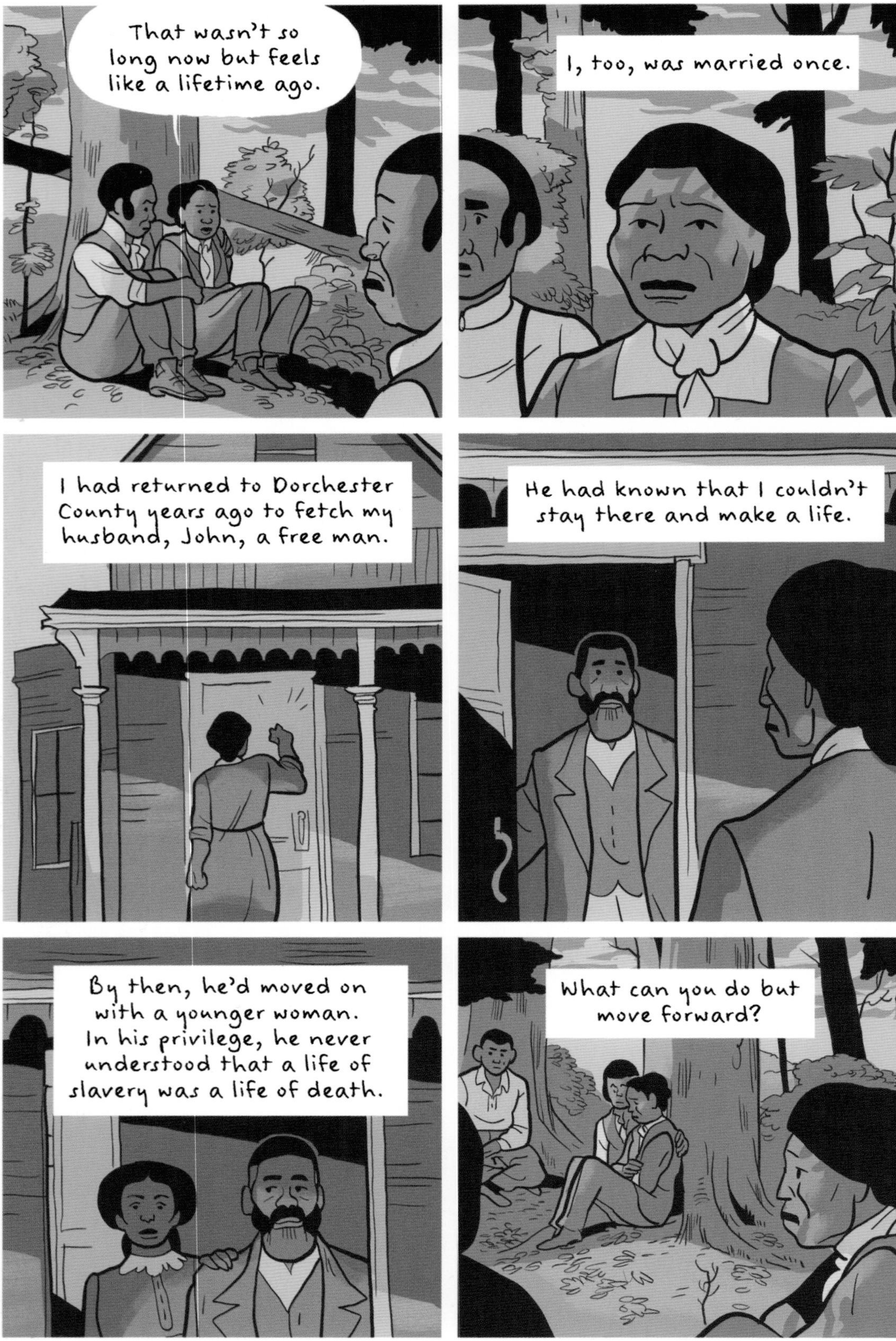
That wasn't so long now but feels like a lifetime ago.
I, too, was married once.
I had returned to Dorchester County years ago to fetch my husband, John, a free man.
He had known that I couldn't stay there and make a life.
By then, he'd moved on with a younger woman. In his privilege, he never understood that a life of slavery was a life of death.
What can you do but move forward?

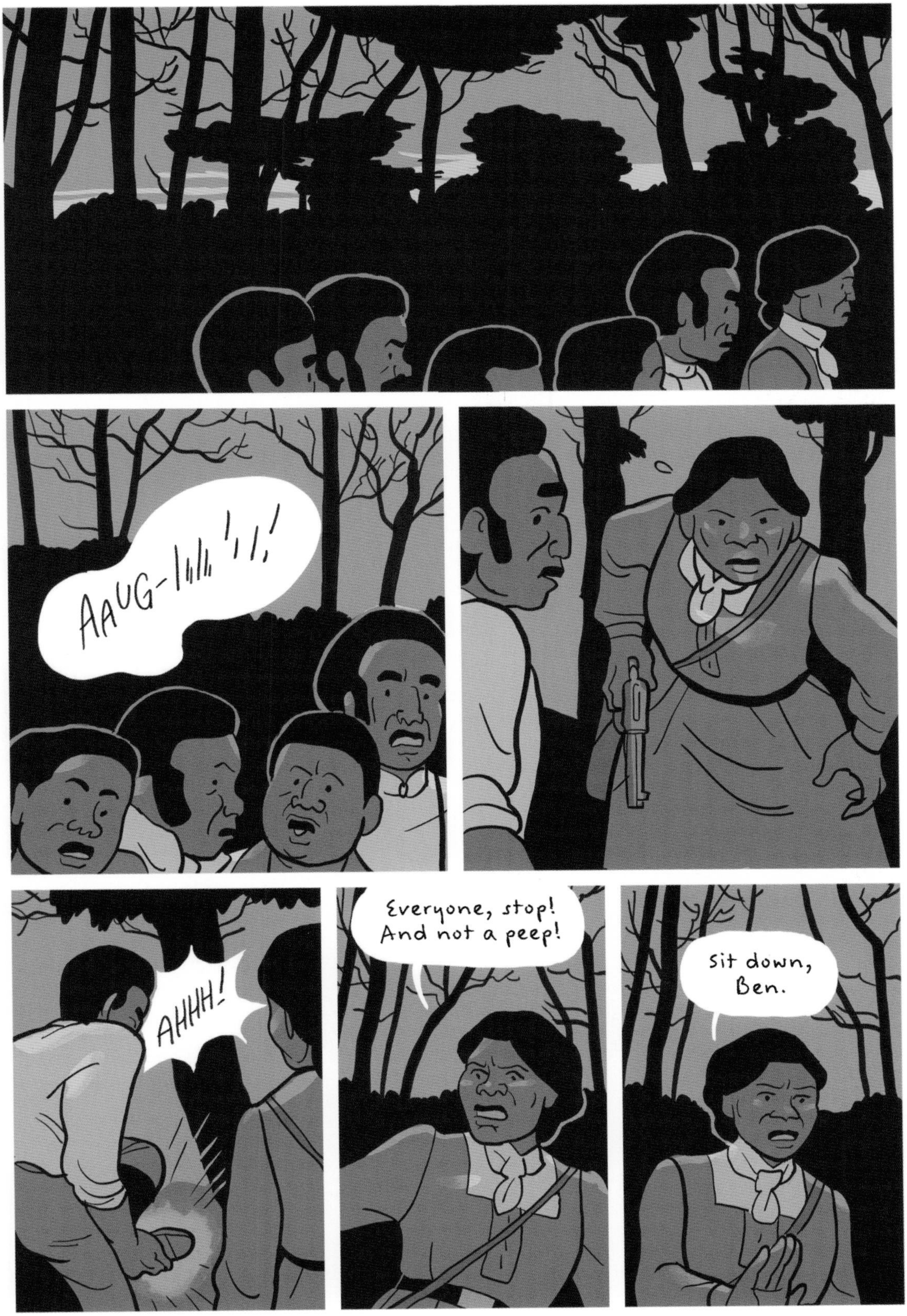
AAUG-hhh!!!
AHHH!
Everyone, stop! And not a peep!
Sit down, Ben.

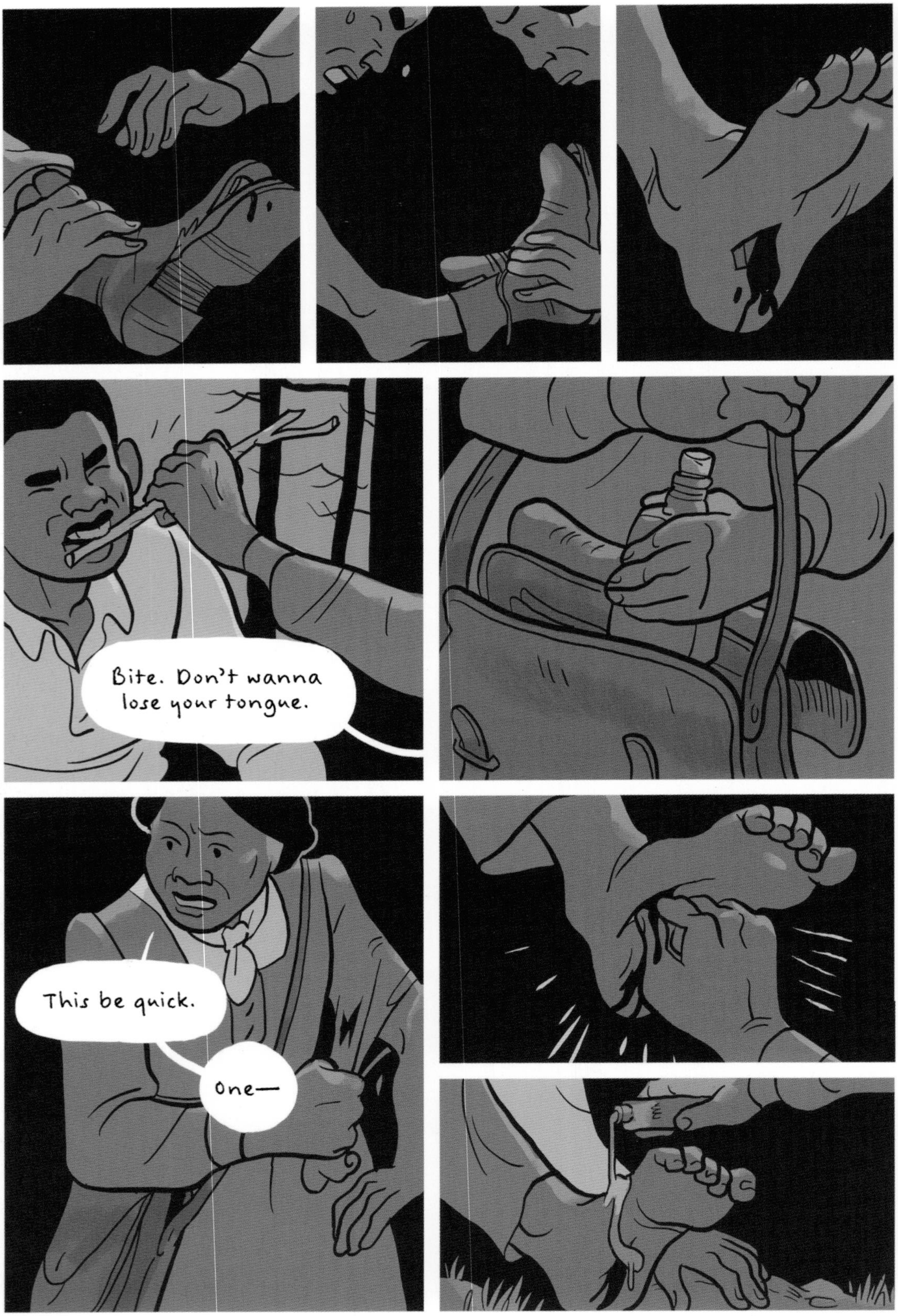
Bite. Don't wanna lose your tongue.
This be quick.
One—

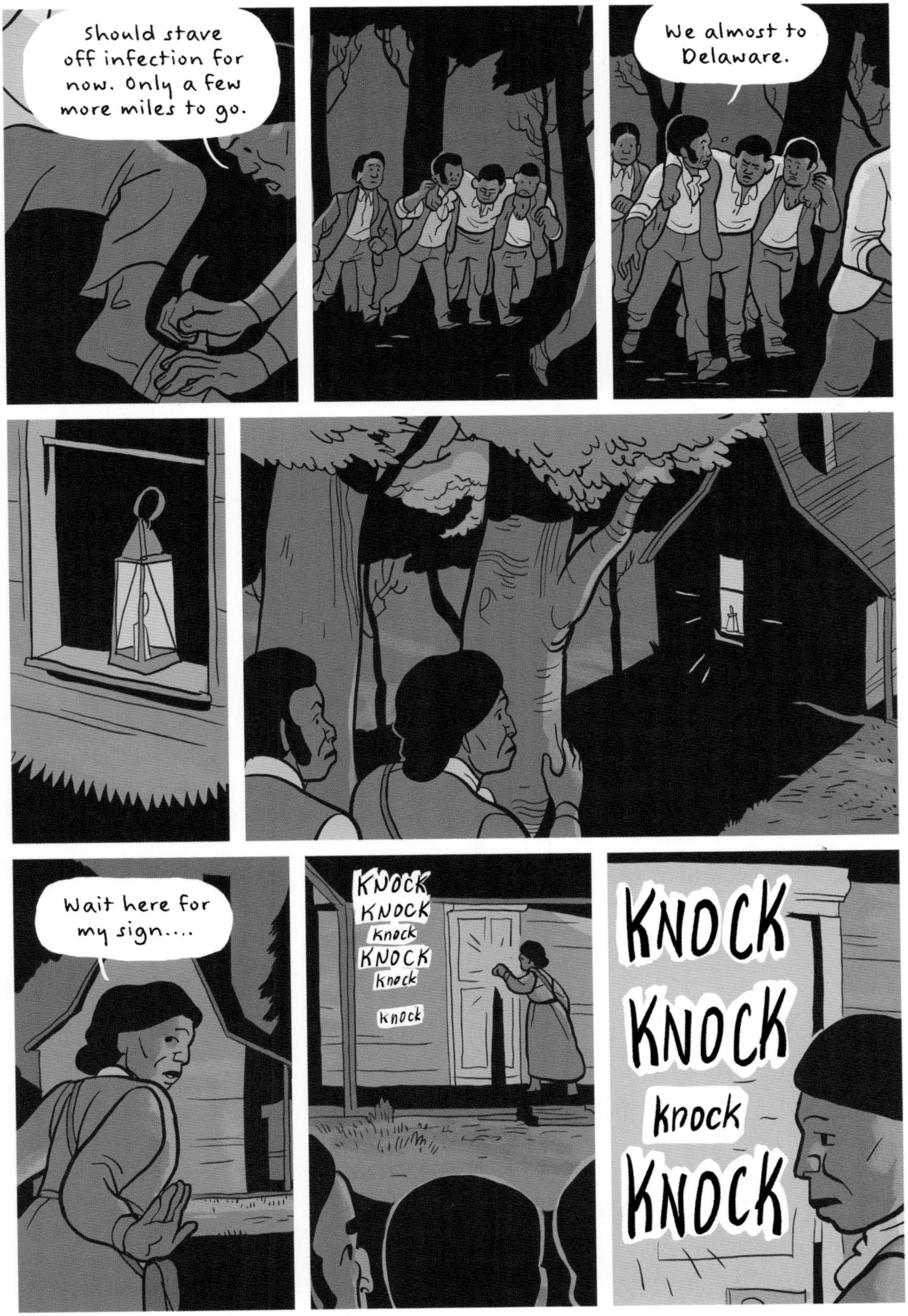
Should stave off infection for now. Only a few more miles to go.
We almost to Delaware.
Wait here for my sign....
KNOCK
KNOCK
knock
KNOCK
knock
knock
KNOCK
KNOCK
knock
KNOCK

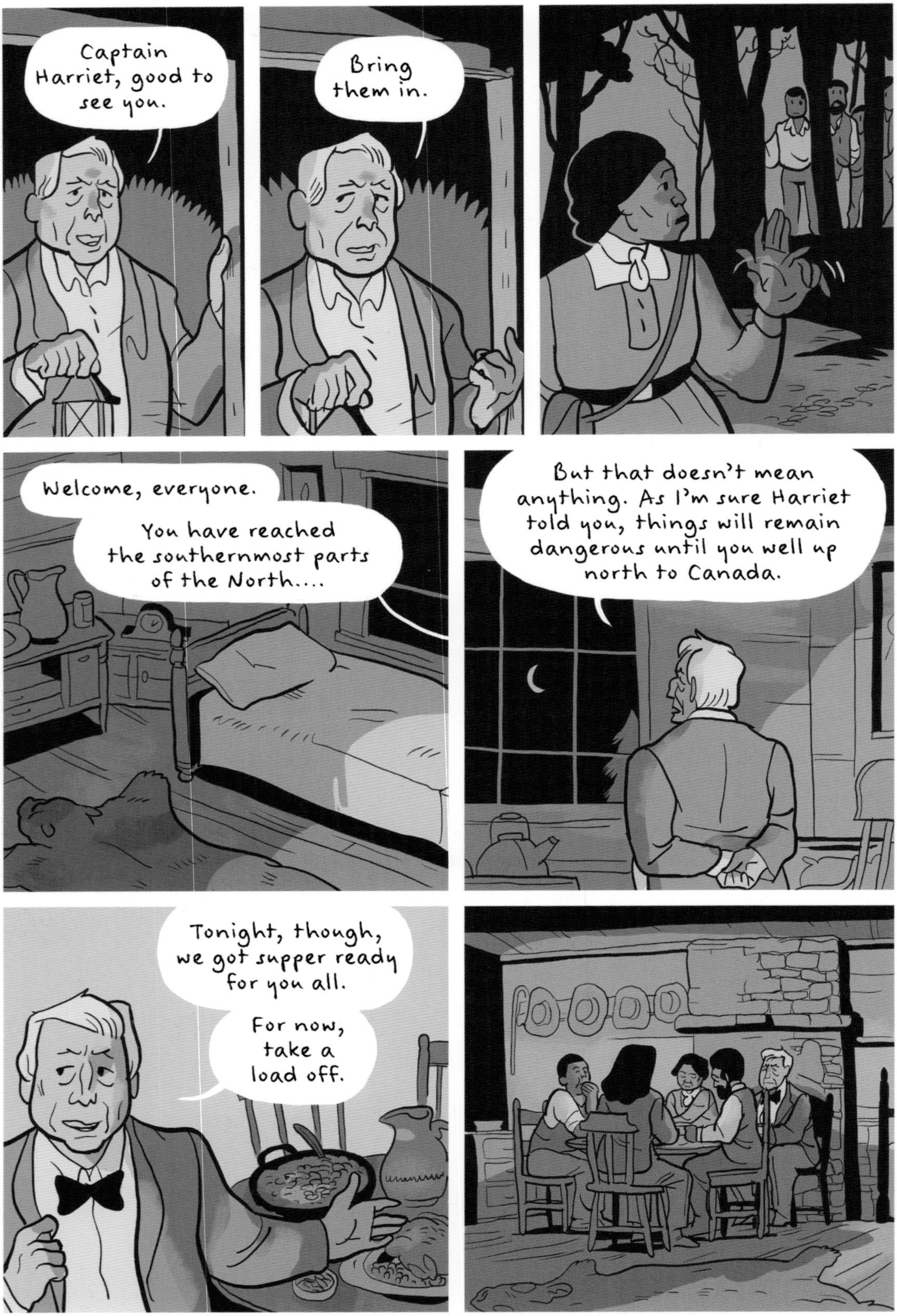

Captain Harriet, good to see you.
Bring them in.
Welcome, everyone.
You have reached the southernmost parts of the North....
But that doesn't mean anything. As I'm sure Harriet told you, things will remain dangerous until you well up north to Canada.
Tonight, though, we got supper ready for you all.
For now, take a load off.

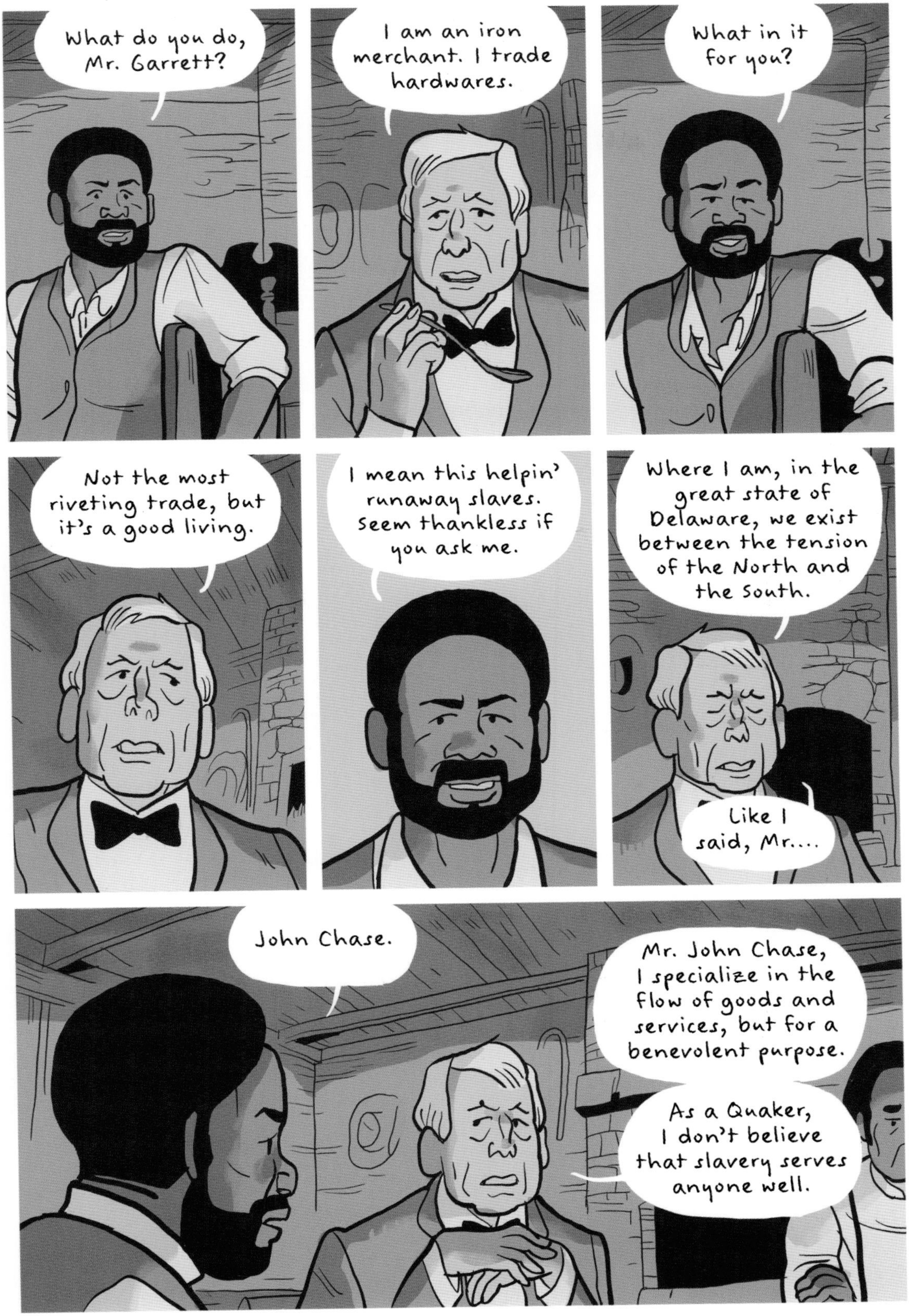
What do you do, Mr. Garrett?
I am an iron merchant. I trade hardwares.
What in it for you?
Not the most riveting trade, but it's a good living.
I mean this helpin' runaway slaves. Seem thankless if you ask me.
Where I am, in the great state of Delaware, we exist between the tension of the North and the South.
Like I said, Mr....
John Chase.
Mr. John Chase, I specialize in the flow of goods and services, but for a benevolent purpose.
As a Quaker, I don't believe that slavery serves anyone well.

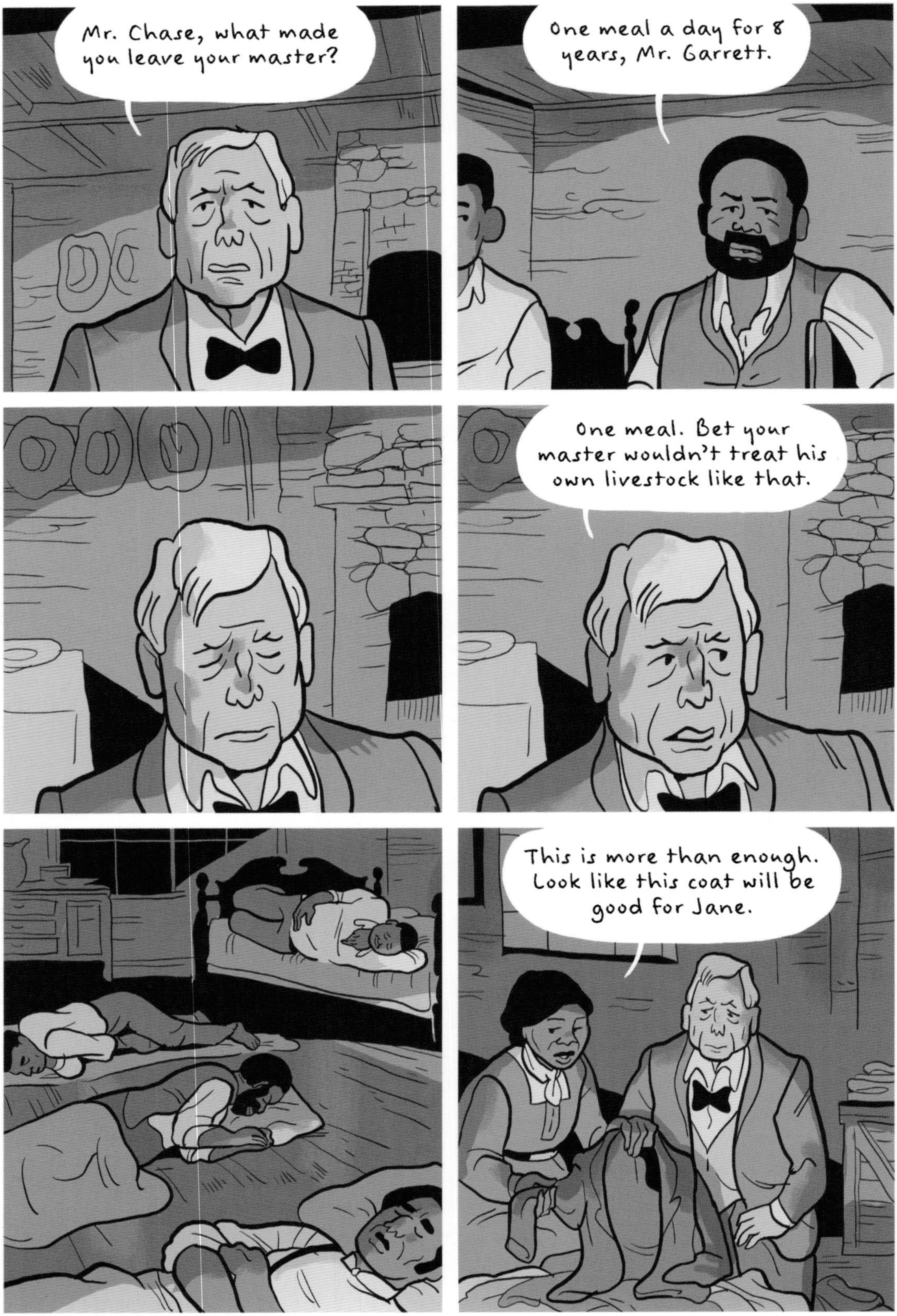
Mr. Chase, what made you leave your master?
One meal a day for 8 years, Mr. Garrett.
One meal. Bet your master wouldn't treat his own livestock like that.
This is more than enough. Look like this coat will be good for Jane.

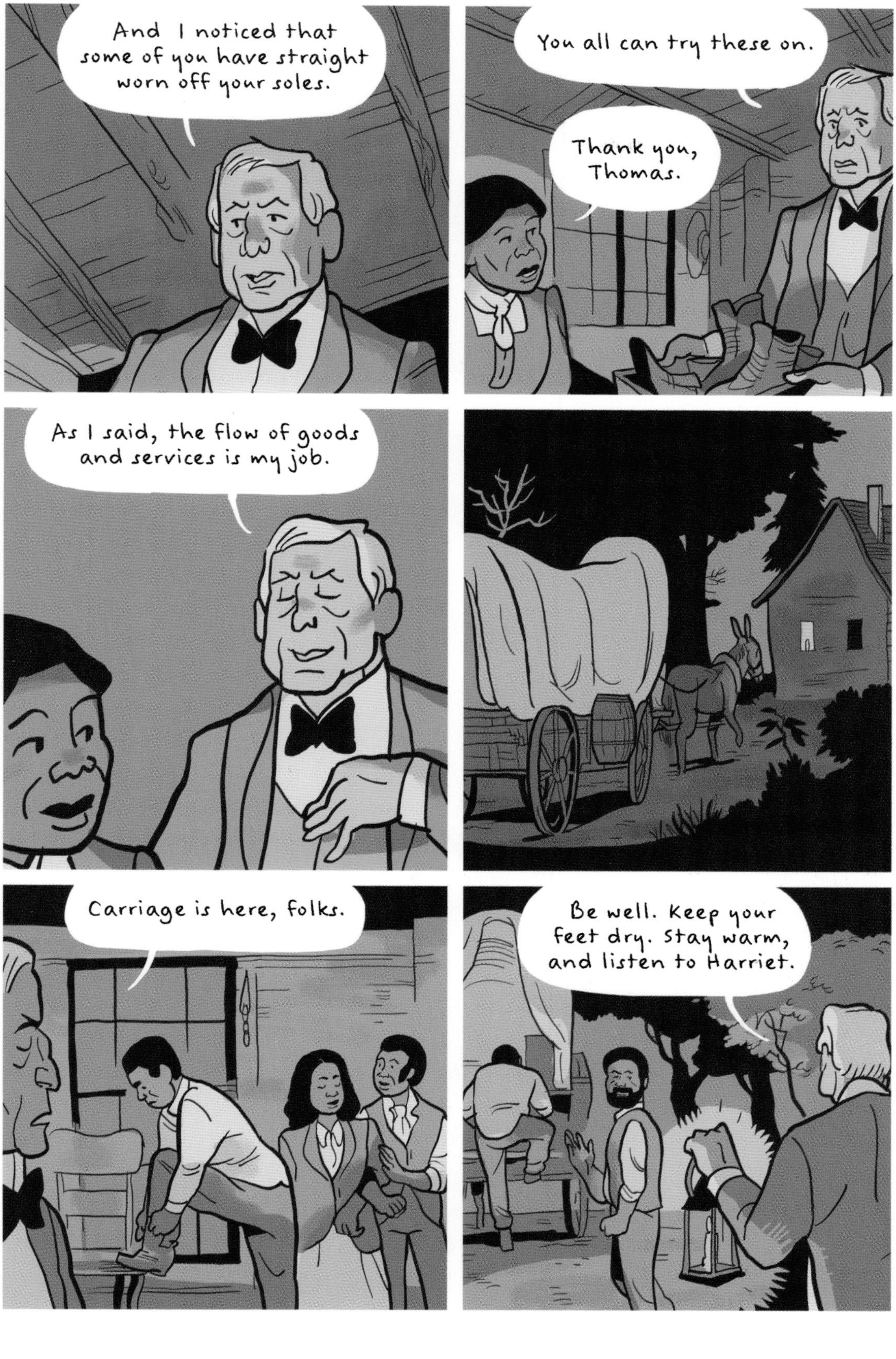
And I noticed that some of you have straight worn off your soles.
You all can try these on.
Thank you, Thomas.
As I said, the flow of goods and services is my job.
Carriage is here, folks.
Be well. Keep your feet dry. Stay warm, and listen to Harriet.

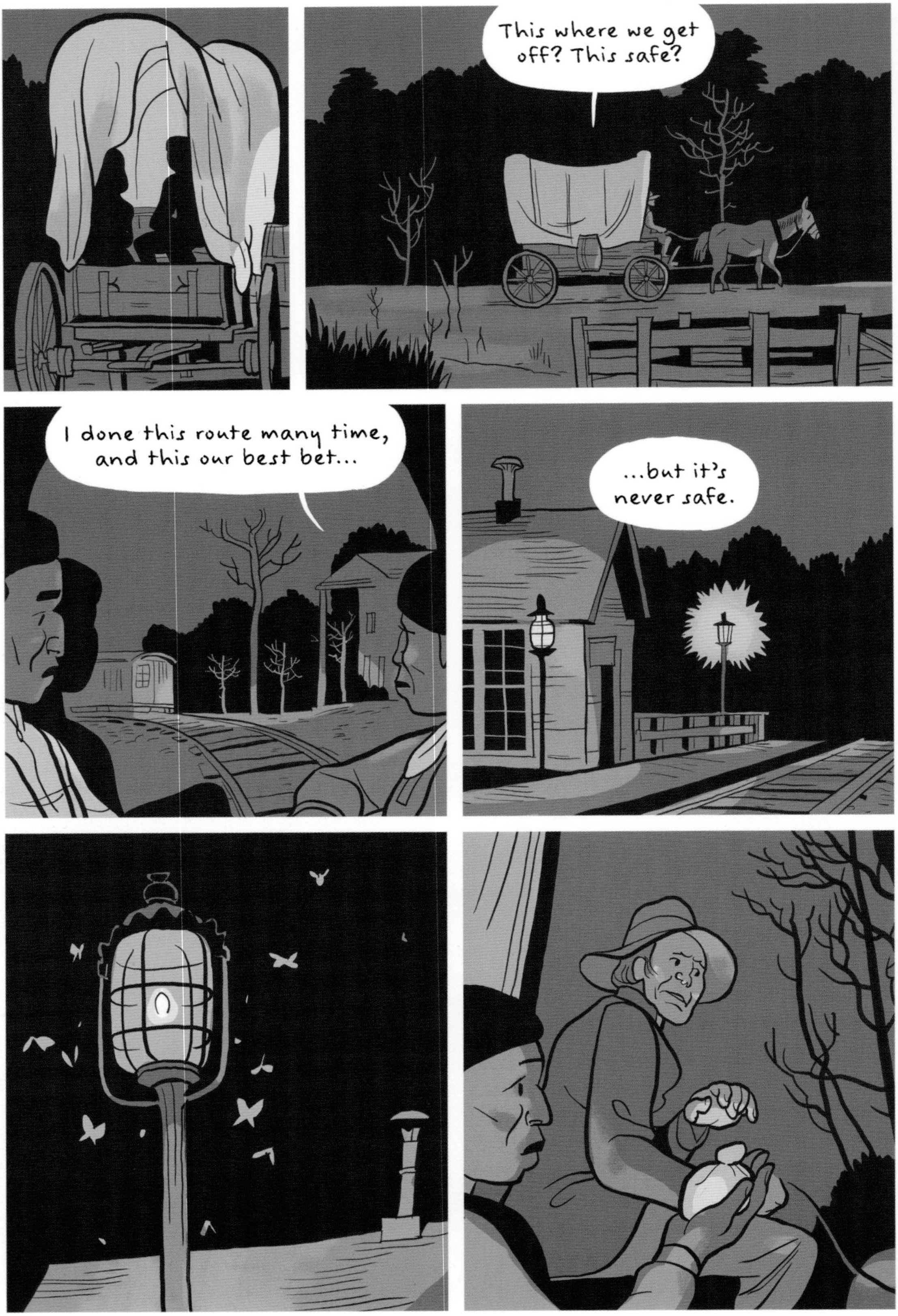
This where we get off? This safe?
I done this route many time, and this our best bet...
...but it's never safe.

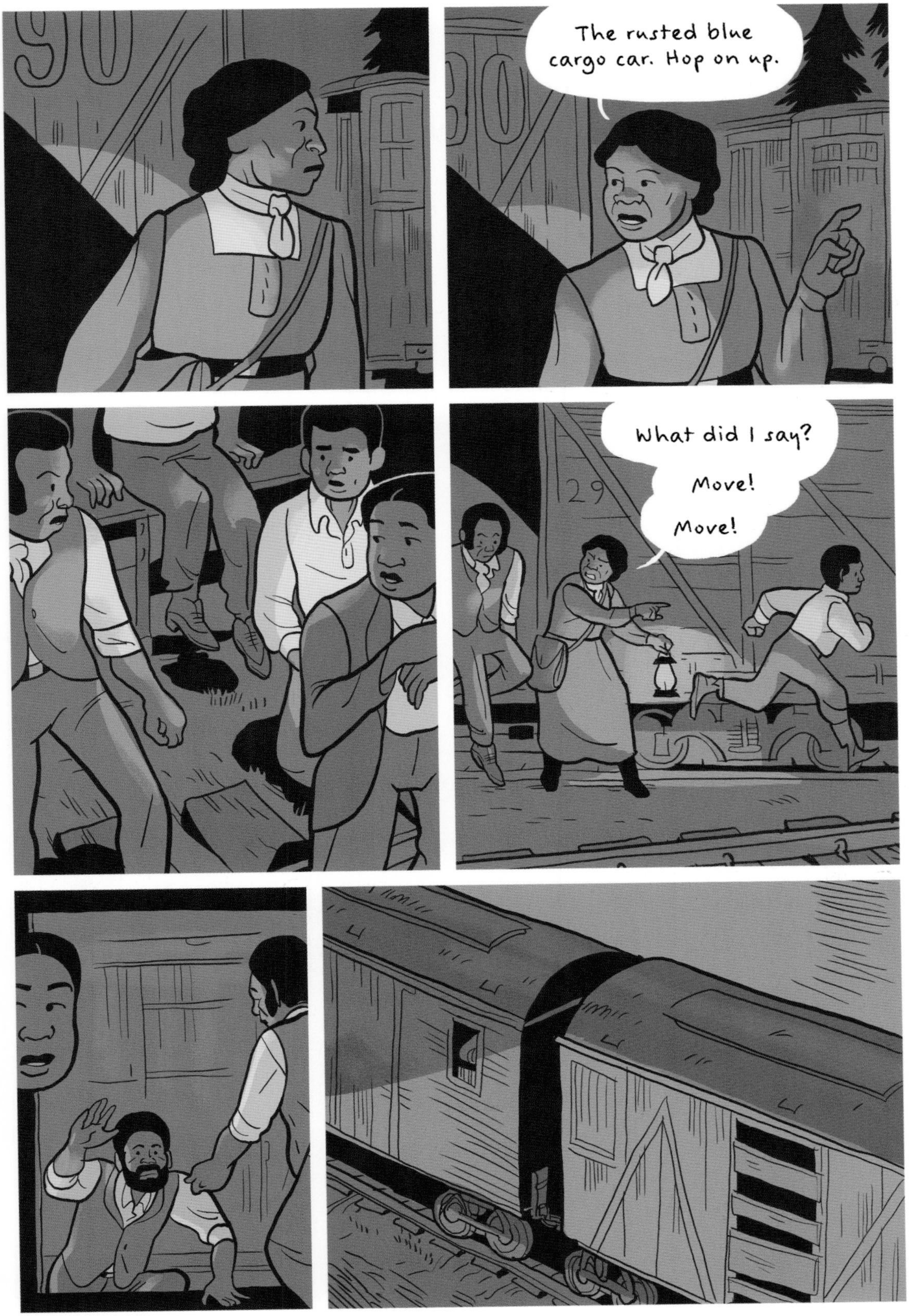
90
The rusted blue cargo car. Hop on up.
29
What did I say?
Move!
Move!

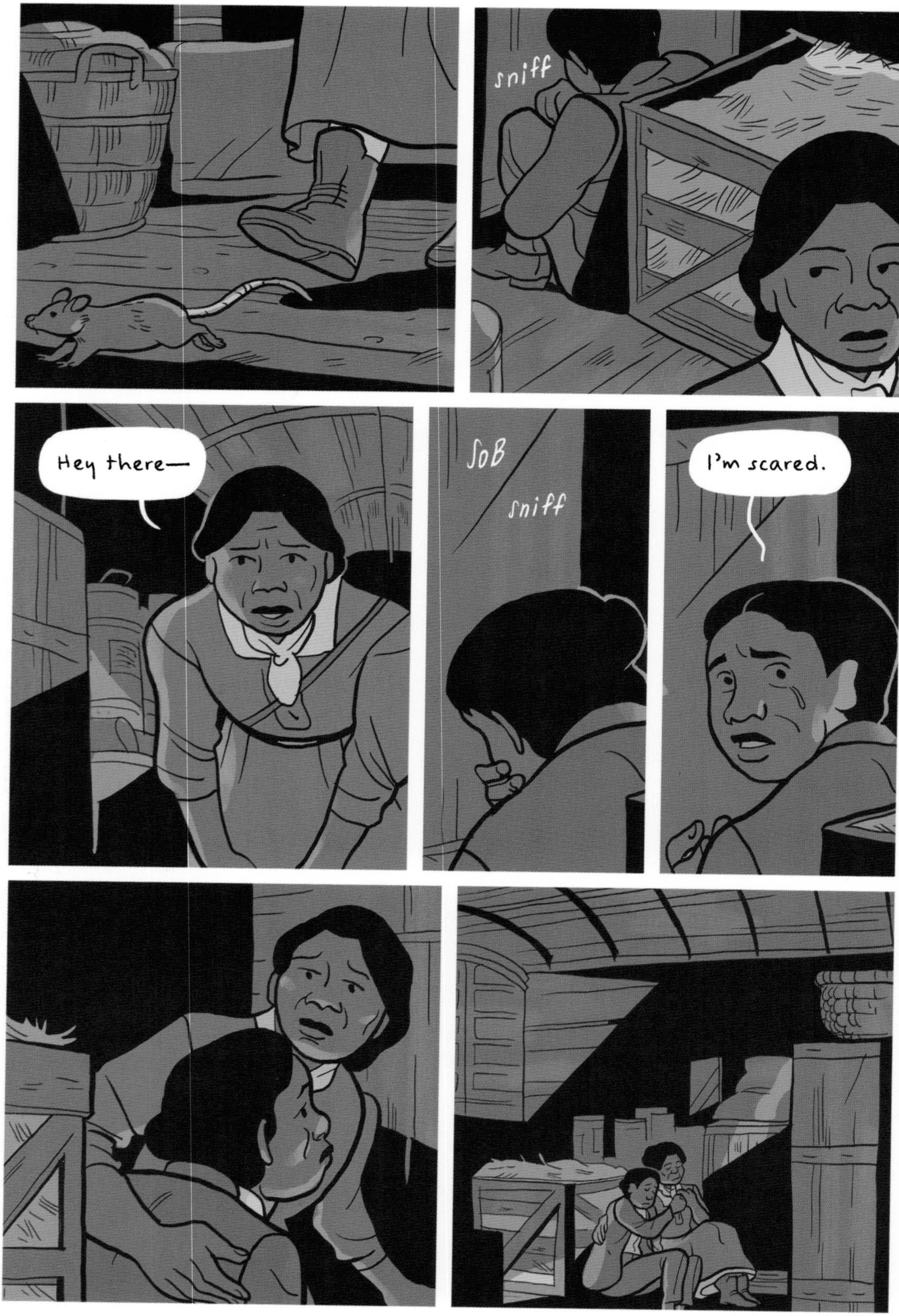
sniff
Hey there—
SoB
sniff
I'm scared.

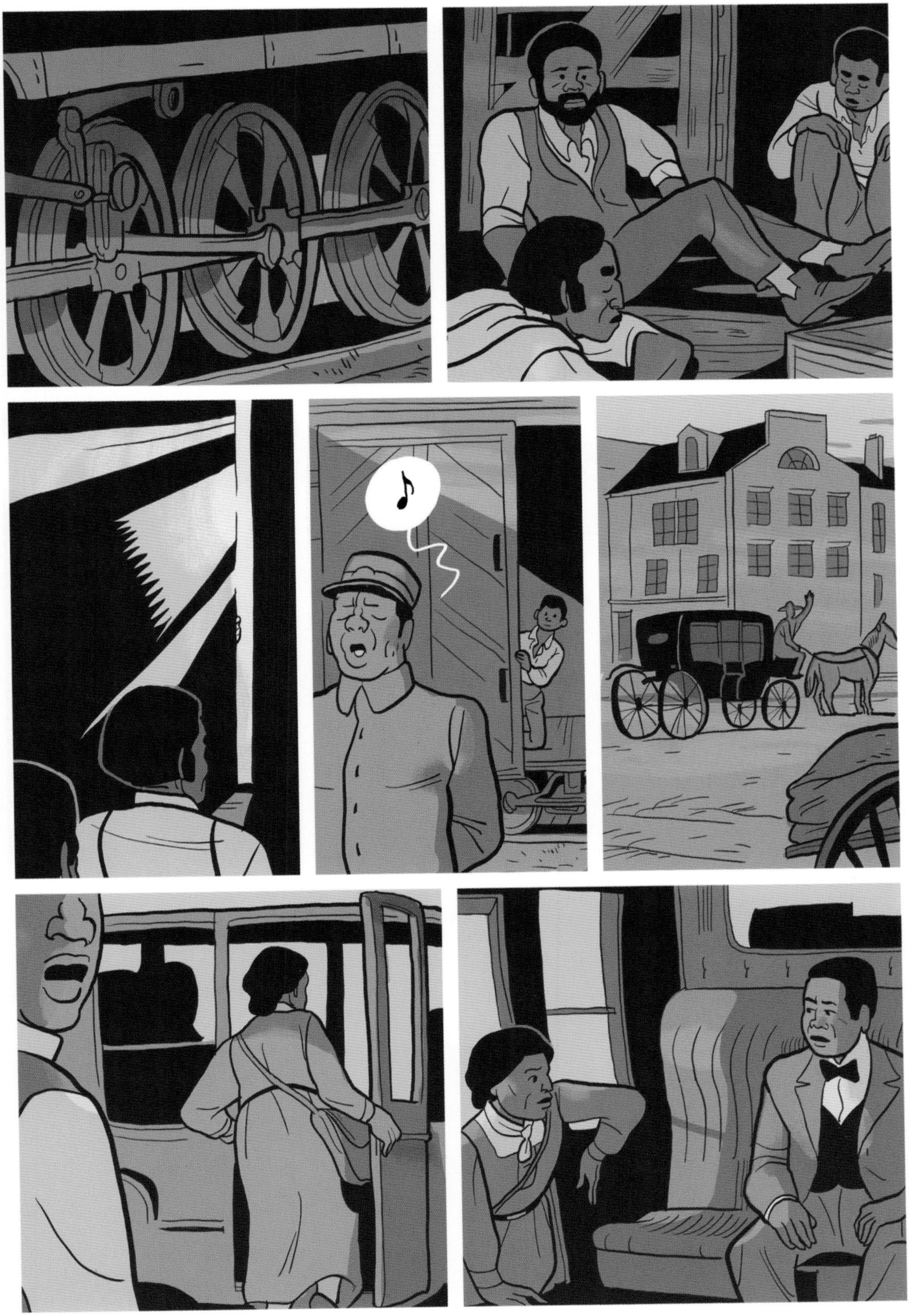

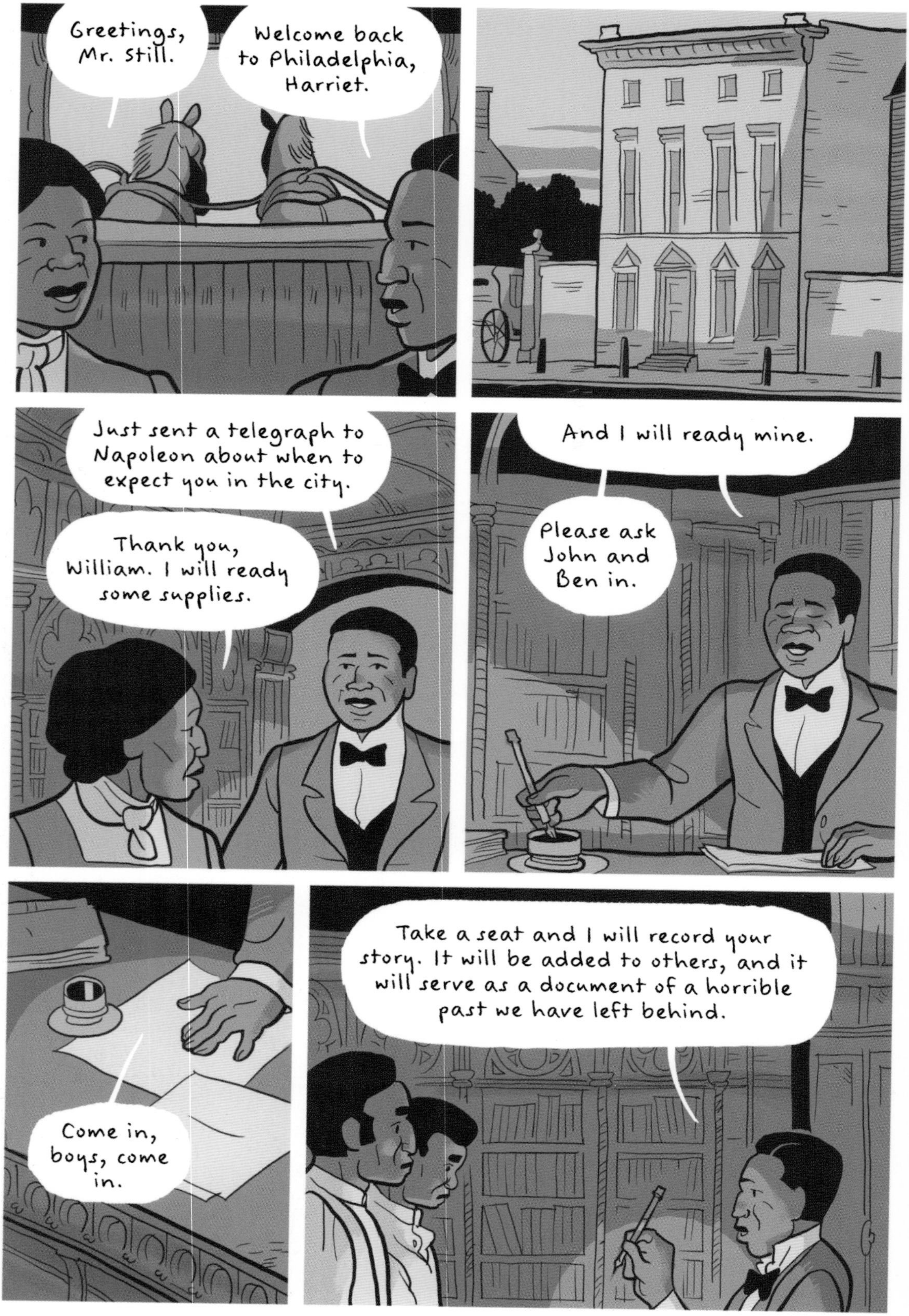
Greetings, Mr. Still.
Welcome back to Philadelphia, Harriet.
Just sent a telegraph to Napoleon about when to expect you in the city.
Thank you, William. I will ready some supplies.
And I will ready mine.
Please ask John and Ben in.
Come in, boys, come in.
Take a seat and I will record your story. It will be added to others, and it will serve as a document of a horrible past we have left behind.

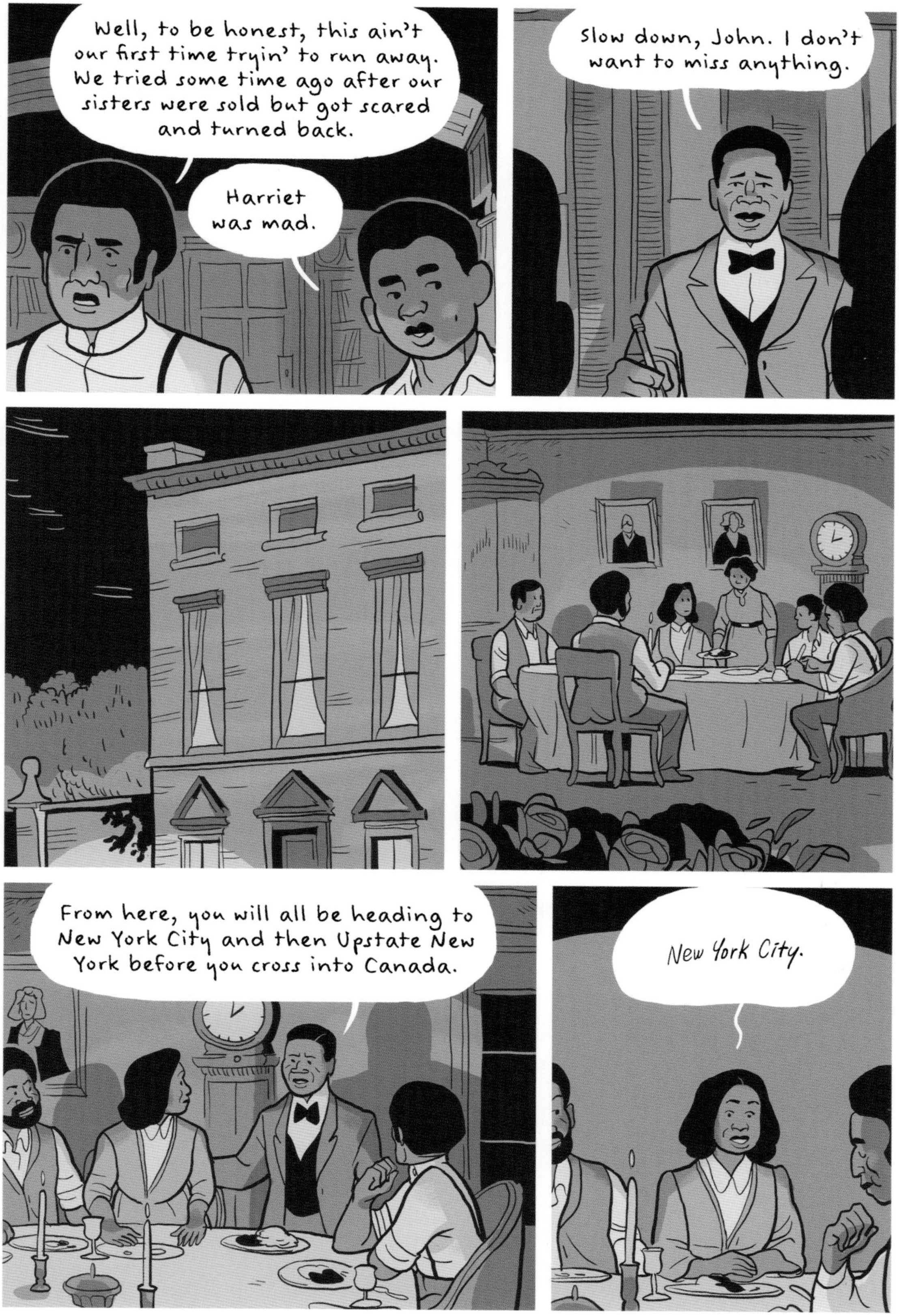
Well, to be honest, this ain't our first time tryin' to run away. We tried some time ago after our sisters were sold but got scared and turned back.
Harriet was mad.
Slow down, John. I don't want to miss anything.
From here, you will all be heading to New York City and then Upstate New York before you cross into Canada.
New York City.

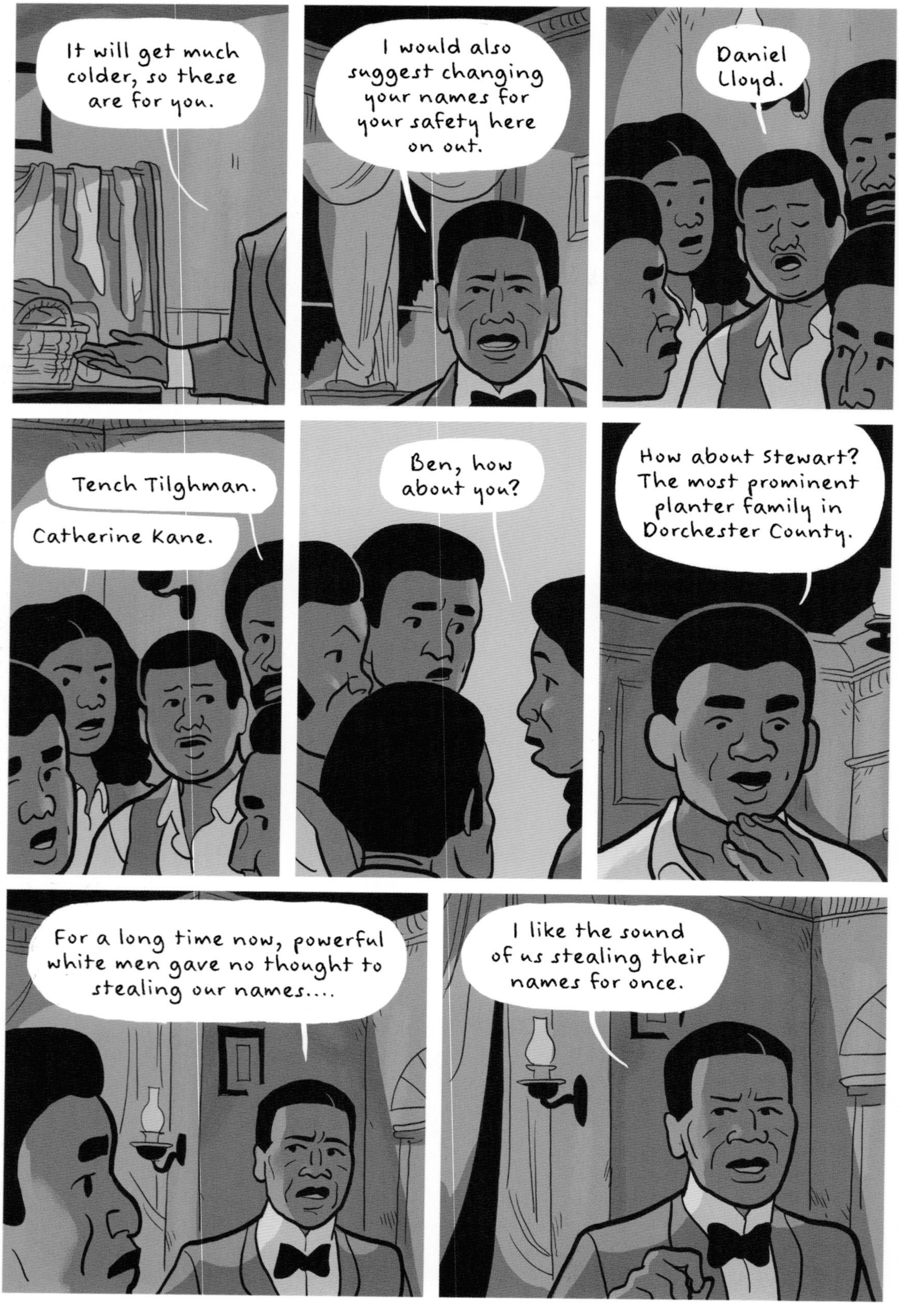
It will get much colder, so these are for you.
I would also suggest changing your names for your safety here on out.
Daniel Lloyd.
Tench Tilghman.
Catherine Kane.
Ben, how about you?
How about Stewart? The most prominent planter family in Dorchester County.
For a long time now, powerful white men gave no thought to stealing our names....
I like the sound of us stealing their names for once.

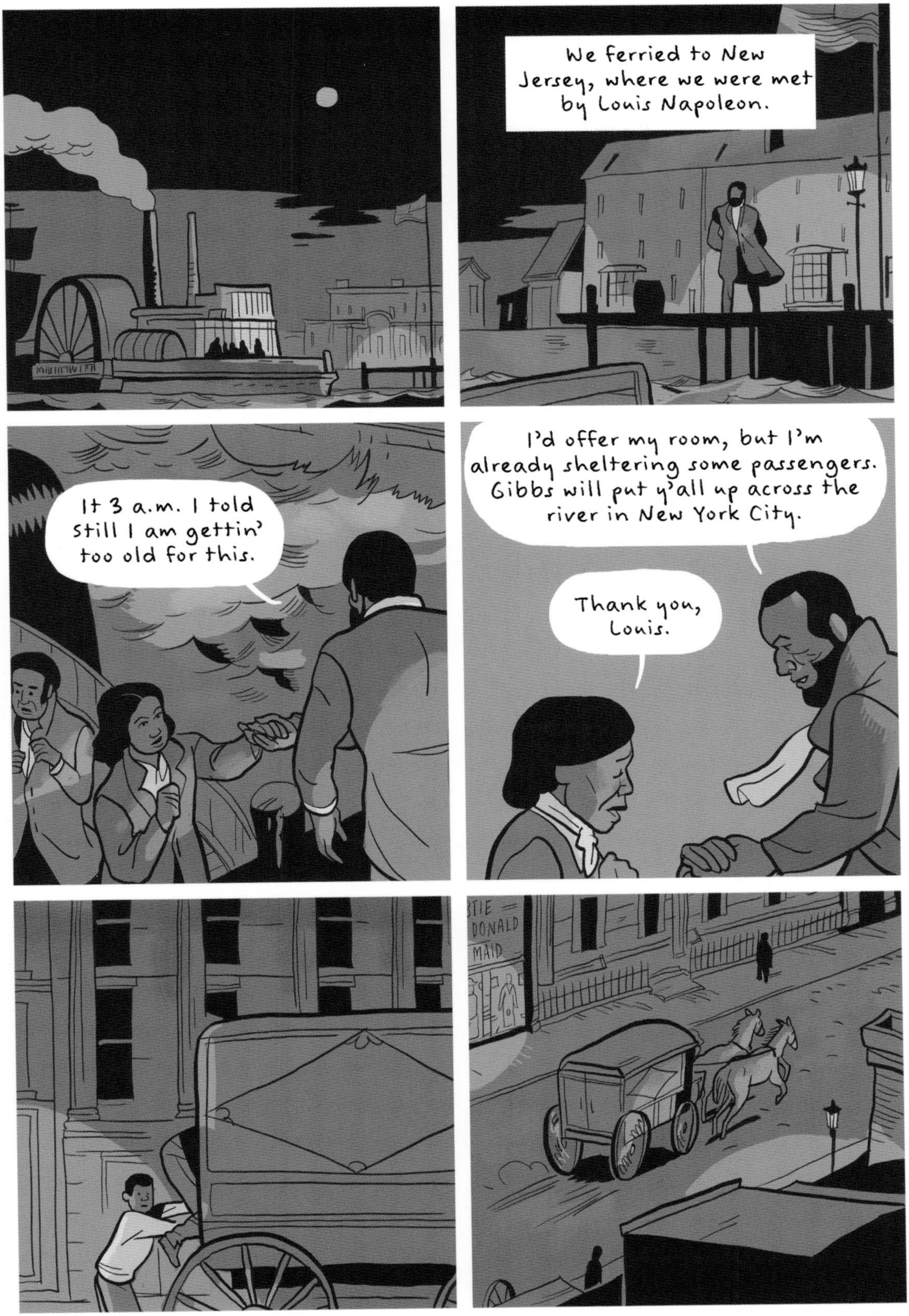
We ferried to New Jersey, where we were met by Louis Napoleon.
It 3 a.m. I told still I am gettin' too old for this.
I'd offer my room, but I'm already sheltering some passengers. Gibbs will put y'all up across the river in New York City.
Thank you, Louis.

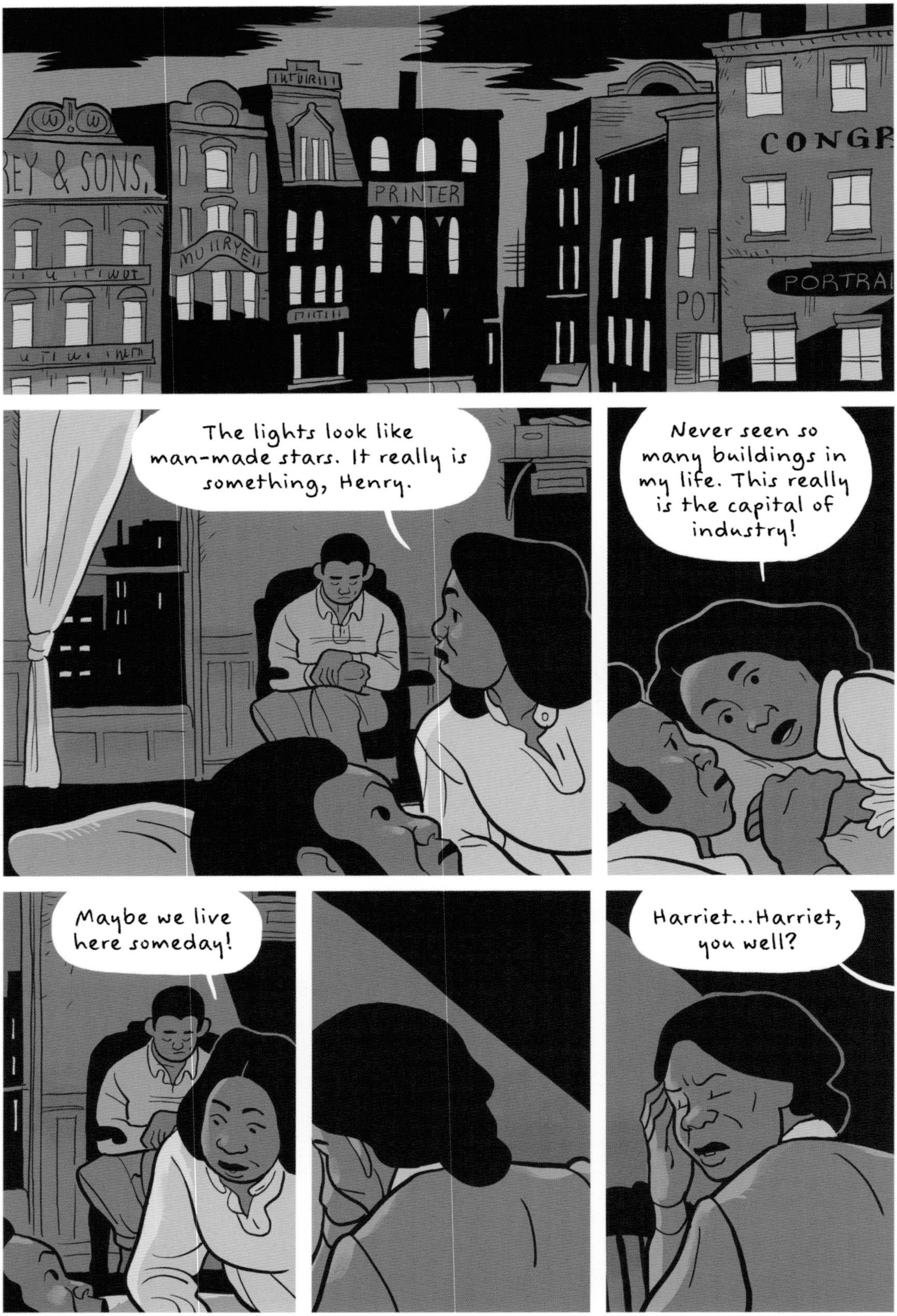
REY & SONS
PRINTER
CONGR
PORTRAI
POT
The lights look like man-made stars. It really is something, Henry.
Never seen so many buildings in my life. This really is the capital of industry!
Maybe we live here someday!
Harriet...Harriet, you well?

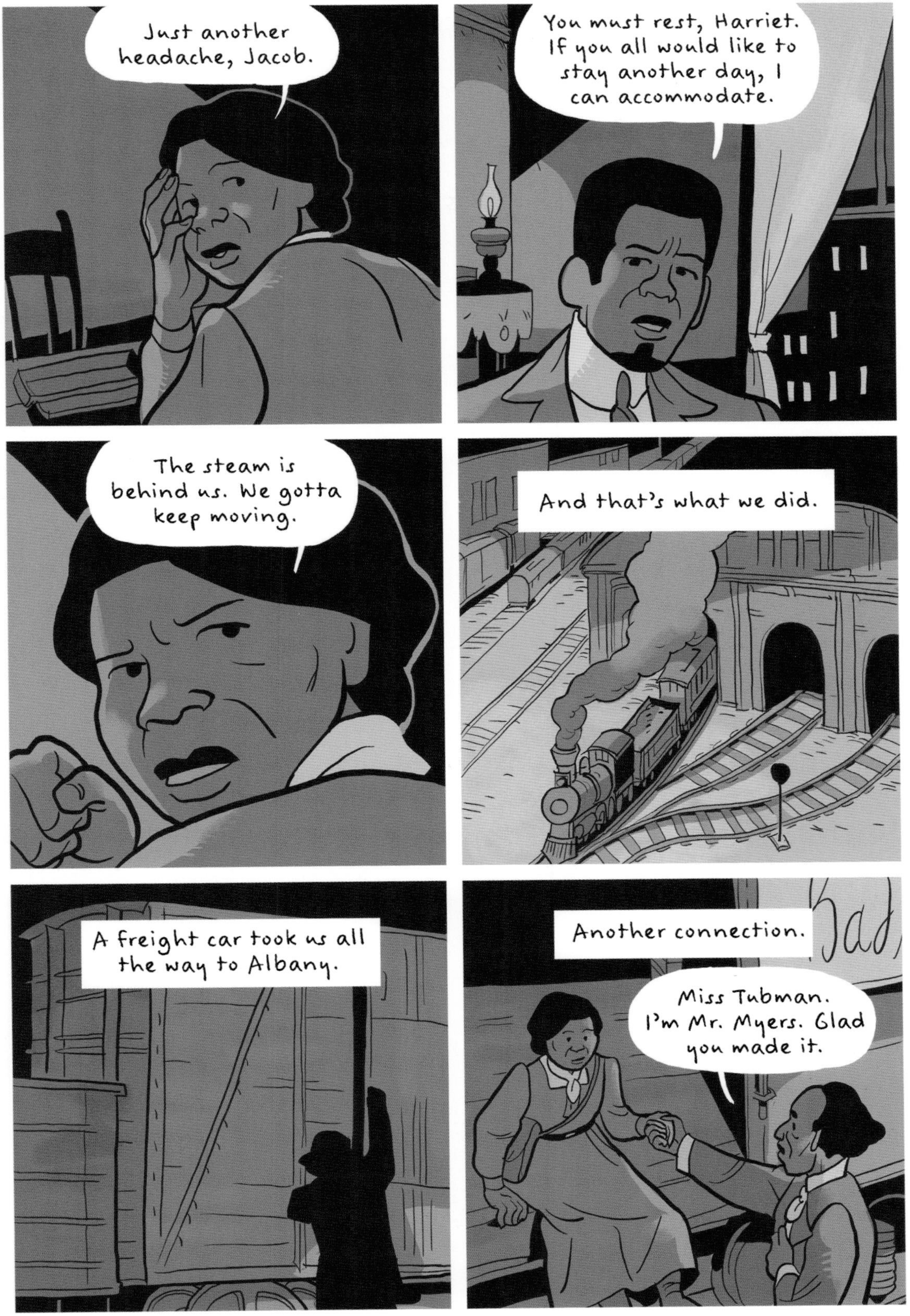
Just another headache, Jacob.
You must rest, Harriet. If you all would like to stay another day, I can accommodate.
The steam is behind us. We gotta keep moving.
And that's what we did.
A freight car took us all the way to Albany.
Another connection.
Miss Tubman. I'm Mr. Myers. Glad you made it.

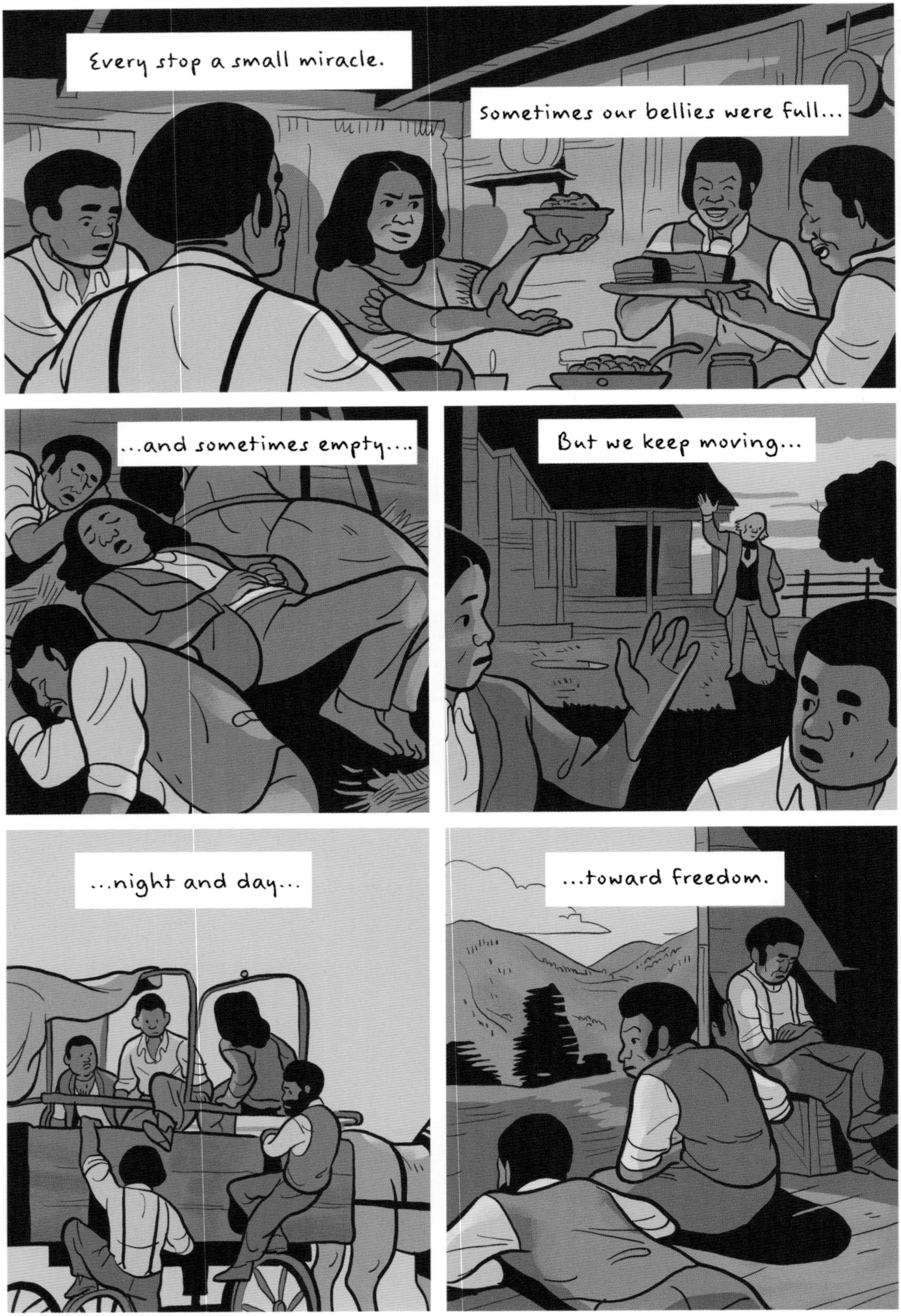
Every stop a small miracle.
Sometimes our bellies were full...
...and sometimes empty....
But we keep moving...
...night and day...
...toward freedom.

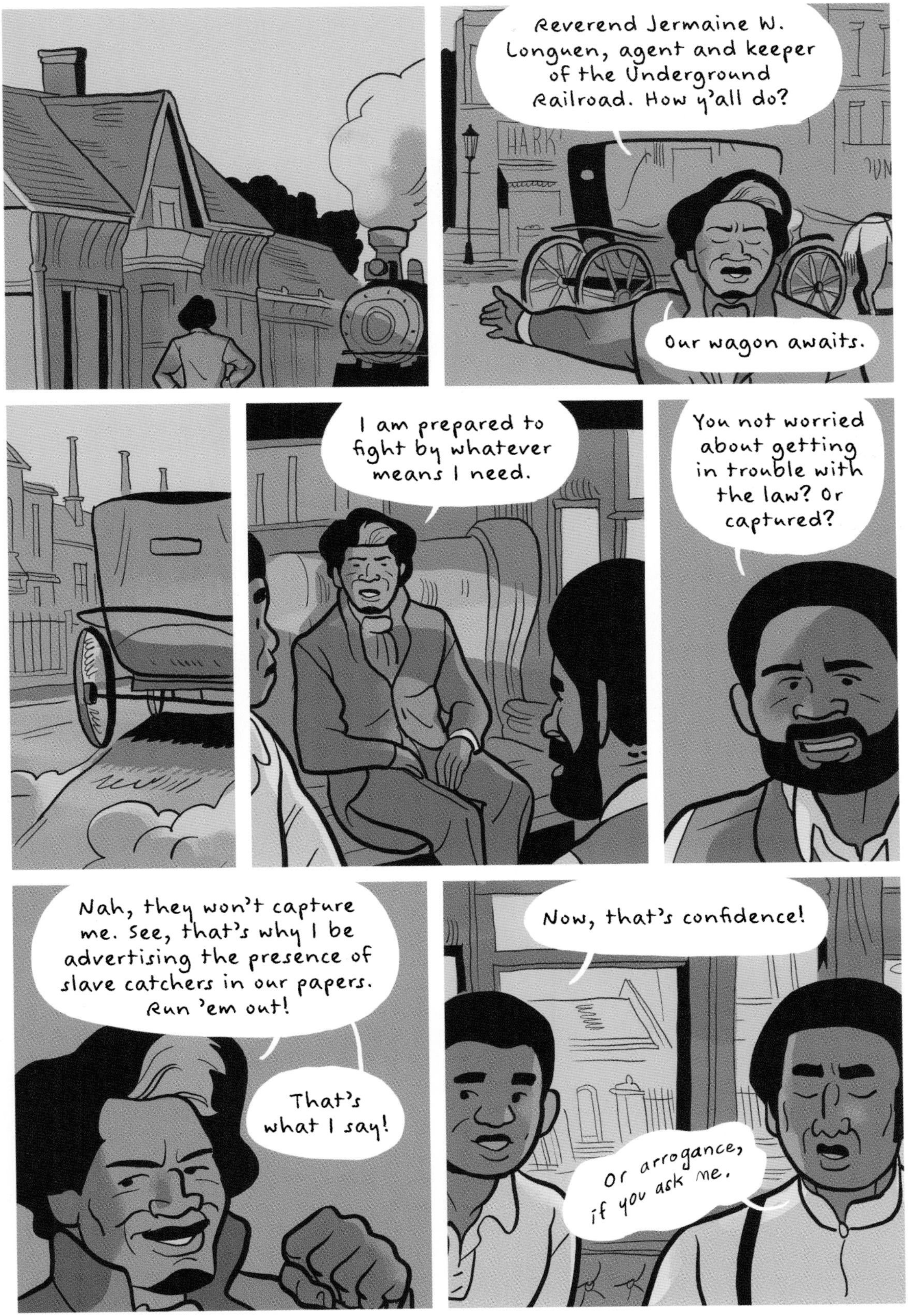
Reverend Jermaine W. Longuen, agent and keeper of the Underground Railroad. How y'all do?
Our wagon awaits.
I am prepared to fight by whatever means I need.
You not worried about getting in trouble with the law? Or captured?
Nah, they won't capture me. See, that's why I be advertising the presence of slave catchers in our papers. Run 'em out!
That's what I say!
Now, that's confidence!
Or arrogance, if you ask me.

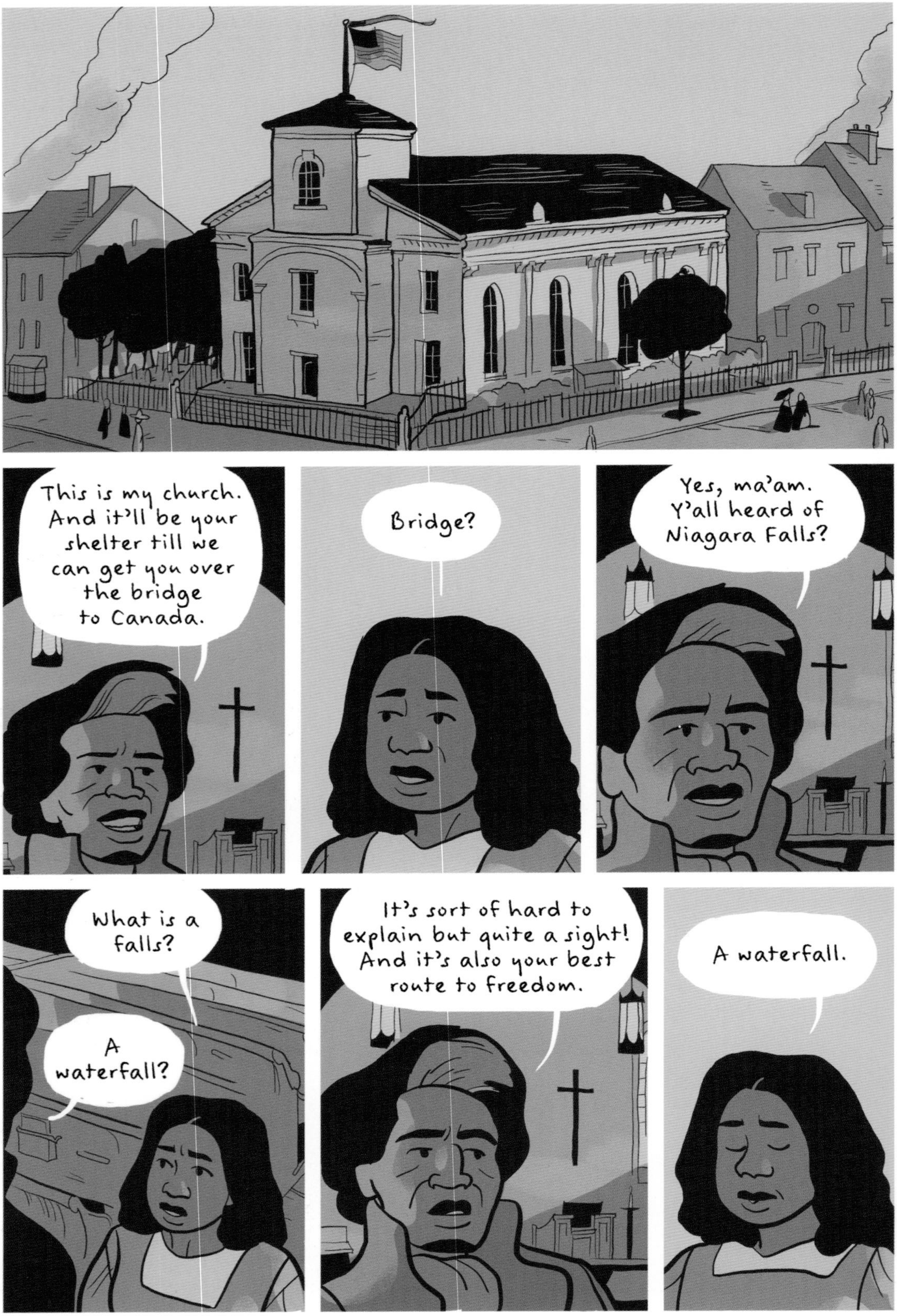
This is my church. And it'll be your shelter till we can get you over the bridge to Canada.
Bridge?
Yes, ma'am. Y'all heard of Niagara Falls?
What is a falls?
A waterfall?
It's sort of hard to explain but quite a sight! And it's also your best route to freedom.
A waterfall.

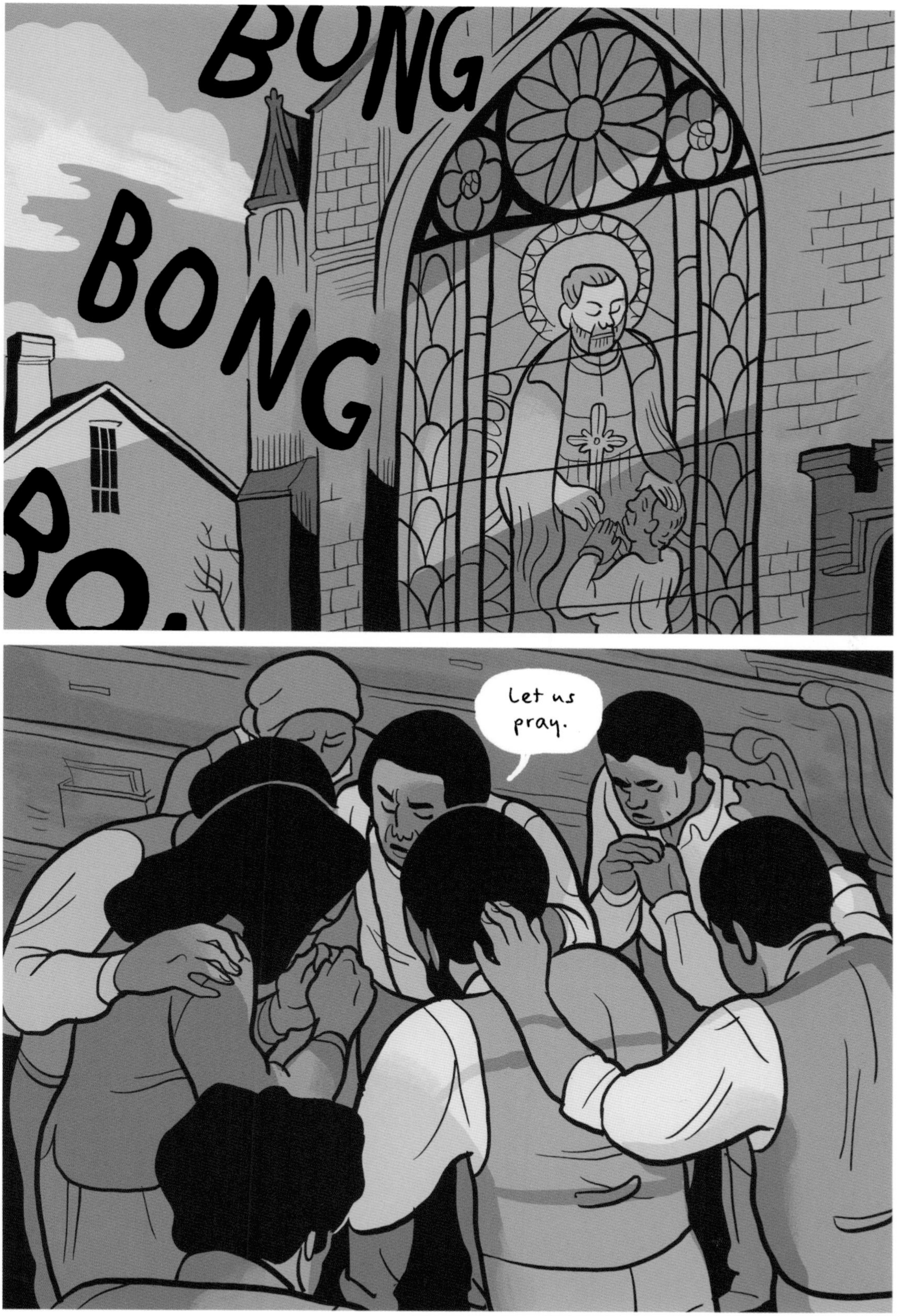
BONG
BONG
BONG
Let us pray.

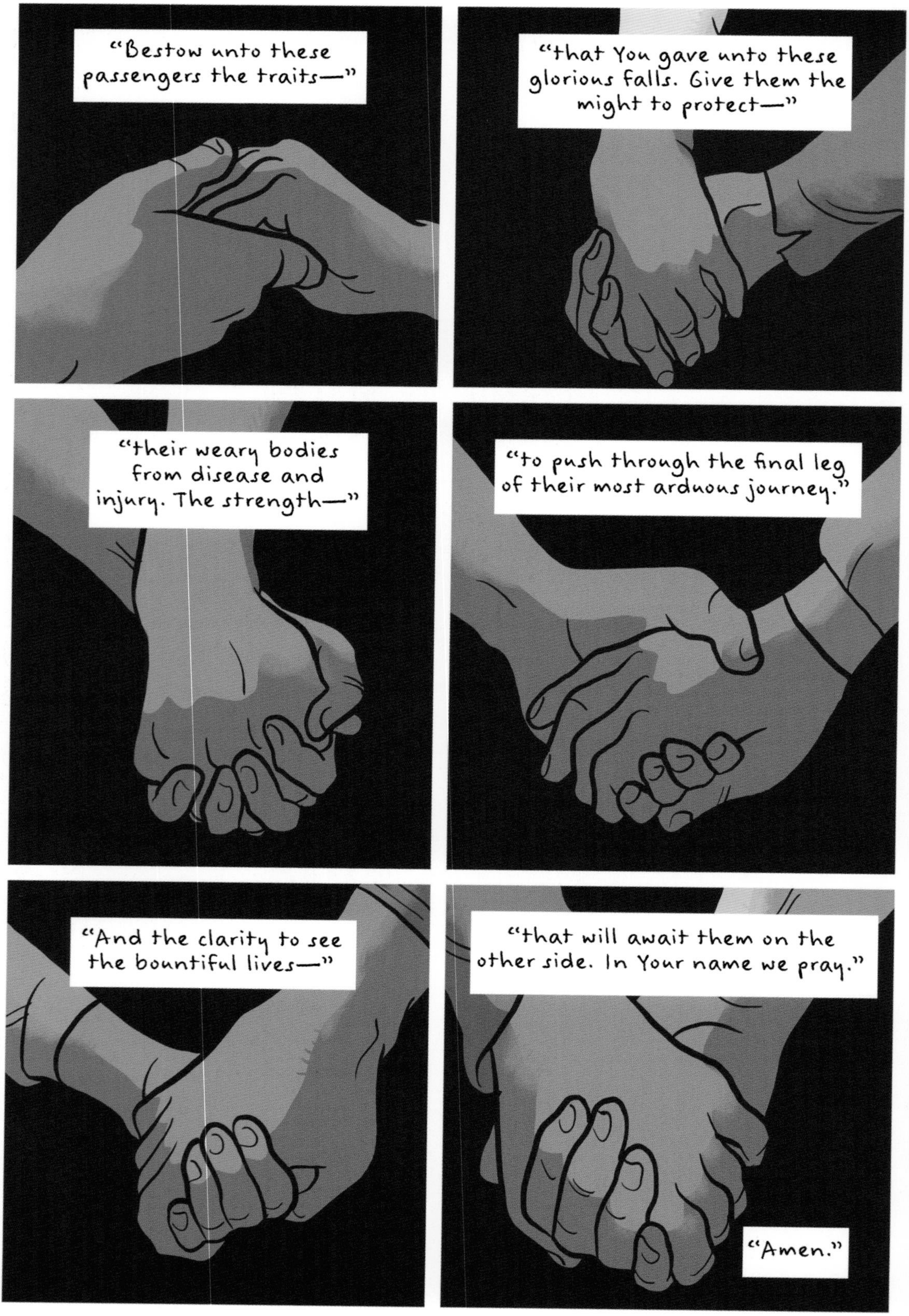
"Bestow unto these passengers the traits—"
"that You gave unto these glorious falls. Give them the might to protect—"
"their weary bodies from disease and injury. The strength—"
"to push through the final leg of their most arduous journey."
"And the clarity to see the bountiful lives—"
"that will await them on the other side. In Your name we pray."
"Amen."

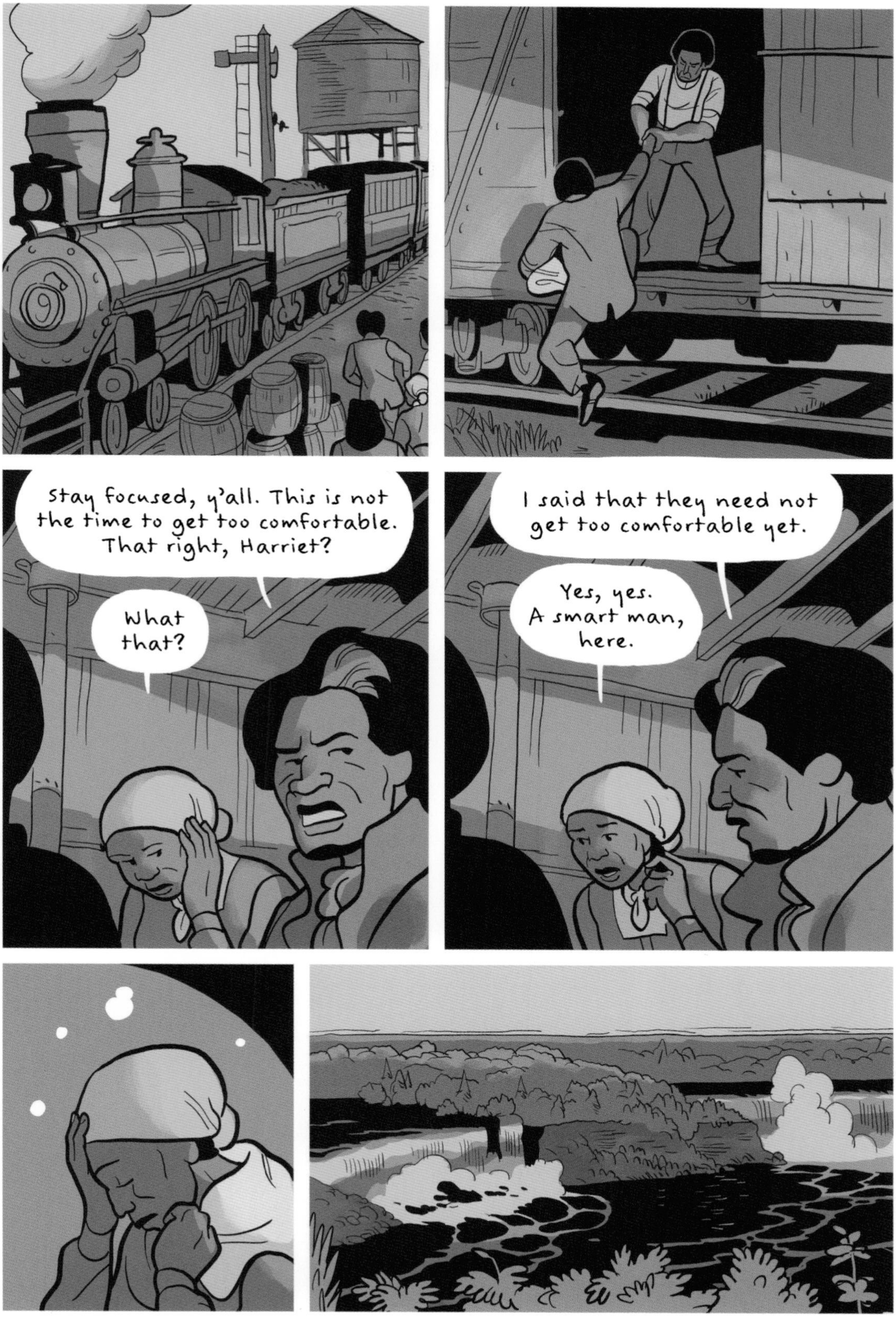
Stay focused, y'all. This is not the time to get too comfortable. That right, Harriet?
What that?
I said that they need not get too comfortable yet.
Yes, yes. A smart man, here.

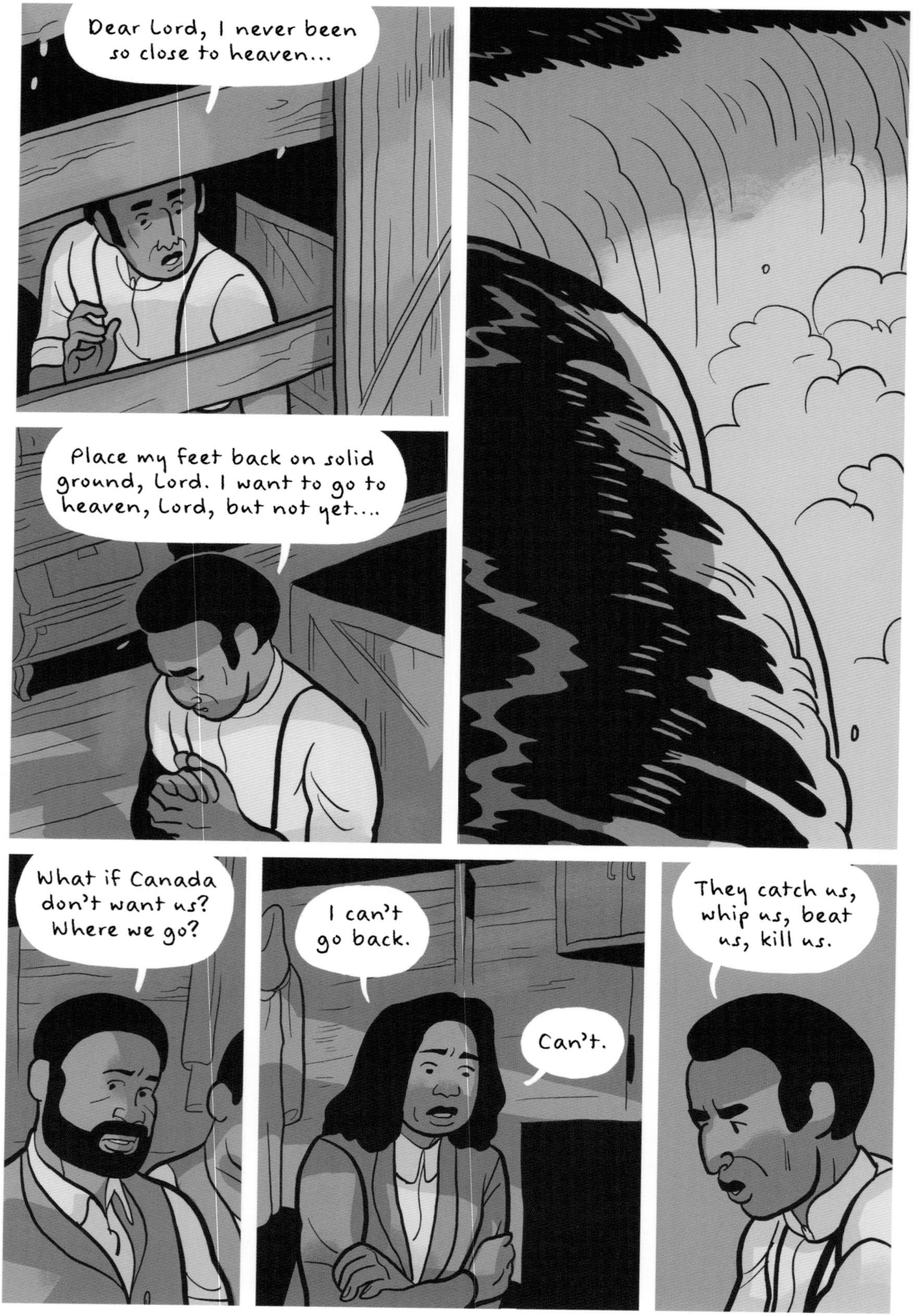
Dear Lord, I never been so close to heaven...
Place my feet back on solid ground, Lord. I want to go to heaven, Lord, but not yet....
What if Canada don't want us? Where we go?
I can't go back.
Can't.
They catch us, whip us, beat us, kill us.

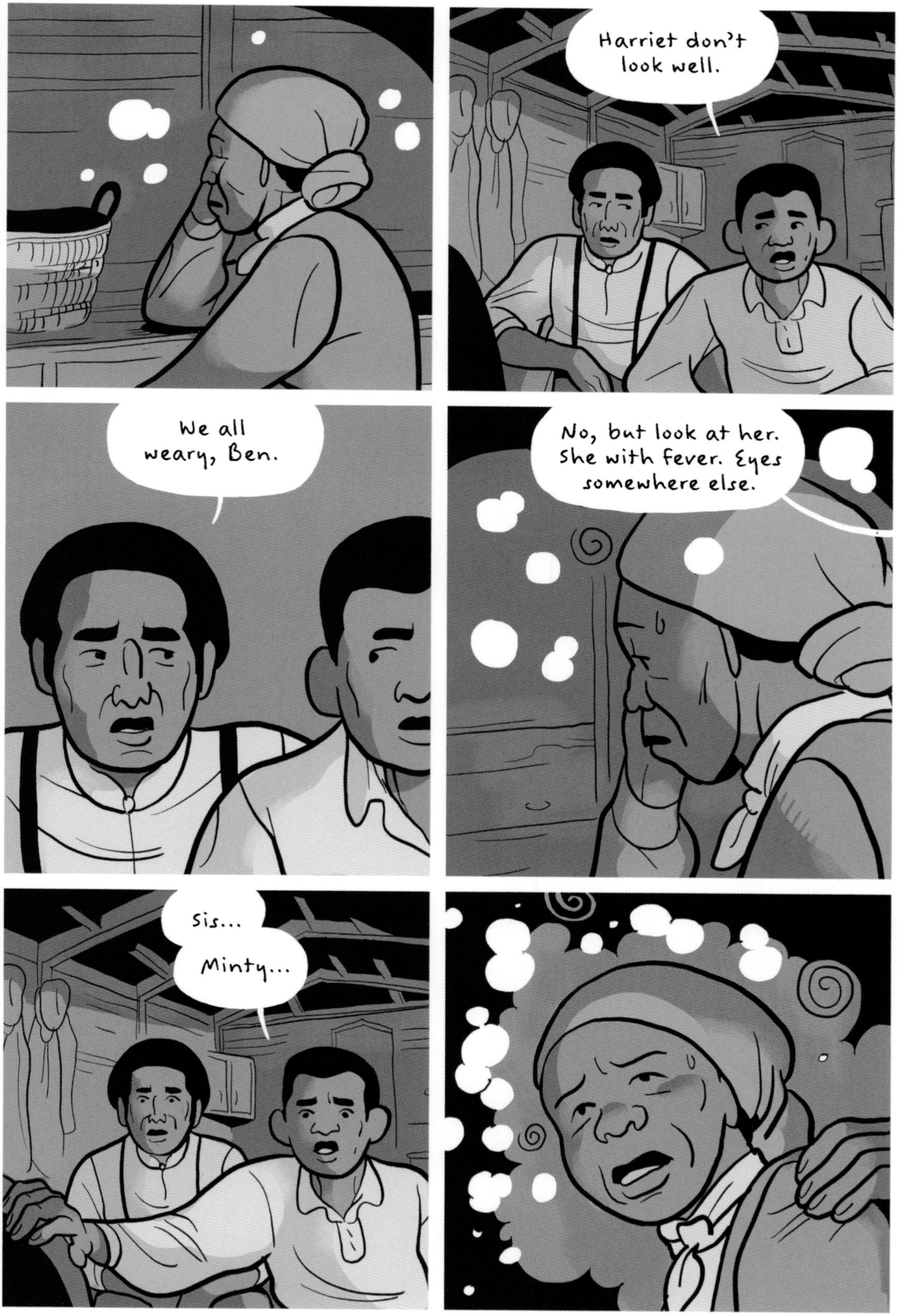
Harriet don't look well.
We all weary, Ben.
No, but look at her. She with fever. Eyes somewhere else.
Sis...
Minty...

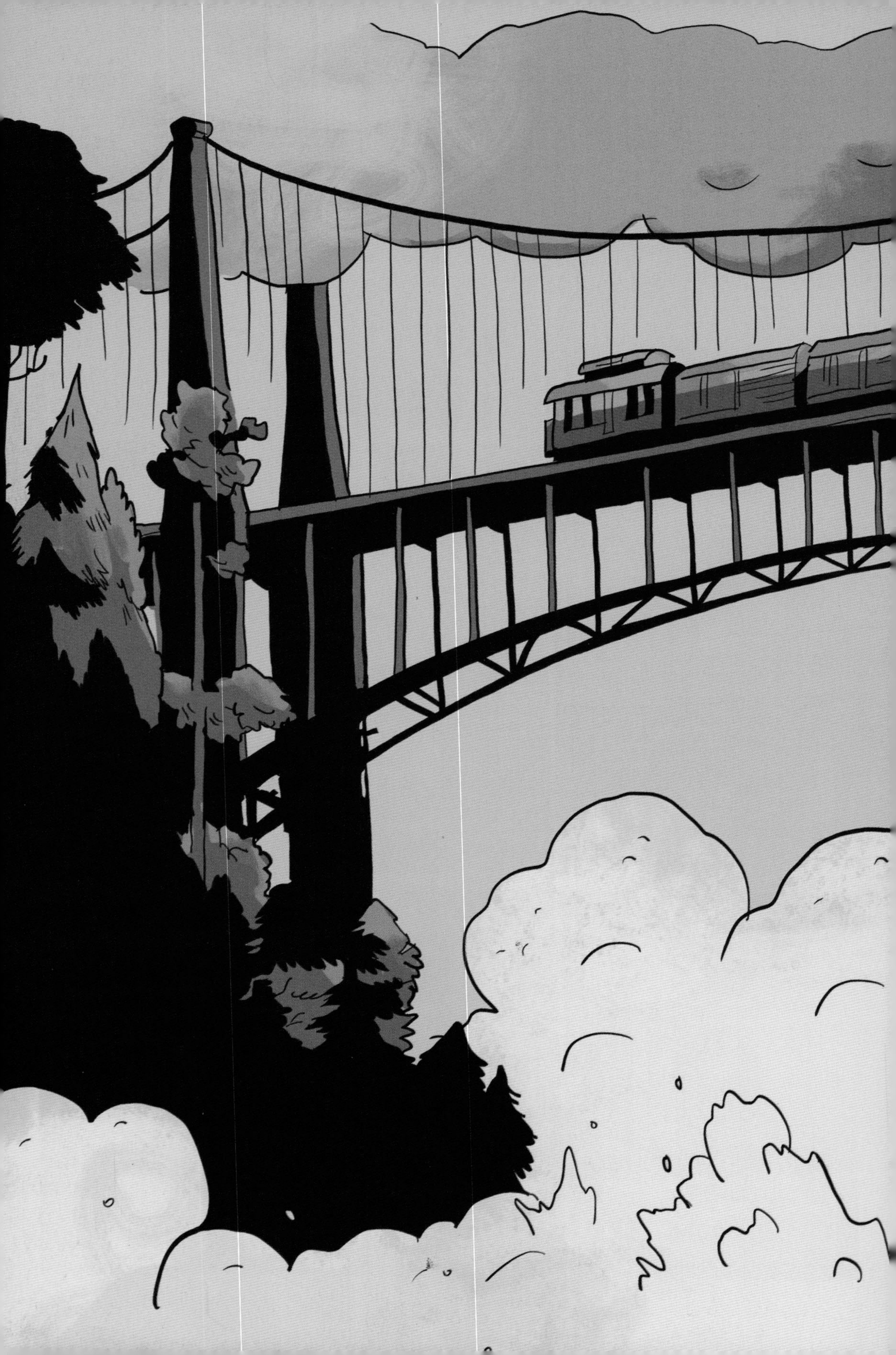

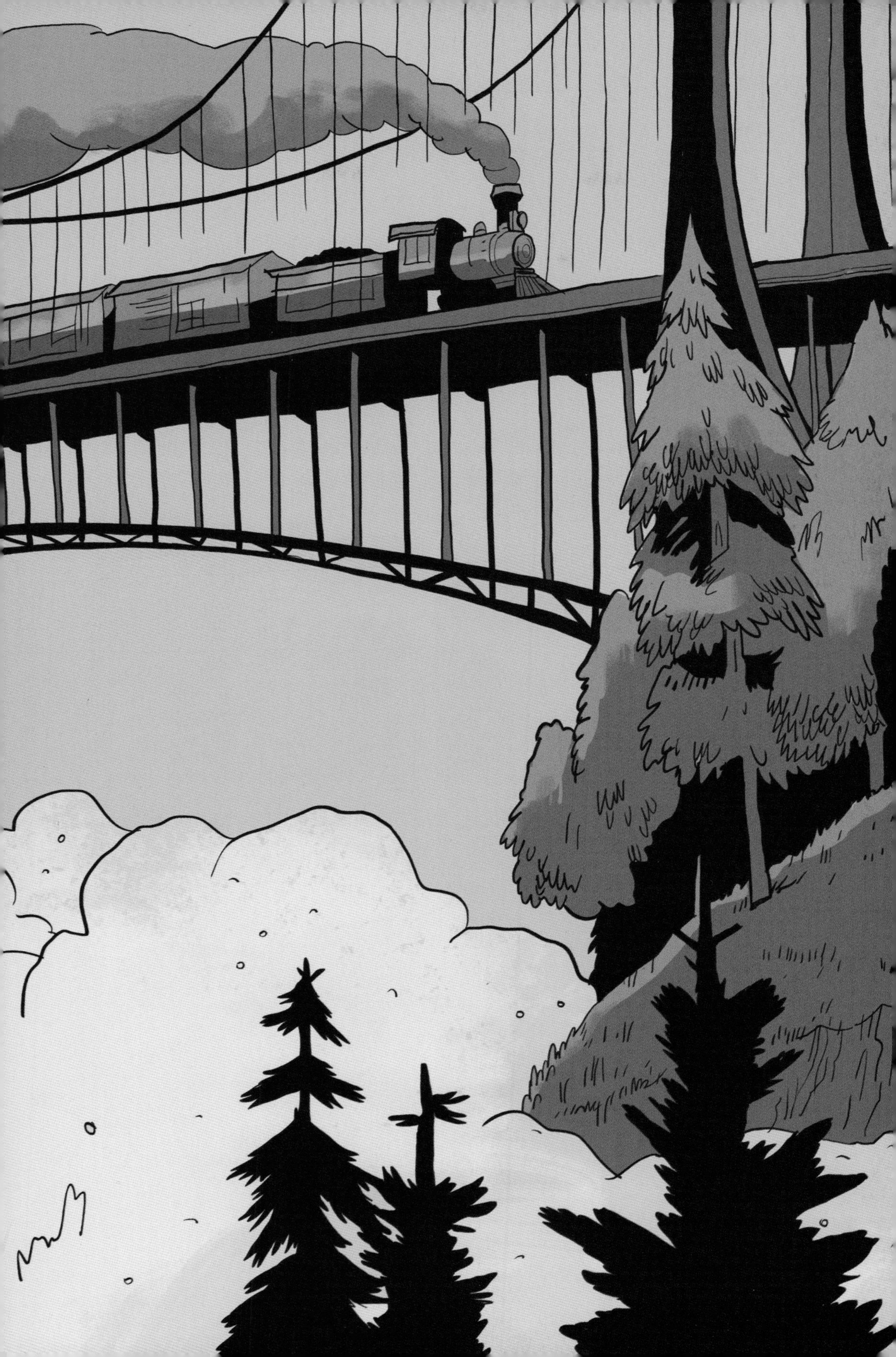

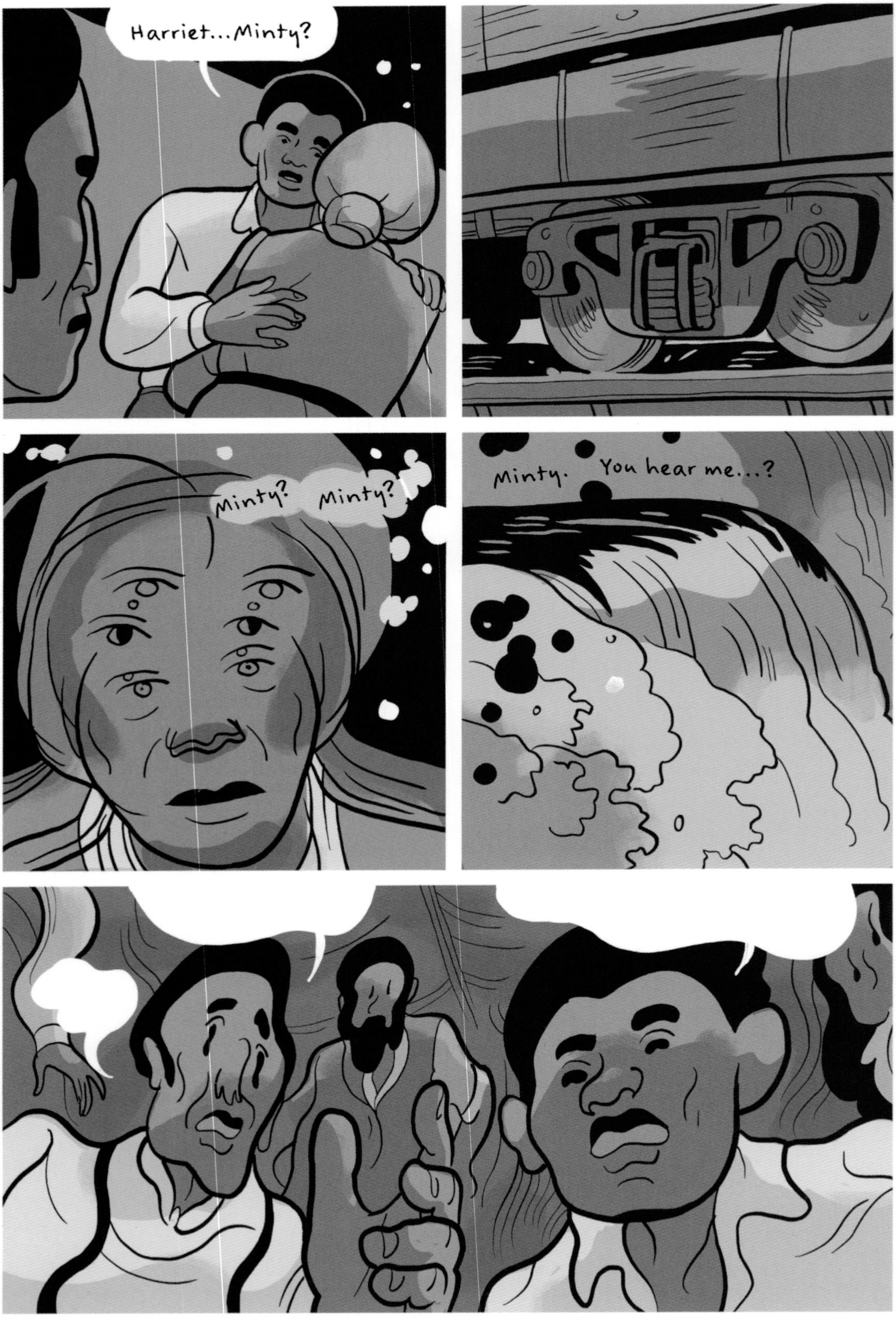
Harriet...Minty?
Minty? Minty?
Minty. You hear me...?

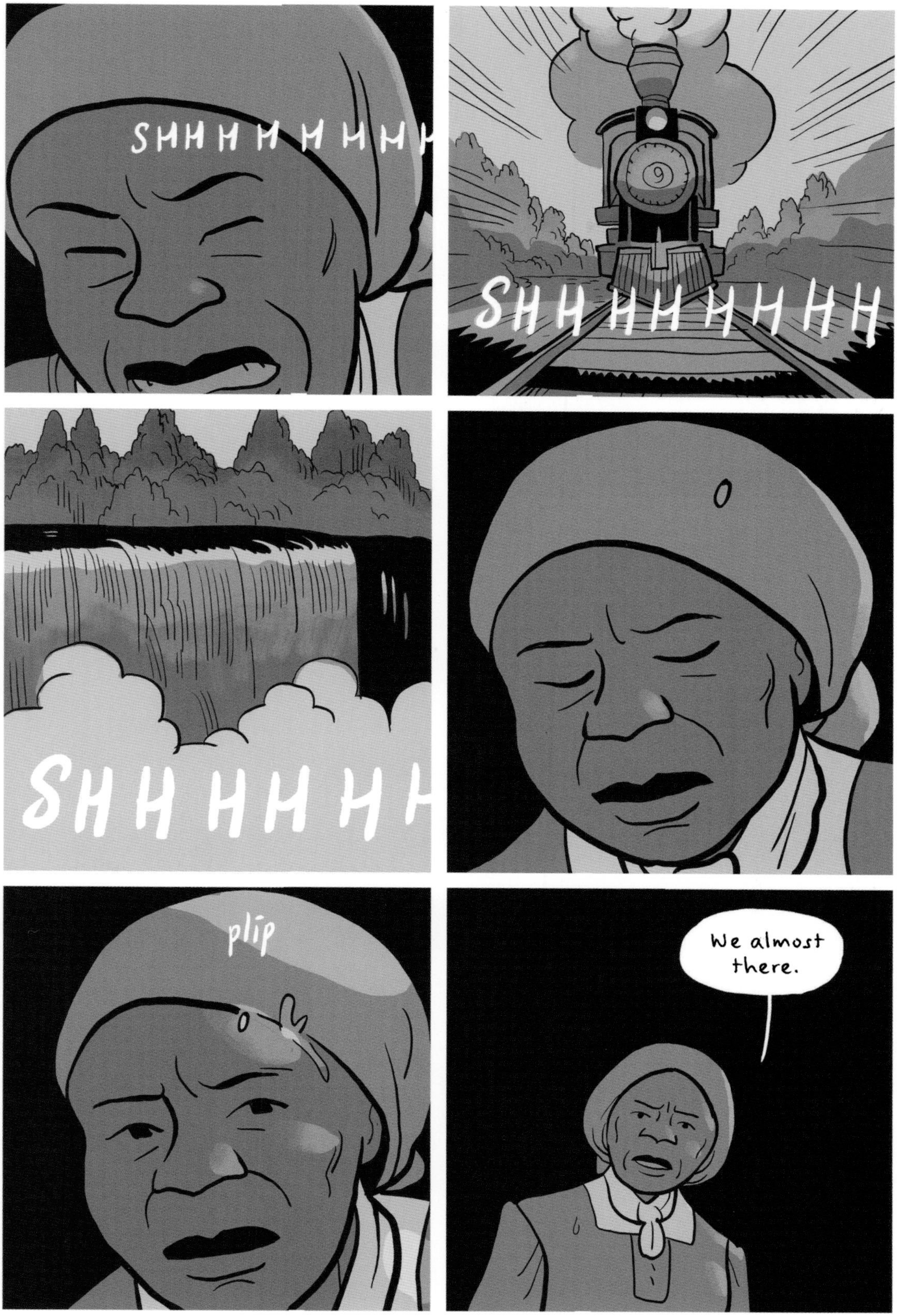
SHHHHHHHH
SHHHHHHHHH
SHHHHHH
plip
We almost there.

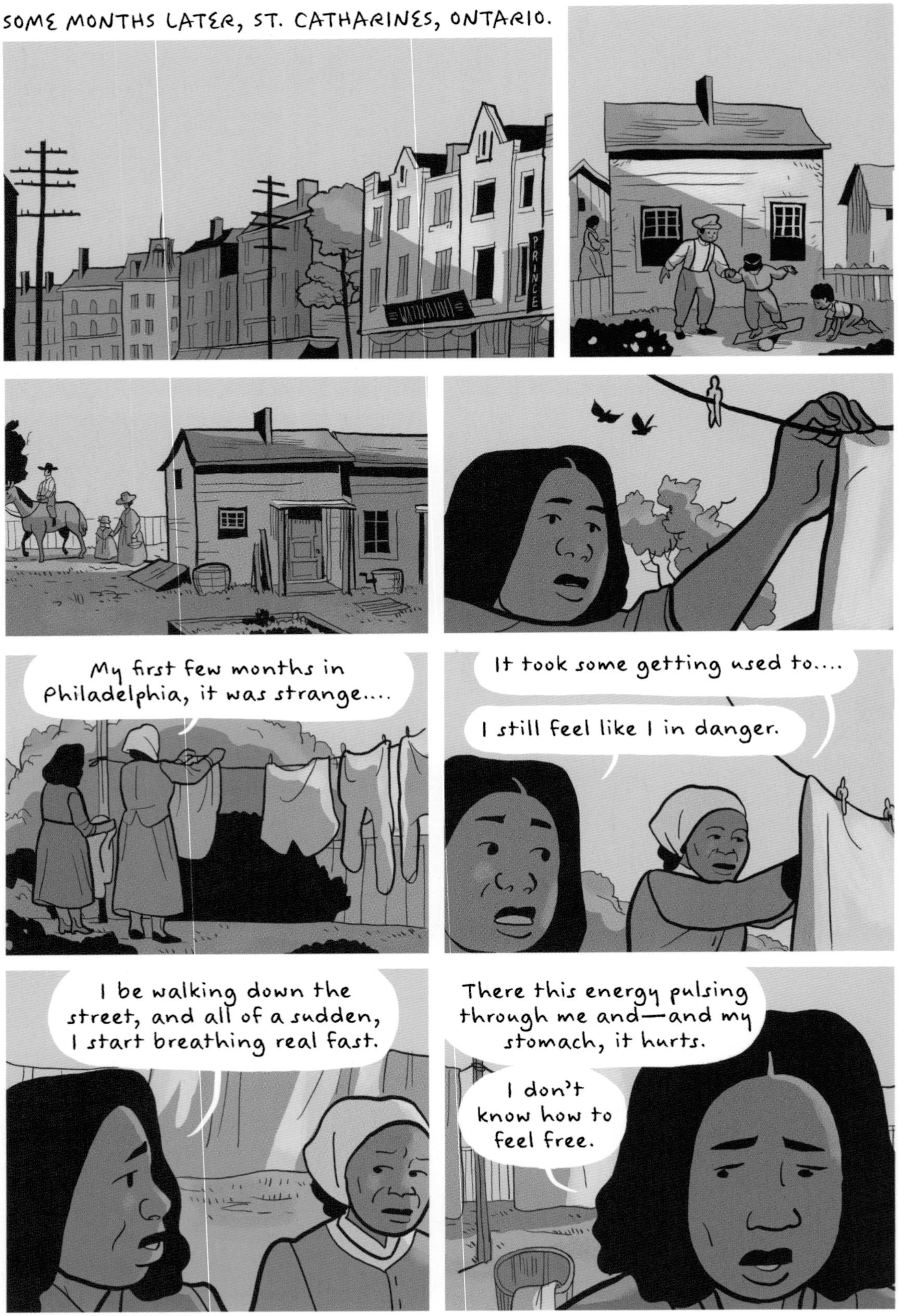
SOME MONTHS LATER, ST. CATHARINES, ONTARIO.
PRINCE
My first few months in Philadelphia, it was strange....
It took some getting used to....
I still feel like I in danger.
I be walking down the street, and all of a sudden, I start breathing real fast.
There this energy pulsing through me and—and my stomach, it hurts.
I don't know how to feel free.

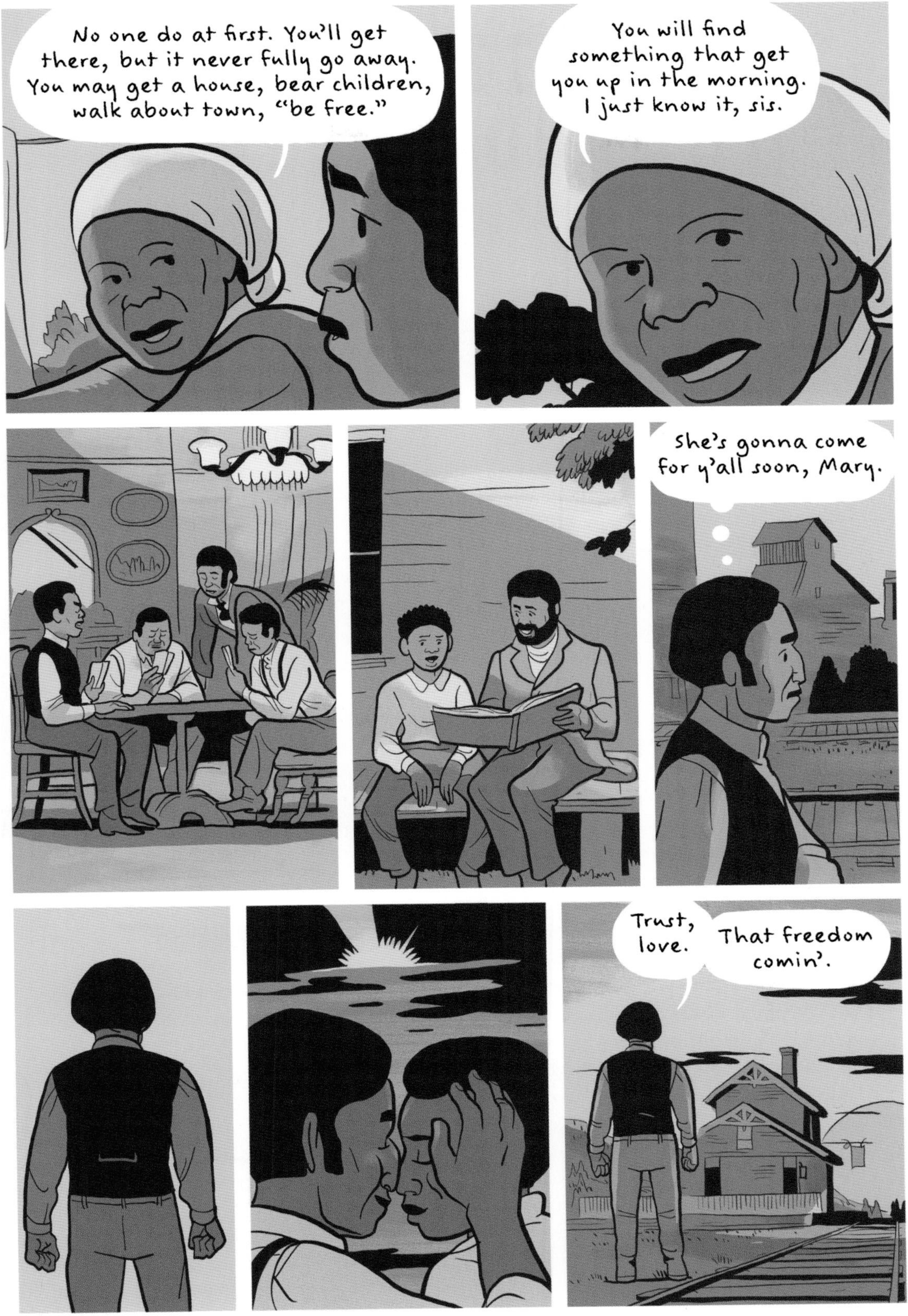
No one do at first. You'll get there, but it never fully go away. You may get a house, bear children, walk about town, "be free."
You will find something that get you up in the morning. I just know it, sis.
She's gonna come for y'all soon, Mary.
Trust, love.
That freedom comin'.

HARRIET TUBMAN
TOWARD FREEDOM

Panel Discussions

PAGE 8:
William Still

William Still (1821–1902) was born in Burlington County, New Jersey, to a mother who was an escaped slave and a father who had bought his freedom. Although Still was born free, he was raised hearing about the trials of slavery from his parents. After moving to Philadelphia in 1844, Still was hired as a clerk for the Pennsylvania Society for the Abolition of Slavery and became a key figure in the Underground Railroad, helping assist fugitive slaves who came to the city. He eventually became the chairman of the Philadelphia Vigilance Committee. Still had little formal education but taught himself to read and write and used these skills to document slave stories, write letters, keep records, and unite formerly enslaved families. He is best known for his self-published book *The Underground Railroad* (1872), a documentation of the lives of escaped slaves.

During the Civil War, Still operated a post exchange at Camp William Penn, a training camp for "colored" troops, north of Philadelphia. Still became a businessman, running a stove store and purchasing a coal yard, and eventually opened the first YMCA for Blacks in Philadelphia. He was also a noted philanthropist and financier, organizing in support of civil rights for fugitive slaves and free Blacks, as well as universal suffrage.

PAGE 8: *Philadelphia Vigilance Committee*

The Philadelphia Vigilance Committee (1837–1844) was a secret branch of the Vigilant Association of Philadelphia, a group founded by abolitionist Robert Purvis (Jacob White). Like its sister organizations, the committee promoted antislavery publicly and raised funding to aid "colored" people in need through membership dues. The committee assisted runaway slaves passing through Philadelphia, providing resources such as food, clothing, shelter, transportation, medical services, and legal fees. The activities of the committee were kept private from the public to protect members, donors, and fugitive slaves from retribution.

A new General Vigilance Committee was established in 1852, with Purvis appointed as committee head. The committee focused its efforts on assisting slaves from states such as Virginia and Maryland and helping them escape to New York State and on to Canada.

PAGE 11:
Brodess Family

Rit, Harriet's mother, born between 1785–1789, was owned by a man named Atthow Pattison. Pattison's daughter Elizabeth had a daughter named Mary Pattison, who married Joseph Brodess, a Bucktown farmer. They had a son named Edward Brodess. Mary was widowed and remarried Dorchester County landowner and widower Anthony Thompson. Mary moved into the Thompson household with her son, Edward; Rit; and four male slaves whom her deceased husband had owned. Rit met Ben Ross, one of Thompson's slaves, and they married and started a family. When Edward Brodess became an adult, ownership of Rit, Harriet, and her siblings was transferred to him. In early adulthood, Tubman and her siblings moved from Thompson's plantation to Bucktown, where Edward had his own plantation. In 1827, Edward married Eliza Brodess.

PAGE 17: *Harriet's Injury and Condition*

Harriet Tubman suffered a traumatic head injury in her youth, which affected her for the rest of her life. Historical accounts detail that she was struck with a metal weight that damaged her skull, leaving her unconscious and bloody. Tubman did not receive immediate medical care following the incident. Throughout her life, she experienced severe headaches, seizures, and bouts of narcolepsy. She was also said to have had "visions," dreams or hallucinations that she interpreted as messages from God. Some modern researchers believe her symptoms to be consistent with a temporal lobe injury, including temporal lobe epilepsy (TLE), which is associated with the sensory regions of the brain, as well as memory and emotion.

PAGE 20: *William Lloyd Garrison*

William Lloyd Garrison (1805–1879) was an influential American abolitionist, journalist, and printer-publisher. He founded the abolitionist weekly newspaper *The Liberator*, which was published from 1831 to the end of the Civil War in 1865. A fierce advocate for the emancipation of enslaved Blacks, Garrison helped organize the New England Anti-Slavery Society and founded the America Anti-Slavery Society. Garrison's strongly held beliefs, including the necessity for women's suffrage, led to a split between him and other factions of the Society leading up to the Civil War.

PAGE 22: *Fugitive Slave Act of 1850*

On September 18, 1850, Congress approved the second Fugitive Slave Act as part of the Compromise of 1850, which was designed to help settle points of contention between the North and South over slavery. Perhaps the largest expansion of federal authority over the states in the antebellum era, this law required that escaped slaves be returned to their masters upon capture. Nicknamed the "Bloodhound Law" by Blacks and abolitionists for the use of dogs to track runaway slaves, this law gave local federal officials authority in fugitive slave cases, even allowing for verdicts to be rendered without trial by jury.

The implementation of this law was met with some resistance from coalitions of free Blacks, fugitive slaves, Quakers, and abolitionists. It also led to widespread fear in northern Black communities. Enforcement of the Fugitive Slave Law led to the migration of thousands of escaped slaves from the northern United States to Canada, where they were not subject to this law.

PAGE 23: *Antislavery Bazaars*

Charity fairs became a means of fundraising along the Atlantic coasts in the 1820s and 1830s. Like bake sales, this form of fundraising was often the primary focus of women's antislavery organizations such as Ladies' Aid Societies. Bazaars, which were often held before Christmas, hosted vendors selling children's toys, sewn goods, foods, and antislavery publications. These yearly events, where holiday gifts were bought and sold commercially, led to the practice of the modern US Christmas shopping season.

PAGE 27:
Harriet's Religion
While young Harriet was required to attend Methodist church services held by her master's son Dr. Anthony C. Thompson, it is likely that she and other members of the Ross family pulled from multiple religious faiths, including Episcopalian, Baptist, Catholic, and African cultural and spiritual traditions. Tubman attended Black evangelical churches as well, such as the African Methodist Episcopal Church, which often interpreted doctrine in favor of the liberation of slaves. Black women preachers, such as Maria Stewart, Sojourner Truth, Jarena Lee, and Zilpha emerged at camp meetings on the Eastern Shore during the mid-1800s, influencing and motivating Tubman as well. It is possible that some of Tubman's hyper-religiosity was consistent with her TLE, but she drew meaning from her religious experiences and visions, believing herself to be an instrument of God who was meant to liberate and guide slaves toward freedom.

PAGE 35:
Tobacco Economy
Tobacco was a dominant cash crop in the Chesapeake region, including Maryland. Cultivating tobacco (planting, harvesting, curing, and packaging) required skilled labor year-round. Fewer slaves were required to farm tobacco compared to crops such as cotton and rice farther down south. As such, slave families in tobacco regions tended to be spread across different plantations. It was not uncommon for a husband and wife to live and work apart in "abroad marriages," with the husband being allowed to visit his children twice a week. This sort of structure led to more spread-out kinship ties compared to in the Deep South, where slave families tended to live and work together.

PAGE 41: *Breaking up Slave Families*
Slave families could be separated at any time for a variety of reasons. The domestic slave trade in the US increased with the growth of the cotton economy following the invention of the cotton gin. As a result, many slaves, particularly young able-bodied men from the upper South, were sold to plantations in the Deep South to work in the cotton fields. When slave masters died, slaves were often sold and redistributed as part of their estates. Slaves could be sold to liquidate assets and pay off debts. Slaves were "gifted" to children or as marriage presents. Mothers were often separated from their own children to care for the children of white families. Slave children were also separated for these reasons. In all cases, these separations were traumatic, causing losses of kinship, support, traditions, and culture.

PAGE 63:
Slave Weddings
Slave weddings were not legally binding or recognized during the antebellum period, although slave owners would sometimes acknowledge them for strategic reasons, such as minimizing interpersonal conflict. Slaves were aware that married couples and families could be separated at the will of slave owners at any time. Despite this, slaves still married and developed their own nuptial traditions and practices. Although the origin is somewhat unclear, one such example is "jumping the broom," where the newly married couple jumped over a broom before witnesses to bond themselves together. This custom fell out of popular practice after Blacks were able to marry legally, but it regained popularity in the twentieth century due to its portrayal in Alex Haley's book and miniseries *Roots*.

PAGE 64: *John Tubman*
John Tubman was a free Black man when he married Harriet (then Araminta) in 1844; it is not known if he was born free or acquired freedom at some point earlier in his life. Marriage between free Blacks and slaves was somewhat common along the Eastern Shore during Harriet's

lifetime, but the status of those marriages was unstable. A 1712 Maryland law stated that a child born into such a marriage would follow the status of its mother, suggesting that if Harriet and John had produced children, they would've been born as slaves. There is no official record of Harriet and John's marriage and little information on how they met, but it possibly occurred when Harriet was working for John Stewart.

PAGE 69: *Quakers*

The Quakers, a Christian denomination also known as the Religious Society of Friends, played a large role in anti–slave trade and abolitionist movements in the US and UK. In keeping with their fundamental belief that all human beings have worth and the ability to know God, many Quakers considered slavery to be immoral and unjust. Although there was some division on how to best deal with specific issues such as adherence to the Fugitive Slave Act, Quakers played a significant role in the Underground Railroad and supporting the formerly enslaved.

PAGE 84: *Niagara Falls Region*

The Niagara River flows north from Lake Erie to Lake Ontario, forming a border between New York State and Ontario, Canada. This region was an Underground Railroad border-crossing location, with many available transportation routes, including through the Erie Canal and the world's first railroad suspension bridge, which operated from the mid- to late-1800s. The International Suspension Bridge (US) or Niagara Falls Suspension Bridge (Canada) connected Niagara Falls, New York, to Niagara Falls, Canada, and was able to accommodate pedestrians, carriages, and locomotives.

PAGE 94: *St. Catharines*

St. Catharines, a town located in Ontario, Canada (then the area called Canada West), was the last stop on the Underground Railroad. Since British authorities refused to extradite fugitive slaves back to the US, Canada became an increasingly popular destination for many escaped slaves after the passage of the Fugitive Slave Act. Towns such as St. Catharines provided more economic opportunity, civil rights, and protections for former slaves and free Blacks. Tubman was based in St. Catharines for ten years, supporting the resettlement efforts of escaped slaves, including family members, and participating in civic and religious life.

Story Notes

"John" was an alias of Robert, "William Henry" of Henry.

The medicines (including for pregnancy) in the story were common during that time period, but there is no evidence of what they did or did not use in these specific cases.

William Still's "sketches" were written accounts, but I chose to have him sketch images for narrative purposes.

It is not entirely clear whether Jane and Ben were already married or just engaged during their journey. I decided to portray them as married to detail slave marriage customs.

Stories suggest that John caught up with the group at the parents' fodder house, later than portrayed in this story.

The timing of Harriet's spells was added for dramatic purposes but was representative of the nature of her condition.

I took a liberty with the timing of the crossing of the suspension bridge. She did cross with a group of slaves, in 1856, but not with this specific group.

Bibliography & Suggested Reading

Bradford, Sarah. *Harriet Tubman: The Moses of Her People*. New York: Dover Publications, Inc., 2004.

Clinton, Catherine. *Harriet Tubman: The Road to Freedom*. New York: Little, Brown and Company, 2004.

Foner, Eric. *Gateway to Freedom: The Hidden History of the Underground Railroad*. New York: W. W. Norton & Company, Inc., 2015.

Larson, Kate Clifford. *Bound for the Promised Land: Harriet Tubman: Portrait of an American Hero*. New York: One World/Ballantine Books, 2004.

Lowry, Beverly. *Harriet Tubman: Imagining a Life*. New York: Anchor Books, 2008.

Still, William. *The Underground Railroad: Authentic Narratives and First Hand Accounts*. Self-published, 1872.

Credits

WHIT TAYLOR is an Ignatz Award–winning cartoonist, editor, and writer from New Jersey. She has authored many comics, including the graphic novel *Ghost Stories*, and is a regular contributor to The Nib.

KAZIMIR LEE has lived for almost equal amounts of time in Malaysia, the UK, and the US. Only mildly discouraged by the preexisting pool of talented Kazimirs in the comic industry, Kazimir adores queer and feminist subtext, ghost stories, brush pens, and pre-9/11 country music.

Series Editor **JAMES STURM** is a cartoonist and the cofounder of the Center for Cartoon Studies.

Acknowledgments

Special thanks to James Sturm for your keen editorial insights and unwavering support throughout. Thank you to Rotem Moscovich, who got us started, and Heather Crowley, who helped move us forward. Thank you to Xia Gordan for your artistic contributions in the early drafts. Thanks also to Luna Skeet Browning for your top-notch visual research and to Rebecca Dalzell for digging into the details. Thanks to Judy Hansen for all your support and to Andrea Colvin for taking the reins. And thank you, Harriet, for your courage in the face of adversity and your fight for a more just American society.

CCS the CENTER for CARTOON STUDIES

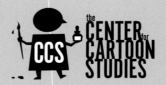

THE CENTER FOR CARTOON STUDIES (CCS), America's premier cartooning school, was founded in 2005 and is located in downtown White River Junction, Vermont. You can find it at www.cartoonstudies.org.

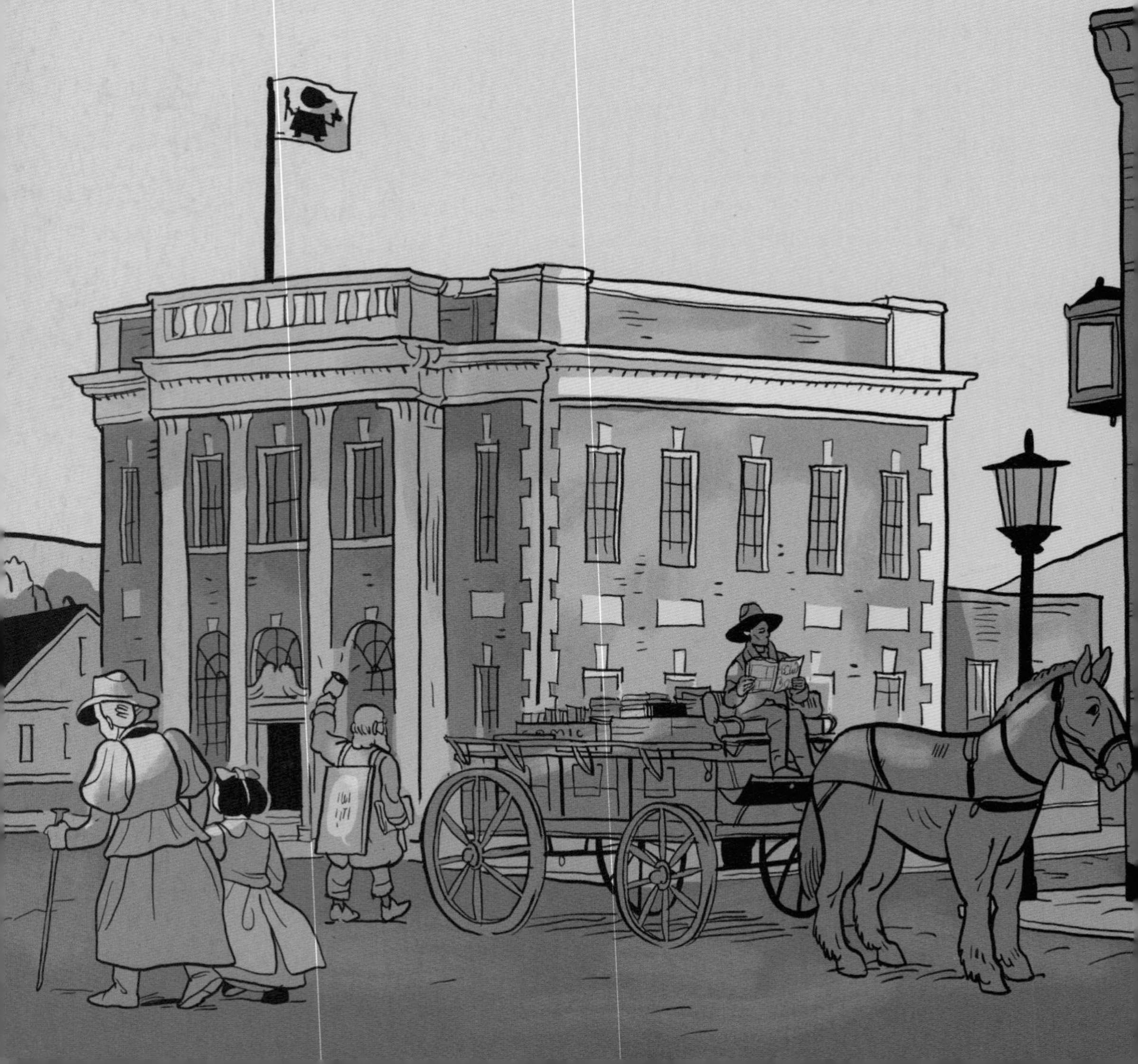